The Making of
a Modern
Psychiatrist

MARK WARREN, M.D.

The Making of a Modern Psychiatrist

Doubleday & Company, Inc.
Garden City, New York
1986

Library of Congress Cataloging in Publication Data
Warren, Mark M.D.
The making of a modern psychiatrist.
1. Psychiatric hospitals. 2. Mental illness.
3. Psychiatrists. I. Title.
RC439.W37 1986   616.89'0232   85-10174
ISBN 0-385-19821-3

*This is dedicated to Lisa,
the one I love.*

None but ourselves can free our minds.
—Bob Marley

ACKNOWLEDGMENTS

Many thanks go to the left side of my brain, which guided all those obsessive tasks, from typing to proofreading, that went into producing this book. The organization, attention to detail and commitment to deadlines could not have been accomplished without its involvement.

Yet none of the creative energy that is so critical to writing could have been found without my right brain. It has been such a pleasure to see it in action, giving a look at the big picture.

Countless teachers, fellow residents and interns have helped the left side in its search for knowledge and dominance. Intellectually speaking, I am in their debt.

The artists and friends who played with me and egged me on, often against quite sensible advice, have enriched my life beyond measure. (Take that, lefty.) The old right side, struggling against an endless education, has its respect back.

Early in the maturation process, long before I could tell right from left, I owed all my thanks to Ann and David Warren. Mom and Dad's support and love have helped to teach me the importance of a whole life. That is what this book is about. To Barbara, Martha, Jim, Tom, Mary, Bob, Anne, Tim, Mary, Bob and Jim, thank you, too.

The fates have blessed my life with Lisa Lystad. Thank you, from both sides of my heart.

Contents

1

Fantasy

"Welcome to Asylum."

The auditorium was bare but for the twelve of us and the thought of welcome was appreciated. The day before, we were all doctors of internal medicine. Today we are psychiatrists. We glance nervously at each other, these people who I will spend the next three years with, this lecturer who will teach me how it all works, this building and this room where it will all happen.

"You are all very lucky to be here."

I guess we are. Being a psychiatrist has to be a pretty good job, as these things go. Although nervous, everyone looks generally proud to be there.

"This is where you will learn not just psychiatry, but how to be a psychiatrist."

A psychiatrist. Is that like being a real doctor? Four years of premed. Four years of medical school. An internship. Two years of practice and learning to be with patients. So now I can be a psychiatrist. Why didn't I just go to psychology grad school?

"Don't ever forget that you are doctors."

Oh.

"You will be dealing with the sickest group of patients you will ever see. You will have to use all your resources and defenses to get through this year, but it will be worth it."

I can tell we're about to get the tradition of excellence speech. This is where we learn that our function is not to learn, but to do well by our institution, which has done very well for itself in the past.

"Asylum was founded in 1890."

Right.

"It is one of the oldest public psychiatric hospitals in America and one of the earliest to be administered by a major American university. Thus, we can offer some of the finest care available to the sickest patients. And since it is a state hospital, ability to pay will not be an issue. We serve an area of over a hundred thousand people, we serve them all well, and you will be on the front line of care."

All alone? Great.

"But you will not be working by yourselves. Remember this rule: Never Worry Alone. Don't go home at night wondering if you've just done something terrible. Talk to someone about every hard decision. Talk to your chief or your attending physician or one of your supervisors. But don't worry alone. You're here to learn this year. You're not supposed to know everything already."

Fine by me.

"And you won't be working all alone on the wards, either. There are nurses to help with patient care, social workers to deal with patients' families and the outside world, mental health assistants to keep the ward running smoothly. Use them to help you. Don't let yourself get isolated."

This sounds pretty good, and I start to drift into a state of shock mixed with hope. At least I should have some support for this year, whatever it may hold.

"You are all looking forward to being therapists, I'm sure."

I suppose. Sure.

"But first you will learn to be administrators."

Like small business administration?

"The administration I am referring to is the working out of a treatment plan for each patient with the staff and the patient. Only after you know what you're doing will you be able to start to do it. Administration before therapy."

Administration? I'm here to be a doctor. Not an administrator. What does this man mean?

"Administration is an integral part of therapy. As you determine how you will treat a patient, you also determine how you will relate to that patient. Thus, you will build an alliance to the patient based on administration."

An alliance? Different ways to treat patients? Don't you just sit them all down and talk to them and they get better and say thank you?

"You will see many different kinds of patients here. People who are psychotic. These are patients who have a problem in the way they think. Their thinking is not rational. Then there are patients with a problem with affect. These people have a mood disturbance. They are depressed or manic. There will also be patients who are none of this. Rather, they will have deep-seated issues in the organization of their personality and cannot cope with the world."

Okay, okay, I get it.

"Don't be surprised if you go through emotional turmoil this year. It's very stressful."

The tapping on my shoulder is not an illusion and I turn to see my chief, Dr. Cooper, looking down at me. I smile and hope she'll go away, perhaps there just to say hello. When I realize this isn't going to happen, I tune in to hear her say, "There's an admission for you, Max. You're first up." A little smile and she says, "Sorry."

Obviously there is only one response called for so I begin to panic. I start to shake and wonder where the bathroom is as Sandra says, "Do a good mental status examination."

"A what?" I respond cleverly.

"A mental status examination."

"What in heaven's name is that?" And so on. And like a good chief resident should, she leads me off into the madness.

"Sandra," I say, "what does it mean that you're my chief?"

"Ask me in a couple of months," she answers. "I just started today, too. Basically, I'll be your boss and immediate supervisor. But I'd like to be your friend. I was in your shoes a couple of years ago. There'll be five residents and me on our team. If we get along, everything will be easier for all of us."

We've arrived at the intensive care unit of the hospital. While in most of the medical world, intensive care means slick, fancy machines and crepe soles, in psychiatry it means that the scene is intense. I am introduced to my patient, a seventy-year-old man lying naked in a puddle of pee. I'm not sure he's alive, but neither is the second year resident, also on his first day of the job, who has accidentally given him enough Thorazine to drop his blood pressure to zero. This I am to learn is a not uncommon side effect of medication. However, Alan, the second year, keeps shouting at me what a great admission this is. But after only a few moments I can focus no longer. There's a woman with a cup in her hand who keeps falling down. She's bleeding all over. There are three folks with boom boxes screaming at each other in the corner. One guy has barricaded himself behind a row of chairs and is eyeing me warily. There are at least a half-dozen people just staring at the situation I'm in. The new doctor, star of the show. Sandra has left me all alone (I thought this wasn't going to happen), and who knows what to do next. The second year resident is mumbling on about what a great admission this is. So I turn to the nurse, part of my team and ask, "What should I do?" Unfortunately she's only been there two days.

So I ask her to clean up the pee and get the patient into a bed and I'll go try and find an old chart and maybe we can figure out what is going on here. This always worked in a medical hospital, and somehow it works here. And three hours later I find my office and pick up the phone to call Zoe.

"Hi, lover," she says. "How's the first day going?"

"Things here are crazy!"

"Is that a joke?" She laughs.

"No, I mean it. It's nutty here. You wouldn't believe the patients."

"Why? Do they lie all the time?"

"That's not what I meant." I can hear her laughing again in the background and wonder if my sense of humor will be the first thing to go.

"Max? Are you still there?"

"Yes, Zoe. I'm just spacing out. It's already been a long day and I haven't met my fellow residents and I've had an admission and things are pretty weird."

"You'll do fine, Max. Don't worry. And we'll have fun when you get home. Okay?"

"I love you Zoe."

"Good. I love you too."

Sandra gets us all together at the end of the day to introduce everyone. We've all met our patients and seen our offices and the day hospital and the intensive care unit and are ready to collapse. Bobby, Denise, Eric, and Nancy, along with Sandra and myself, make up the crew. It seems like a nice group, but who can tell? As we shake hands and get acquainted, a man, who introduces himself as Sam, enters the room and makes an appointment to see us all. After he leaves, I ask Sandra, "Who was that guy?"

"That's Dr. Watson. He's the attending physician. The man in charge of the entire ward. Don't worry about him. He's a good man."

Great. Okay. One less thing to worry about. But how many supervisors will I have here?

"Here's a list of your supervisors," says Sandra. "You each get me and Sam, as well as five others."

"Seven," I croak. "That's like a day a week of full-time supervision."

Bobby looks up at me and grins. "Max, we're going to need it."

Zoe is standing at the door waiting for me when I get home. She gives me a hug as I walk inside and I feel calmed, the anxiety of the day melting away in her embrace. I relax. I remember when we met, eight years before. She was a knockout. For months I would dream of her, not knowing what to do with all the emotions I was feeling. Luckily, she was having similar feelings and suggested we get married. Now, holding her hands I am filled with the pleasure I've found only with love.

Standing on tiptoe Zoe gives me a kiss. "I finished all my applications," she says.

"That's great. Any offers for interviews, yet?"

She looks disappointed. "Nothing in the mail today. You don't have to ask me. I'll tell you when I get one." I catch the tiny frown she makes with the tip of my finger and she breaks into a wide smile. "Don't worry, Max. I'll get into medical school."

"I shouldn't worry? I thought you were the one who was worrying."

"Well . . ." She lets it trail off.

"Well, what?"

"I think we're both wrapped up in our new activities. Psychiatry is going to change our life. And if, I mean when I get into medical school, we'll be that much busier."

"We'll always have each other," I say.

"I was worried about you today." Zoe looks at me and puts her arms around my neck. "You sounded so sad on the phone."

"I wasn't sad. Just confused. The theories of mental illness don't have much to do with what I saw at the hospital."

"Same as always, Max."

"I know that. But I hope every day isn't as crazy as this one. I don't feel like a doctor. I feel like I need one."

"To teach you theory?"

"Hardly. To ease my troubled mind."

"Med school or no, Max, I can take care of that."

On a hot summer day, Simon checks into the hospital. He doesn't know I've been doing this less than a week. But I do. Simon is in the arms of the police, his hair in a tangled mess (hair is always the first thing to go). He looks disheveled and frightened, being held by four men while he tries to crawl out from inside his skin. Eyes bulging, skin pulled taut, fire pouring out of him, he seems a man who is seriously angry. Not to mention huge, at least six feet four inches, three hundred pounds. He's a monster on the loose. Simon looks at me and says, "Doctor, I'm going to explode! Don't you understand? Oh my God! This is real. This is it. Where am I? Don't you know who I am? I am Mozart! This is illegal. Where am I? Where am I? Help me! Help me! Don't be destroyed! You will be destroyed and so will everyone! Where am I? Where am I? You can't do this to me!" I have no prepared response for this. I believe him. He starts pounding the walls with his fists, already bloodied from earlier outbursts.

So we send him to the intensive care unit and put him in a seclusion room. It's about six by nine feet, stark white walls, no furniture, just a mattress on the floor. The windows are barred, and the door can be locked, when someone is trying to kill you or themselves or something. But the next morning the door is open and I enter to see Simon pacing the room, waving his arms wildly, mumbling to himself.

"Hi. I'm Dr. Jackson. Remember me? We met yesterday."

"I remember you burning in a sea of flames. I am not mad! I am the great. I am the grand. Bland. Sand. I am the greatest musician of all time. I am Amadeus! I can destroy the world in a second or give it strength. Short or tall. Big or small. I am cursed!"

"Please, tell me more."

"Are you the doctor? This is amazing! This is mad. Do you want to know me? Powerful things will happen with me. Me! Be! See?" Simon starts running around the room and shaking his fists over his head. He begins mumbling to himself and then punches a wall. The room shudders.

Edging nearer the door, I ask him, "Do you have trouble with your anger?"

"Yes!" he yells, this huge haggard man, rising to his full height and then continuing to expand. "I am angry my father is so angry and your anger is killing me!" He looks very sad. "I have such talent! I am incredible!" he shouts. "I have the power!"

"And that seems to be a problem?"

"Oh yes," he says, rubbing his hands together. "I've had problems with people. Oh yes. You know it's very easy to kill. Oh yes it is. I sing and I dance and I fly. I have a respect for people. Oh yes I do. And who are you? Are you my new killer? Will you torment me or will you love me?"

"I'm your therapist."

"My therapist? Who is there under the disguise? I don't need a therapist! Get out of here! Don't kill me! You make me crazy! You murderer! You swine! You've come to kill me!"

I'm stumbling backward out of the room at this point. Although Simon has been talking and yelling at me for only ten minutes, I am totally lost in his rap. He is standing on his toes now, and the fire within is streaming from his eyes. Hair fraying wildly, mouth open in a silent shout, he moves toward me. "Simon," I bellow. "We want you to feel safe!"

"Then get out of here you murdering scum!" he screams. Pushing me out the door he rushes into the hall, only to be grabbed by the mental health assistants and placed back in his room, now with the door securely locked. In a daze, I shuffle back to my office, wondering what the hell just happened. Doesn't he know I'm here to help him? Doesn't he recognize my skills? Why do I feel I don't have any? I close the door to my own office, my private seclusion room and look around. It's bigger, has a rug, my desk, pictures on the wall. And books in the corner. Scholarly books by those in the know. Books that will help me deal with this madness.

I look up manic-depressive illness.

> The essential feature is a distinct period when the predominant mood is either elevated, expansive or irritable and when there are associated symptoms of the manic syndrome. These symptoms include hyperactivity, pressure of speech, flight of ideas, inflated self-esteem, decreased need for sleep, distractibility . . . Although elevated mood is considered the prototypical symptom, the predominant mood may be irritability, which may be most apparent when the individual is thwarted . . . Manic speech is typically loud, rapid and difficult to interpret . . . If the mood is more irritable than expansive, there may be complaints, hostile comments and angry tirades . . . A common associated feature is lability of mood, with rapid shifts to anger and depression . . . When delusions and hallucinations are present, their content is usually clearly consistent with the predominant mood . . . God's voice may be heard explaining that the individual has a special mission. Persecutory delu-

sions may be based on the idea that the individual is being persecuted because of some special relationship or attribute.*

Well, that sort of describes what's going on here. Not exactly,
but it gives me something to work with. A working diagnosis, so
to speak. But if I can't talk to him on my terms, because of the
delusions and such, what can I do? I ask my chief. "Sandra, can't I
just decide to let him ride out the storm, wait a few days and see
what happens?"

"He's your patient, Max."

Sam, my attending physician, disagrees with this. As I sit in his
office, much more nicely furnished than my own, he turns and
speaks gruffly. "Don't you think Simon needs medicine?"

Twisting in my chair I try to formulate an answer. He prods me
gently. "Tell me the truth, Max. I want to know."

"Jesus, Sam. I don't know. He just got here and he says he
doesn't want any."

"Well, Max. That's pretty common with manics. They are un-
aware that they are sick, quite often. But he needs the medication.
Otherwise, he may be here for months."

"Well okay, Sam. But why not leave it up to him? Let's observe
him for a while. If it takes a month, well then that's not so bad. I
don't want to force drugs on him."

Sam shakes his head at me and says, "Naturally. We can't force
drugs on him or anyone else. That's a job for the legal system.
But we ought to think about guardianship through the courts so
that we can get him out of intensive care. I hear he's causing quite
a stir up there." He looks at me gravely.

"But Sam, that's just like we were forcing him to take medications. We're just using a judge to help us."

No sympathy is forthcoming for my plight. "Look Max, I understand how you feel. Nobody wants to use force. But we may
have to." I start tapping my fingers and staring out the window.
Sam continues. "He can't live in the ICU. We need the bed. And it
doesn't do him any good. People are in pain when they're psy-

---

* Taken from Diagnostic and Statistical Manual of Mental Disorders, Third Edi-
tion. Washington, D.C.: American Psychiatric Press, 1980.

chotic. They don't like it no matter what they say. We owe it to Simon to do everything in our power to help him."

Mental illness certainly is strange, I think. What other disease causes you to avoid treatment? Someone with a heart attack will submit to the most outrageous indignities in the name of "health" or "getting better." But a manic? Simon had gone through five thousand dollars the week before coming to Asylum. He had spent it on a gold-plated saxophone. He had plane reservations to Vienna, but spent his nights prowling graveyards, looking for buried treasure. He was in love with a subatomic particle. He thinks he's Mozart. And as far as he was concerned there was absolutely nothing I could do to help him. But untreated he could die. He can't get himself food or shelter. He hasn't a penny to his name now. And he puts himself in constant danger through a series of crazy activities, like standing in the middle of traffic jams and exploring the inner workings of garbage trucks at night. But where's the illness? Is it thinking crazy or acting crazy or feeling crazy or just doing things that cannot be tolerated, either by him or anyone else?

But he doesn't want help. Is that a disease, the inability to tell anything is wrong? So the police drag him into the hospital and now I'm supposed to get him to take drugs to get better. There are just too many questions left unanswered. And Sam keeps talking.

"I'll give you some time to get him to take medications on his own. That's all you should talk to him about. Remember, administration before therapy."

Tough to forget that. This certainly isn't insight-oriented therapy.

Every week or so I get to spend a night in the hospital. All the residents rotate the task, so that there's always a doctor in the house. It's a different kind of pleasure. There really are few experiences like waking up at seven in the morning at a mental hospital, completely bent from a night of admissions, angry staff, medical freakouts and so on. Highlighted by secluding my new patient, Manny. Seems he attacked three staff members at once and was deemed to be a bit out of control. PCP *(phencyclidine)*, a hallucinogen, they tell me. Then we had an hour of rounds, which I got to spend discussing Manny and the other court case that I admitted the night before. Both of my new patients were sent by a judge, both have assault records and worse, and both have stories that are so sad it makes me want to cry. At the same time I get filled with an enormous anger. So I sit here with conflict and all anybody wants to talk about is what meds I'm using and getting the patients out of here. AARRRGGGHHH!!!

"What was that Max?" Rounds are over and I seem to be mumbling under my breath. Kathy, the head nurse and I suppose a very nice person, seems to be interested. Turning toward her I think, "Aah. Maybe I can get some support here."

"Hi, Kathy. I'm just trying to deal with all the emotion around this place."

"Well, you don't seem to be doing very well at it."

"What do you mean?"

"I mean I'm angry at you and I think you've been treating my nurses badly. I spend all day trying to get everything in working shape and then you botch it up with your own headaches and poor communication. I don't know what is going on, but if you can't communicate better, you're in real trouble."

"What are you talking about? Kathy, I like you. I don't want to make your life harder. You know that. What happened?"

"You yelled at Bailey yesterday for giving the wrong drug. She had made an honest mistake. No need for you to go off the handle."

"Look," I say, "I'm tense, too."

"I know that." She appears to calm down a little and we walk over to the nursing station for a cup of coffee. "I didn't mean to yell. But you have to work with the nurses, not treat us like a bunch of staff who are superfluous. When we don't work together, everyone gets pretty tense."

"I won't argue with that. But don't yell at me. I'm just learning how it all happens."

And then it's off to work for me, seeing a few patients, making two dozen phone calls to social workers, the chiefs, nursing homes, shelters and who knows what else. Finally I get home to see Zoe. Standing in the doorway I call out, "Zoe, love of my life. I need you. I just had the worst day of my life."

She cracks a smile. "Oh? I think that makes eight worst days you've had this month. You must be in real trouble."

We sit together on the sofa and I try to arch my eyebrows. Instead, I look hurt. "Thanks, Zoe, thanks a lot. You don't understand how it is."

Now it's Zoe's turn to look hurt, which has a nice pouty quality to it. "Hey. If you don't like it, just quit. No one is making you do it."

"But I do like it. It's just so hard sometimes."

She smiles and holds me. "I know, Max. Let's not talk about it tonight. I made us a beautiful dinner and we can go out and go dancing afterward. Or maybe just stay home."

Ah! Home sweet home. A few beers and a daiquiri and I know she is right. Being in love solves lots of problems. If more patients had love they wouldn't need so many drugs.

So why am I drinking?

"Sandra," I say, sitting in her office, eating M&M's, "how am I going to cope with Simon?"

"Well, Max, you have to understand that he is acting like a one year old. He is in an unremitting oral phase, wants to be taken care of and needs constant proof of our love."

"Whoa! What does that mean in standard English?"

"It's like this. Someone who is manic is out of control. Look at how much pain you would have to be in to find a mental hospital a realistic alternative. By coming to Asylum in the first place, Simon is giving us a big message: 'I can't handle it out there. Will you please take care of me?' "

Oh. "So how do I do that without also taking away his freedom to make his own decisions and be himself?"

"Well, that's a very fine line, one that may not even be there sometimes. Because you need to figure out what is going on inside of him, when all you get is garbled messages. That's part of what makes mental illness so horrible. The illness prevents you from getting the treatment that would be most useful. Simon has already decided he may be better off crazy than well. What you need to do is to show him a third way. But first you've got to slow him down enough to talk to."

"Fine. I'll buy that. But what am I going to do? I don't want to sound like a broken record, but it's very difficult for me to say to someone, 'I know what's good for you, don't worry about it.'"

"Look, Max. This isn't like any other situation you've ever been in. Give it some thought. If a diabetic wouldn't take his insulin, what would you do?"

"I guess try to explain to him that he was killing himself. But it's not the same thing."

Oops. "Think about it, Max," she implores. "If Simon wasn't here he could be dead. He has a potentially fatal illness. If there was someone else to take care of him, he wouldn't have come here. You may not want responsibility for his life, but he sure isn't taking it on himself."

I try to relax and put my feet up on her desk. "Alright, that's true. But I don't want to force meds down his throat. I don't want to lock him up. I don't want to be another power trip he has to cope with. Damn! That's his major issue."

"And yours, too?" she asks softly. "You're his therapist, not his father. Your job is to do the right thing, as any doctor would. You know he would be incompetent if he wouldn't take his insulin. Why is this different?"

Well, that's another good point, and one I have been known to puzzle over. "But Sandra. Isn't there any other way besides forcing meds? He really doesn't want them and I think he should have the right to refuse."

"If he was one year old and was your child, what would you do?"

"I don't know. He's not one year old. Kids you make stay in their rooms."

"So? Why not do that now?"

"Make him stay in his room?"

"Sure. Long before drugs the only way to treat manics was through space restriction. If being with other crazy people stirs him up, then pull him back. If he's right and doesn't need meds to pull out of this, then let him burn out without driving you or anyone else crazy, too. You need to remember your own sanity. You're his doctor. If you can't treat him then where is he?"

In the doghouse, which is where I feel at this point in the day. I need time to figure all this out, but everything moves so swiftly here. Admissions every day, dozens of meetings, endless phone calls. A week or two off and it would all seem so clear. But we know better. After a month of working with Sandra I can tell that she really wants something done and fast. Deadlines from Sam slip past with his indulgence, but the heat keeps coming from all over. And as Sandra has grown more comfortable with her job, she keeps more and more on top of mine. She continues saying to me:

"Max, you're doing an okay job and I'm happy to be working with you."

Scratching my head, I lean back in one of the 1930s institutional chairs that fill Asylum and wait for the rest of the sentence. When it doesn't come, I respond, "It sounds like there's a 'but' that goes along with that."

"I guess so," she tells me. "I've heard a lot of reports that you're having trouble with staff members."

"Ah hell, Sandra. People make such a stink about everything. It's nothing, really. It's just so hard to get any emotional support in this place."

She leans forward at me and says, "I think that may be some of your doing, not just this place."

Feeling angry, I snap back, "What do you mean by that?"

Sandra doesn't back off. "I mean that support is there but you're not asking for it."

"Now wait a . . ."

Speaking soothingly now she puts her hand on my arm and says to me, "Give me a second, Max. I didn't say you were a bad person. I know that you do a good job and are good with other people. But how is anyone going to know how to relate to you if you won't share what is going on inside you? No one here is a mind reader, even if the patients think so."

Pulling my arm away, I flash angry again. "Low blow, Sandra. But what do you want me to do? Explode? There's so much tension here."

She reaches out to me again. "But that's no reason not to get angry. All you need to do is express it directly and appropriately. If you're passive or act it out, people will just be angry back and you'll never get any help." She lets go of my arm, pushes her hair out of her eyes and gives me a blank look.

My look of puzzlement won't go away. "But everyone is so busy with their own problems that they can barely see that anyone else is in pain."

"Max, give them a chance. Your fellow residents are a pretty good group. And people notice and care about you more than you may realize. Try reaching out. There's no need to carry all this alone."

So now we're talking about trust and friendship and the group and when it gets to be five, I am so very tired and am not sure whether I went into psychiatry to have my personality reconstructed. I'm glad that Sandra likes her job.

Sunday morning at Asylum is not a pretty sight. My eyes will barely open, the wallpaper is peeling, the mice sense that they have the majority on the weekend. Say a few prayers and try to believe that it is all not real and then close those eyes back again. There's a joke at the hospital that goes this way: "How can you tell the doctors from the patients?" Answer: "The patients go home." This is especially apparent on a Sunday. Where is my newspaper? Where are the lox and bagels? Hey, I'd settle for football. But instead I am hung over in a mental hospital, trying to open my eyes.

Sunday in a mental hospital. So you have to get down to it and do all the nickel-and-dime things like calm down riots and see what the patients have on their minds. Well, Magda, my other court case, loves being at Asylum, although soon she must leave. And why shouldn't she like it? Thirty-eight years old and it's the best mother she ever had. I asked her to tell me her life story to help with writing her court letter and then became sorry when I heard it. All the horrors—rape many times, abandonment by everyone, the life of a smack freak, ODs, hunger, life on the streets. Violence, lots of violence. And it stretches over her thirty-eight years like it was forever, with no breaks, no relief, no space in which to grow. Someday, will all this end? I ask myself, "How can Magda and I be from the same planet? What kind of crazy universe made such insane circumstances?" If you ever want to feel privileged, hang out in a mental hospital.

Simon approaches. He's having a good day and is out of his room. Still thinks I want to kill him and can't put a coherent sentence together. But my limits plan must be a modest success. He hasn't hit anyone. And if he never goes to sleep and seems to be on speed all the time, well, at least he's interesting.

"Dr. Jackson," he shouts at me, "I'm just fine. I'm composing and I'm playing and the world will be a wonderful place." Then his face changes and he growls, "But you are the soul of the devil. And soon you will explode. I'm okay. Yes I am. Did I tell you about my family in Vienna? My awful friends? You're no help to me. You're a murdering swine. Begone!"

As always, he has caught me without a response. So I leave. Anyway, Sunday is not the time for therapy sessions. Simon and I have plenty of time to try to talk during the week. Usually we can last about three minutes before he loses it totally. But at least he's getting to know me. This is what my supervisors call building an alliance.

But even though I leave Simon, I stay in the ICU, since it's an opportunity to go to snack time. It's the mental hospital's version of a rap session, except most participants are psychotic. But as we sit there eating cinnamon toast and drinking tea I can finally drift away from all the labels and hear these people. Julie talks of her family and how she misses them and reads some poetry. Lucy collapses in the corner but listens intently. Billy and Mary, with a combined IQ of less than one hundred, demonstrate sibling rivalry. Stick tells us of his anger at women and hard feelings. Which leads to why he killed his wife. And sure a lot of it is crazy but it still reminds me of a college dormitory. And in that same crazy way, it all makes sense.

When I talk to someone who is psychotic, the first feeling I get is horror. One of the schizophrenic patients constantly hears voices in his head, saying over and over, "You moron, you moron, you moron, you moron, kill, kill, kill, kill . . ." Like an endless nightmare. But I can only observe and hope that even for these patients a quiet moment can be found. Sometimes, the depth of the pain seems too great.

There is a new patient, Ella, on the ward. She was brought in because she was hearing voices. The voices she heard were small children, crying because no one would pick them up to play with them or feed them. They just kept crying and crying. But no children lived in Ella's house. They only lived in Ella's head. And they continue to cry, over and over, because now, as it has always been for her, no one will pick her up.

Monday morning, as every other one for weeks, I ask myself, is Simon competent or not? Should I let him refuse medications and hang out in the hospital acting crazy, or should I get the court to declare him incompetent and force him to take drugs? I've been at the hospital long enough to see other patients helped by the powerful antipsychotic medications. Or at least calmed down enough to leave. But going to court seems such a strong alternative. I'd much rather go with negotiation.

Sandra suggests that I should at least have a family meeting and see if Simon's folks will lend a hand. So we all meet in my office, a very bedraggled Simon, his father, the architect, all spiffed up in a three-piece suit, looking just great. His mother is there, a businesswoman, also looking good. A little too made up, perhaps, but they are visiting their son in a mental hospital. For the first time. They have been divorced for the past fifteen years, with Simon living with Mother, while Father was basically no-where to be found. New York. But a check comes every month. And of course I'm there, along with Elyse, the social worker for the case.

The general idea is to have two therapists with each happy family, so that the family dynamic has a harder time sucking in the therapist. If one of us is getting pulled into the vortex of the family, the other can rescue. So we all sit there, wondering where to begin. No one looks real happy about the whole scene. Simon's dad keeps looking at his watch as if he'd much rather be flying back to NYC. The silence becomes prolonged, when Simon can stand it no longer. He turns to his parents, sitting side by side and shouts, "You're so ugly! You ruined me! Both of you! When I see you I feel like I'm going to explode! I hate you!" His voice is a high-pitched whine, piercing and shrill. He turns the volume up and hones in further. "I'm a big boy now! I'm strong! I'm strong. You have to leave me alone!" His eyes begin to glow as his parents start to slide under their chairs. They seem to shrink as Simon grows in size. He leans toward them as they retreat and yells, "I hate you! I hate you! I hate you Mommy! I hate you Daddy!"

Mom and Dad look as dumbfounded as I. This twenty-year-old saxophonist, who is now pounding his fists on the wall, is doing a marvelous imitation of a two year old in a tantrum. And the only response that the parents have is to pull away. Which is understandable. Simon's energy fills the room like a dam burst pouring from the reservoir and it is an awful sensation. We all gape in horror and I think, "How can I get out of this?"

Father reacts first. He explodes in anger and starts screaming, "Shut up, Simon! Shut up!"

Simon is set off again, and then Mother joins in. Within seconds they are all screaming at each other as Elyse and I stare in shock.

In my mind I tick off the options: commit him, restrict him, force him to take meds. This scene of madness has to stop. There is no way to turn this man loose on the world. I forget about rights and feel like I have to do something. Anything. Taking him by the arm I lead him from my office, up the stairs to the ICU and through the door. He acts as if in a daze from the moment I touch him and follows docilely. As we reach the door, he turns to me and says, "Thank you very much, Dr. Jackson," then walks into the unit.

Elyse and his parents sit in my office, as she tries to help them deal with the weird stuff and I wander on down the hall. So maybe he's not competent. I don't know. They all seem nuts. How do you decide? AARRGGHH! What to do, what to do?

Luckily for me, not all patients are like Simon. Following all my hassles with him, seeing Alexandra is almost a relief. I say almost, because sitting with her can be one of the most boring experiences life has to offer. But wait. I'm supposed to find all my patients interesting and fascinating. Each has a marvelous story to tell, if only I could adjust myself to them. Yeah, sure. Alexandra's idea of a session is fifteen minutes discussing her eating habits, followed by fifteen minutes on what I think she looks like. But hey, at least she's not psychotic. A little obsessive. A lot obsessive. Quite frankly, these sessions are not fun. So I lean back and look professional and listen and hope that someday this gets better. After ten minutes of silence she leaves, which is okay by me.

I go home to an empty house. Zoe is at work. A pity because I am full of things to talk to her about. Although it may be good she's not there. "Psychiatry? Is that all you want to talk about?" she'll say. "God, I remember when you were interesting. Now you sound like one of your boring patients." Oh well. That's worth remembering too. She doesn't want me to obsess about the hospital. Takes up too much of my time, time I should spend with her.

The pains and rewards of a two-career family are well documented, I suppose. One of the joys is getting drawn into activities that you would otherwise have never heard of. If it wasn't for Zoe's interest, I never would have been able to take a two-year break from medicine working as an ecologist after my internship. It was her turn to pick where we went. And somehow, it was as an ecologist that I discovered psychiatry. Or rediscovered it. After listening to one of my ecology and health talks at the ecological institute, a tall, dark man with sunglasses approached me and said, "You would be very happy in psychiatry."

"Oh yes? Why?" I had previously told Zoe that I wouldn't go back into organized medicine for all the tea in China, or something like that, but I'll always listen to a good offer.

"Because there are a lot of people like you in it. People who care about moral and ethical dilemmas. Confused people."

Well, that sounded good, so I started my new career, no great loss to the world of vegetables and came to Asylum. But history comforted me little tonight. I just missed Zoe very much and felt sort of sad until she got home.

After rounds, I decide to begin the day with Simon. It's back to ground zero after his explosion.

"Simon?" I start softly, "I'd like to discuss your new treatment plan," referring to our limit-setting program. I was pretty sure he'd go for it, since I had complied with his wish for no medications.

"Up yours, Daddy. You liar, you asshole. I'm the king here. I'm the greatest composer who ever lived. I hate you. You're nuts. Ruts. Butts. You never try to help me. You're not a doctor. You're a magician, you're the fool." Tauntingly, he turns his back.

Should I plead? "Simon. This is the plan we agreed on earlier. Don't you want to get out of here?"

"You're not my doctor. You're a murdering swine. This is a terrible hospital." He starts pulling on his hair, then whirls around to face me. "You are a swine. The air is mine. Nothing will help me!"

"But, Simon . . ."

Putting his face three inches from mine, he blurts out in rapid sentences, "You're the one who is sick. I've never been better. Hi. Bye. Get out. Get away. You ruined my life. You're so sad."

And so it goes. Weeks of work lying in shambles. I take my problems to Molly, a favorite supervisor who I see at her home. She has a one-year-old child, a cute little button who crawls over to say hi. A nice house away from psychotics. What a dream.

Holding her baby in her lap, she tells me, "Max, he doesn't know if he can trust you. He thinks you may be in cahoots with his parents, or perhaps just his father. So he needs to test you." The child crawls onto the floor and starts to pull on my leg. "The important thing for you to do is to be honest, to tell him when you don't understand. When he says he wants freedom and then acts

out to get restricted, let him know what you see." She scoops up
her baby and starts bouncing him on her knee. How I envy that
child.

"But I feel his anger and sadness. How can I deal with my own
conflicts and his at the same time?"

"Let him know how it is. If you pick up on his feelings, be
honest with both him and yourself. He's exciting, sad and terrifying. He is very insane right now. But he is also a person in great
pain. He needs you to understand that." And baby is fast asleep.

So can I relate to a person in great pain? It's supposed to be the
stuff that makes up lives. But I want to hear Simon's pleas for
dignity and honor, and I fear the sameness of all these treat-
ments. I fear the regularity of lives outside the hospital. The
moments that I treasure are of Zoe and me just fooling around,
with our love and ourselves. How much of Simon's universe do I
mess with? How do I know how to help him keep what he wants
and leave the rest?

Remembering Sandra's admonitions, I decide to take my am-
bivalence into rounds. Get some backup or whatever. "This case
has really got me down," I say to the group.

Irwin, one of the nurses, responds, "What do you mean?"

"It's a difficult case."

"Well, it is for us, too. You're not the only one here struggling
with this."

"I know that. I just wanted to share some of my thoughts."

"Well," he says, "the management of this case has been lousy."

"Could be. I guess that upsets us all."

"If only you could get it right, this would have been taken care
of long ago."

"What does that mean?" I demand angrily.

"That if the resident doesn't know what to do, then it's impossible for the rest of the staff to do their job. Which," he adds,
"they know how to do."

"Now wait one second . . ." I begin, but Sandra cuts me with a
curt, "Stay out of this, Max." Then she turns to Irwin and asks,
"Just what is your idea of the treatment plan?"

"It doesn't look to me like there is one."

"Have you checked the chart?"

"Not lately."

"Then do so. You'll find that Dr. Jackson has written out an extensive treatment plan explaining what is going on." She flashes me a glance and I nod.

"That doesn't change my point," Irwin continues. "This case is a mess and it's not the fault of my staff. This stupid attempt to restrict Simon without forcing him to take meds is a lot of work for us and gets nothing done. He's been here for almost a month and he's as crazy as ever."

"We'll stick with the plan," Sandra replies. "If you want to have a meeting to discuss a new idea, let's have it. But talk to me, don't bring it up in this way." She turns her head, changes the subject, and I moan inside. That was fun.

Sandra grabs me after rounds and takes me to her office. "Max, what the blazes is going on with this patient?"

"Sandra, I don't think it's the patient, although he's a pain in the ass. Everyone in this hospital is angry all the time. They have to spend all day on a ward filled with people like Simon. They get no space, no quiet, and feel unsupported. It's awful up there. It makes me pissed off, too."

"What!" she shouts. "Whose side are you on anyway? I work my butt off supporting you and that's all the thanks I get?"

"I didn't mean that, Sandra. Of course I appreciate your help. But you cut me off today and I could have handled it."

"Maybe, Max. But Irwin was wrong and so were you. A manic patient needs limits, reduced access, and reduced stimulation, and if that makes people angry I'm sorry. But that's the way it has to be."

"Believe me Sandra, I'm starting to agree with you." Now that our anger is out, we can relax and lower our voices to normal tones. "My past few days, hell, the past month, has been awful with Simon. I don't know what to do."

"Max," she begins, "you know what to do. You just don't want to do it. There is no way that Simon is going to get better as long as he feels that he can manipulate the system. You have to let him know that you are serious about limits. And that means letting him know that if he can't follow them you'll go for guardianship and get him on meds and out of the hospital. If he can do without them, fine. But it's not working. He's crazier than ever and, as you pointed out, the whole staff is going nuts."

"Yeah, well thanks." I shift a little nervously. I hate being wrong. "And I'm sorry I was angry at you."

She smiles and says, "You don't have to be sorry. I'm just glad you didn't keep it inside." Hearing that makes me feel better.

Sam echoes Sandra. "Go for guardianship. It's painful to be psychotic. You don't do him any favor by letting him act crazy for months. When he's sane, he'll remember, and it will be another issue to deal with. Medication works. We're doctors, not faith healers."

Well thanks, Sam. I guess. There are many days when faith healing seems like a very noble profession.

Okay. So now I'm going to seek a guardian for Simon, go to court, and get him out of the hospital as quick as I can. And I don't even really know what the issues are that brought him into the hospital. Damn. I want to be a therapist, not a policeman. Administration before therapy, I remember.

Simon is not happy when I tell him what we have in mind. He goes totally wild, tries to hit me again, and gets secluded. As Sandra would put it, he is asking for limits. And I'm just the guy to do it.

I want to go home. But there are six more patients to see, my group therapy and residents' meeting. I always look forward to the latter, since that's where we can let our hair down, get dirty and revel in the joys, such as they are, of our work. But today we're all too burned out. We sit around eating chocolate chip cookies and drinking Cokes and gurgle unintelligibly. Sometimes it's hard to say anything.

Denise drives me home. A fellow resident who I'm just beginning to get to know. She has the gift of constructive interpretation and usually has a few criticisms of my emotional makeup to offer in the hope of defusing whatever I feel. But today she wants to tell me of her confusion, anger, and frustration. And how much everyone she works with means to her. And I am glad someone else is dealing with heavy issues, too.

As I daydream I am wondering which of my sins will catch up with me today. Now that I'm a psychiatrist I have taken to wondering what this means. Am I ambivalent about the profession? Do I want to share my inner burdens? Do I want to prevent myself from messing up again? Heaven only knows. But this is all too similar to my patients. And I suppose to everyone else in the universe. I hope.

I really don't want to work today. It's Friday and too late to get anything started. All that's left to do is survey the wreckage left after a week of emotional blasts. Zoe is at Asylum though, working at her volunteer job. We arranged it so that we could hang out at work. She gets a résumé builder for medical school and I get to play a little hanky-panky at lunchtime. Which beats being cranky at home.

Simon, however, is in a fine fettle. He has withdrawn his threat to leave Asylum, which means I won't have to go to court to keep him in the hospital. At least not yet. He feels he has made his point by giving us notice that he can leave the hospital and doesn't want to force the issue. Neither do I. He has also agreed to take medicine, is out of his locked room and is as peaceful as a lamb when I speak to him.

We sit on a couch in the dayroom and I ask, "Simon, how are you?"

"Better," he replies, twirling his fingers. "I want to get out of here, but I'm so depressed. What can I do? No one will hurt me, will they? I just want all these horrible thoughts to go away. Can you help me?" he pleads. Does better equal being depressed?

"I'll do my best, Simon. I really think the medicine will help. It's been hard for us to talk up till now."

He swallows hard and asks, "If I take the meds can we talk more?"

"I hope so," I answer and really mean it. "We have to learn to cope with each other."

Dr. Halloran thinks differently. All people need is a little less dopamine. Or a little more of something else. Maybe money. It's all in the chemicals, you see. The molecules tell you what to do. His molecules make him very slick. But as an outside consultant, his concerns are not the same as mine. "You see, mental illness is simply a disorder of the neurochemical pathways. It's very easy to understand once you know what the chemistry of the brain looks like. Yes, all these people have had horrible lives. Frankly, most people have horrible lives and they don't end up in mental hospitals. No . . . there is something profoundly wrong with the chemistry of these individuals. And with the right medications we can change them. They don't need talking to, they need chemistry."

I am forced by my chemicals to raise my hand and make a point. "But they have so many problems and issues they have to straighten out. They still have so much to deal with, even when they're medicated to the gills."

The good doctor is not impressed. "That's not their illness, that's their life. Since when is being unhappy an illness? Since when is not being able to work an illness? Cure the disease. The rest is society's problem."

Sam wasn't totally in favor of this approach when we met for lunch at the coffee shop. While not much physically, the coffee shop is a sight to behold. Six feet of counter with the standard Coke machine and Fritos, it's staffed by patients, who do a good but slow job, even if the change can be variable. The clientele is also varied, being a mix of the hospital hierarchy in their three-piece suits and the patients from the chronic wards, the treatment "failures" who live at the hospital. Guess who is more ill at ease.

Ernie is always there, his tongue hanging out, shirt hanging out, cup of coffee in his hand. His familiar greeting is, "Got a quarter?" He rasps this out through burned-out vocal cords, the result of too many cigarettes. On the hundredth request you give him a quarter and he thanks you by asking, "Got a dollar?" Julie is always present. The fattest woman I've ever seen, at least five hundred pounds, she never talks, just makes the universal hand signals for, "Got a quarter?" Leo is only three feet tall, is totally blind, and has no teeth. But with a voice straight from the opera, he gets your attention. He loves to stand around going, "Oh, oh, oh." I'm not sure what it means, but if you respond incorrectly, he spits at you. And so on. The action at the coffee shop never stops.

But we're used to this by now, so ignoring it all, Sam tells me, "Sure their biochemistry is all messed up. But there's more to it than just that. The same argument Dr. Halloran made cuts both ways. There are lots of people with abnormal chemistry who never get to the hospital. Look at identical twins. Some get psychotic, some don't. Environment, upbringing, genetics, stress, all are important. Who can say which is most crucial for any one patient? Medications help many patients. For some that's all you can do. But look at Simon. When he calms down and deals with his underlying depression, he'll have lots to talk about. You've won a battle over meds, but it's only the first step. Now you've got to be a doctor. Find out what made him sick and help him get better."

One of the ways we accomplish this learning is by presenting the patient at what is called a case conference. So today I present Simon to Dr. Friedrich, a middle-aged analyst who reminds me of my father. Great. Smiling, controlled, acting as if this was a normal experience, he listens to my tale of Simon. As I explained his birth, moves, school, battles with Mother, rejection by Father, involvement with his saxophone, delusions about Mozart and so on, Dr. Friedrich listens and writes. He never does stop smiling. Then, in the moment we are all waiting for, Simon is brought into the conference. There are about fifty people watching the spectacle, and the ones who are paying attention and not being beeped out for something else are waiting with anticipation. For this is the high point, when the consultant will interview the patient. All Dr. Friedrich has to do is meet, diagnose, and suggest a treatment for the patient in the next twenty minutes. Now then, Simon knows about this conference and has in fact been banking his whole treatment on it. He expects much better things from an expert than some first year resident.

Unfortunately, I don't know what's about to happen, since

Simon can still be somewhat manic at times and twenty minutes has been my limit with him since his admission. He walks in and sits down.

And takes off. "Hello, Dr. Friedrich. How are you? Who the hell are all these people?" He twists in his seat to eye us all. "They never help. They only try and hurt me. When I was a little boy, all the bad things, it was so bad, you remind me of my father, he wanted to help me but then he left and then there was only Mother omommyomommyomommyomommy!" He starts crying and puts his head in his hands, then suddenly stands up and yells. "Where is that Dr. Jackson? He's a swine!" And he continues to take off from there. And on and on for about ten minutes of incredible anger till Dr. Friedrich interjects, "Yes, Simon, it's horrible here and no one understands you."

Simon turns to him and blurts out in a startled voice, "That's right, Dr. Friedrich. I'm glad someone understands."

And so they go on for another fifteen minutes while Dr. Friedrich holds the mania in check while learning more about him and his depression in half an hour than I have learned in a month. So that's why he's a big cheese. Maybe I can be a big cheese when I grow up.

Sandra pulls me aside when the conference ends. "What did you think?" she asks.

"I thought he was great. I feel like an imbecile."

"Did you see how he finessed the symptoms and dealt with the underlying issues?"

"You bet. It looked like a miracle."

"It's not, Max. Just hard work and listening. You'll get it." She pats me on the back and walks away. I ponder this as I walk to my office, only to discover Magda, the thirty-eight-year-old court case, is waiting for me.

Wearing hot pants which expose way too much of her body, she looks as if she's trying to sell something, which for all I know is still her major occupation. I invite her in, invite her to keep her halter top on and ask, "What brings you here?"

"The judge says I have to see you. You recommended treatment for me in your letter to him, so seeing you is part of my treatment. You have to get me off drugs."

"Is that what you want?"

"Oh, it's okay." She leans forward on my desk. "Maybe this is a chance for me to get to know a respectable guy. All I ever meet are muscle heads."

"Sounds pretty bad, Magda."

"Well, you know, I could go for you. But I bet you're married. All the rich guys are married." And I feel the office walls closing in on me.

"Do you know what therapy is all about, Magda?"

"Nah. Let's just talk."

So I give the canned spiel. "There are a few rules and guidelines we follow. About the only thing that I require is that you tell me what's on your mind, what you're thinking. Other than that, the only other rule of therapy is to think of therapy as a safe place, somewhere to say what you feel without having to worry about dire consequences. That way you can have a chance to think things out and have insight into your ideas and emotions. One other thing. You may have feelings about me. One of the best things about therapy is that you can talk about a relationship while it is happening. And you can see that talking about it and feeling things isn't the same as acting on those feelings." Whew.

I memorized that my first day. Rarely has anyone heard it. But it makes me feel safer. Usually, the patient will go on as if I've just coughed. Magda is no different.

"So you won't help me? You bastard! Well screw you. I'm leaving." And she did.

Supervision with Molly follows, luckily. I'm lost in the dreamworld of what my psychiatric practice will someday be. I'll have a small but cheerful office. It will be filled with plants and other living things. On the walls will be colorful pictures of beautiful places. There will be a photo of Zoe. And a small etching of Freud. Patients will come and sit on the leather chair or perhaps lie on the sofa. I'll lean back, put up my feet and talk. "So you're unhappy." I've added a barely distinguishable accent to my voice. "Oh yes Doctor," the patient will say. "I've always had this fear that I would kill my father and marry my mother. It torments me." "Well," I intone, "that's perfectly understandable. It's normal and natural. Don't worry about it." A look of relief crosses his face. "I don't have to worry about it? Oh thank you Doctor! I'm cured! Hallelujah!" "It was nothing," I respond, tapping my pipe on my hand. "Please give the check to my secretary. I'm going to take a walk and contemplate my triumph."

Molly says I'm doing fine with Simon, bad with Magda, and I sure do have a strange group of patients. She suggests I daydream less.

At home that night I have a treat waiting for me. Zoe has made us reservations for dinner and drives us to the restaurant while I try to reorient to the world I used to inhabit.

"Max," she says, "let's try to talk about something else besides psychiatry tonight. Okay?"

"Sure, love. What do you have in mind? How about sex?"

She giggles and pats me on the knee. "Later, Max. You can wait. I have my first medical school interview tomorrow and I need a pleasant distraction."

"And that's me?"

"Well," she asks, "do you think you're up to it?"

"I think I can handle that. I used to be a pretty fascinating person, you know. In the good old days."

"Don't worry, Ace. You still are."

I can feel my whole body sigh. "Thanks, Zoe. Thank you very much."

When I enter the hospital, I feel as if I have somehow cleared a hurdle. I don't know what it is or where it was, but there is a subtle change. Simon and I work out another deal, whereby I'll get the guardianship while he voluntarily continues meds. The day he stops, he's either discharged or we go to court, depending on how crazy he is. I wrote it down and we both signed it and that's that. It feels good, too. Simon says, "I knew you never wanted to force meds on me. Someone else must have been forcing you." Very insightful, these manics.

Barely out of my session with Simon, I run to make my juggling group. All the residents have to do a group of some sort with the patients so I chose juggling. I go into my rap on how it's relaxing, good for coordination, takes your mind off your problems and so on. The first question anyone asks me is, "Do you do this because psychiatry has no future?" Finally, someone asks me to throw a club behind my back. Unfortunately, I can't.

In the group is Shirley. Shirley is a ninety-pound, five-feet five-inch woman who manages to have the dopiest look on her face I have ever seen. Said to have an IQ over 160, she never made it through tenth grade. She is twenty-four and has been at the hospital for four years. Basically, here is the way that Shirley has the world figured out. When she was a child, her sister arranged for her to have electrodes planted in her brain that would allow her to hear spy messages from the Russians. All the voices she hears in languages that she can't understand are part of the message system. And although this is painful for her, there is a payoff. Because she is a very important person in our strategic defense system. And she will be rewarded someday with great fame and fortune. If she tolerates the pain now. She is deluged in her mind by existential questions. Perhaps the answers will be her reward. Shirley is totally convinced that I have some of these answers. So she likes to be near me in case I can solve them with my special knowledge. How I've joined the action in her head still escapes me. She's the sort of patient who makes Freud look like a genius. She says things like, "Last night I dreamed that Mom was dead and I was all alone with Dad." She carries around a diagnosis of schizophrenia.

"Well, Shirley, what do you think that dream means?"

"That my transmission will soon end?" She never looks at me, always averting her eyes. Her position is one of someone with no place on earth. At least not until her mission is complete.

"Well," I respond. "I don't really understand what you mean."

She shifts from leg to leg while juggling and burps. "How are we related?" she asks. This is what we call a loose association. How did she get from A to B? It's also pretty crazy.

"What do you think?"

"Well, I don't have one of those things, you know, a penis. And you probably do. Sometimes I see like a man."

"Shirley, you're a woman."

"How do you know?"

"I'm a doctor. It's my job to know. But I guess you're unsure about who you are."

"You must be nuts to say that."

Oh. It's pretty hard for her to juggle, too.

As I drive home I notice that the sun is lower in the sky and the hottest part of summer has ended, and I have survived the start of the academic year. There are many parts I can barely remember, but I have survived. I seem to have learned something. And what I need is a celebration. What I get is a weekend with Zoe, whose interview for med school went very well. But she too is anxious and we go to sleep very early.

2

Denial

In the dream I am in Rome, traveling to the outskirts of the city.
Zoe and I are in a car that no one is driving. We arrive at a
beautiful home in the country outside town, and when we go
inside it is filled with artists. I notice that this is a small cottage
with a garden in the back. Zoe has gone into the yard to stand
among the trees. The house begins to fill up with water and I try
to find the door, but can't. I begin to pound on the windows, but
no one can hear me.

I sit up and look around the room. Still in Boston. Definitely
not Italy. Zoe has been awakened by me and rolls over to say
hello.

"What's the matter, Max?"

"I had a horrible dream. You were there and some other people, and I don't know what was so scary. I can't remember all of
it."

"It'll come back to you if it's important. Don't worry."

"I am worried. My sleep has been awful this week. All these
dreams of being trapped or losing someone or going crazy.
What's happening to me?"

"You need a good night's rest. I'll give you a backrub if that'll help."

"I don't think so, love. Maybe we can just snuggle for now. I'd like to hold you."

"No trouble there, Max. I'd love to hang on to you, too."

Asylum is nothing like Rome. And as I drag myself in on a cold rainy Friday, the last thing I want to hear is Sandra, saying, "Max, I've got another admission for you."

"Damn, Sandra. I can't stand it! This is the third admission this week. I think there is some sort of plot against me."

"Calm down, Max. You're too excitable. Anyway. I think you'll like this patient. Her name is Ecaterina."

So I climb the stairs to the ICU to see what this next adventure holds. But did Sandra say just another admission? That hardly describes Ecaterina. Tall, lanky, and strikingly gorgeous, her hair freshly coiffed, made up to look like she is off the pages of *Vogue*, she sits in the dayroom of the hospital, looking furious and furiously about. About thirty-five years old, she has maintained her seductiveness. Curling her legs up under her dark gray suit, she tries to huddle on the wooden chair. Gradually, as I watch her across the ICU, her fury is replaced by fear, as if she has realized that this is real and her presence here is serious business. I walk on over and introduce myself.

"Hi. I'm Doctor Jackson. I understand your name is Ecaterina."

She tosses her head and runs her hands through her hair. Turning toward me very slowly, she eyes me as one would eye someone selling flowers at the airport. Barely moving her lips, she replies, "What did you say your name was?"

"Dr. Jackson."

"Oh." And turns her head away, again with deliberate speed, and says no more, as if the issue is somehow settled.

"I'm going to be your doctor while you're here." Another great intro line.

For a third time she rotates her lovely profile into my sight. "That won't be necessary. I have a psychiatrist."

"Who's that?"

"I don't believe you need to know."

At this point she has deigned to give me the benefit of her face for the entire discussion. Which I appreciate. Not only is she beautiful, but this also affords me the opportunity to try to watch her and try to set up a line of communication.

"Maybe I don't, but it might be helpful."

"I don't think so." And still only the lips are moving.

"What brings you to the hospital?"

"Is that any of your business?" There is a not too subtle sneer in her voice.

At this point I am tempted to check the address on the front of the building. Unless this woman has the fixed delusion that she's Queen Victoria, there is a crucial piece missing from the puzzle. But some guy is naked in the corner and there's three old people wandering around looking for a nursing home and lots of other minor scenes of recognizable madness, so this must be the place. I try again.

"It's my business if you want it to be. Generally, each patient in the hospital is assigned a doctor when they are admitted and that doctor is in charge of their care while they are in the hospital. I'm that person for you. So it certainly would make your life and my job easier if we could talk."

She starts to twirl a piece of hair between her fingers and then smooths her dress out. I notice at this point that there is a nice figure to go with the face, albeit a bit thin. "Very well." Her tone is a bit less sneering and she begins to move her face as she talks. Which is something she does very well.

"What is it you want to know?"

"I'd like to start by finding out why you are here."

"I'm here because my mother is an idiot."

"Yes?"

"She doesn't understand me."

"Can you tell me more?"

"She thought I wanted to kill myself."

"What gave her that idea?"

"I said I was going to. But I didn't mean it. And she should have known that. It's not the first time I ever said that to her."

"What happened the other times?"

"Well, the last time I slashed my wrists." She pulls back her sleeves to show me two long scars running across her wrists. "And another time I tried to hang myself." She pulls down her dress collar and shows me, around her neck, another scar.

"But you weren't serious this time?"

"No. Of course not."

"What makes this episode different?"

"I just took pills. And then I went to work."

"Doing what?"

Lifting her chin she peers at me down her nose. "I'm an actress. I dance and I sing. Usually I'm onstage, but now I'm working, temporarily, as a waitress."

"You usually work onstage?"

"Yes." And her voice takes on a pleasant lilt as she leans forward and smiles at me. "I lived in Hollywood all my life. I always wanted to be in film. When I was fourteen I got my first part. I was very good. And very famous. That's when I changed my name. Perhaps you've seen me?" I shake my head. "No matter. I was very well-known."

"What happened?"

"It's an awful business."

"Yes?"

"They screwed me. They tried to kill me. They made me very sick."

"Sick?"

"Very sick. I had to retire and nurse myself back to health. That's when I got depressed and tried to kill myself. So I had to move to Boston."

"But you had lived in LA all your life?"

"No. That's not what I said. I moved to Hollywood to be in the movies. I was wonderful. OH GOD! WHAT'S THAT!"

I whirl around and see a patient standing there, smeared with feces, hair that looks like a barbed wire fence with combs sticking in it, holding a stuffed doll. The monster looks at the two of us and then screams in some unknown tongue, religious, I suppose. Then runs off down the hall, chased by two attendants. Nice of her to say hello. Although Ecaterina has other thoughts on her mind.

She's sitting with her head between her hands, rocking gently back and forth, sobbing quietly. I call her name a few times and get no response, then touch her shoulder to get her attention. She looks up at me with a start and then turns her head away. As she tries to put the best actress look that is left to her, I apologize. "I'm sorry for the interruption. I hope you weren't too frightened."

With her back to me she answers, "No, no, I'm alright. It's just that . . ." Her voice trails off as the tears begin to flow.

"You seem so sad."

Facing me, she rubs her eyes and hair. "Well, there's a lot to be sad about." With a gallant toss of her head and shrug of her shoulders she has transformed herself into Ingrid Bergman in *Casablanca.* "Things have been very bad for me. My mother left when I was a child and my brother is quite ill. I had to work to support him. Men find me very attractive, but all they want is sex. And when I tried to tell my mother about any of this, she locks me up in a hellhole like this."

There are enough holes in that story to make Swiss cheese, but I am wondering still why this woman is here? "Why are you here?"

"It's because I don't have insurance and no psychiatrist."

"No psychiatrist?"

"No. I don't have one."

"Should you? Isn't that why you came here?"

"Of course not. I had one, but he wouldn't see me anymore."

"Why not?"

"I have no money to pay him, if you must know. You can see how bad things have been for me." She sighs.

"It sounds as if they've been very bad."

"I shouldn't have to put up with all this." She gestures around the room.

"I agree." I look around with her. "How did you end up here?"

"I'm just so depressed." She runs her hands through her hair. "The future looks so bleak. I have no future. I'm a total failure at everything." I expect her to start to cry, but the look on her face is more one of pain.

"You feel like a failure, despite all your accomplishments?"

"My accomplishments are shit!" she shouts. "I've got nothing. I've got no one. When I think of the future I see myself on skid row, an alcoholic, a bum. All alone." She begins to wring her hands. At the same time her appearance starts to unravel in an inexplicable way. And she looks terrible. "Look at me! I'm ugly and awful. I'm too old. I have no security, no people, nothing. I'm a failure, a wreck." Finally she cries, but it comes out in huge, gasping sobs, each one taking all her energy to expel.

I sit in silence and watch her. Tall, blond, smart and beautiful. And sad. I don't think I'll be letting her out of the ICU tonight.

When her tears trickle down, I take her to the examining room with a nurse for her physical. Somehow I don't trust this woman. She undresses and puts on a hospital gown, then says to me, "Don't you think I look great?" She has regained her composure and is back onstage.

"We can talk about it later. I want to do a physical now and then I'd like to talk to your previous doctor. Do you mind if I give him a call?"

"That bastard? No way."

"It'd be helpful for me."

"Who cares?"

"I do."

"Big deal. I haven't seen him for a year and he stays out of it." Wonderful, I think. Am I the next to go?

"Sam," I ask, "what kind of crazy patient is Ecaterina? She doesn't seem to be bonkers. And she isn't what I'm used to seeing as depressed. I can't figure her out."

"What do you mean, she's not bonkers?"

God, can't anybody just answer a question here? "I mean she's not delusional, not hallucinating, doesn't think I can read her mind, isn't convinced the CIA is after her, you know, that sort of thing."

"So she isn't psychotic?"

"That's right. What is she?"

"She sounds like a personality disorder."

"Well that goes without saying."

"What?" Sam seems confused by my answer.

"She's got a strange personality."

"I mean her diagnosis," Sam replies. He pulls out the diagnostic manual and thumbs through it. "She could be a borderline personality disorder.

> At least five of the following are required:
> 1. impulsivity or unpredictability in at least two areas that are self-damaging, e.g., spending, sex, gambling, substance abuse . . .
> 2. a pattern of unstable and intense personal relationships . . . (consistently using others for one's own ends)
> 3. inappropriate, intense anger or lack of control of anger . . .
> 4. identity disturbance, manifested by several issues relating to identity, such as self-image, gender identity . . .
> 5. affective instability: marked shifts from normal mood to depression, irritability, or anxiety . . .
> 6. intolerance of being alone . . .
> 7. physically self-damaging acts, e.g., suicidal gestures . . .

What do you think of that definition?" Sam asks me when he finishes reading.

"Well, I think that a lot of people I know would fit in there somewhere. Hell, who doesn't do things impulsively, angrily, and with lots of emotion sometimes."

"But, Max, that's the key word—sometimes. Everyone has some personality problems. But some people live their life that way."

"I don't know, Sam. It sounds pretty vague."

"Well, listen to this one." He begins to read again.

> "Histrionic personality disorder:
> Behavior that is overly dramatic, reactive and intensely expressed, as indicated by at least three of the following:

1. self-dramatization
2. incessant drawing of attention to oneself
3. craving for activity
4. overreaction to minor events
5. irrational, angry outbursts or tantrums

Characteristic disturbances in interpersonal relationships as indicated by at least two of the following:

1. perceived by others as shallow
2. egocentric, self-indulgent, and inconsiderate of others
3. vain and demanding
4. dependent, helpless, constantly seeking reassurance
5. prone to manipulative suicidal threats, gestures or attempts."

"I don't know, Sam. She has a lot of those characteristics, too. As do many of my friends. Certainly someone isn't crazy because they have bizarre interpersonal relations?"

"Max, we're not just talking about personality traits. We're talking about personality disorders that ruin your life. Not all depressed people try to kill themselves, you know. Well, not all people with strange personalities have personality disorders."

I begin to protest again, but he lifts his hand to stop me. "Keep an open mind, alright. Now, how are you going to treat her?"

"You don't want me to give her meds do you?" I ask in an outraged voice.

Sam grins as he knows he's got me. "No, of course not. I just wondered how you'd handle her suicidality."

"When she says she isn't suicidal, I'll believe her."

"That sounds fine," he says. "Let me know how it turns out."

Zoe and I spent Saturday driving around the New England countryside. We saw a marvelous parade in Connecticut. Dozens of bands were playing and the bass drums were a sight to behold. And I thought of nights in the country and stars that held me in awe with their brilliance. Every month during the new moon I would see the Milky Way. The countryside was deathly quiet and I'd always be a little afraid of the dark. Sometimes the quiet would be broken by the whistle of the wind or of a cricket leaping out of my way, rubbing his legs furiously. And I could stop and think and not feel rushed. There was so much less insanity, both within me and outside of me. Now I feel anger and confusion. I don't know the boundaries and rules of what I'm doing. I am not sure how much of what I do is for anyone's health. But I know that for my patients, it is all too real. I do not know if I am angry for them or for me.

"Hi, Simon."

"You swine! You murderer! I don't want to talk to you, you idiot! Don't you know who I am?" After a weekend of introspection, it's back to the basics. He's depressed and manic together. Or perhaps just sad and angry.

"Simon," I ask in my calmest voice, "what's going on?"

"Who are you? Who are you? You're scum! What are you going to do to me?"

"Simon. I'm just here to talk. I'm Dr. Jackson. I'm your therapist. What are you so angry about?"

He still won't sit and I still have no idea what caused this outburst, but at least he backs a few inches away from my face and stops shouting. "Look at me. I'm sad. They're all so sad. They need more. Why won't you help them?"

"I agree they're in a lot of pain, Simon. I'm afraid you might be in pain also."

"I am. I'm so sad sometimes. I just want to die." He begins crying.

"How can I help you?"

"You can't!" he explodes. Then he breaks down again. "I want you to. But I'm so afraid. I cause so much agony to my father. My life is so horrible."

"That's an awful feeling to have."

"It is awful. How can I live anymore? How?"

He sits down and breaks down. "Oh God, yes . . . I want . . . I want . . . Don't you know who I am? Help me!" I try to talk to him for a few more minutes about his feelings but he is inconsolate. And I don't know whether to be buoyed by the communication or bummed by the fact that the only place it led to was depression. So I saunter over to see Ecaterina. I find her lying in bed, her breakfast untouched at her side. I knock on the open door and ask if I can come in.

She smiles weakly, barely lifting her head. "But of course. I would so like to have the company of an intelligent person. My night here was awful. I must look a wreck."

"Do you feel a wreck?"

"Oh? Want to play psychiatric games so early in the morning?"

"How do you feel?"

"I feel great. Who wouldn't? After all, I'm in a state mental hospital, you keep me locked up, and I feel depressed. But good news, Doctor. I don't feel suicidal, anymore. So you can let me out of this place."

"Where will you go?"

"What business is it of yours?"

This one takes a moment, but I'm not sure of the stock answer. If she was psychotic, it might not be a reasonable question, but now I don't know. "I'd feel more comfortable knowing."

"And I'm supposed to cater to your comfort? That's a new twist. Or maybe not."

"You certainly don't seem as depressed as you did yesterday."

"That was yesterday. Today is today." She sits up in bed and reaches for her robe. Again I see her dancer's figure, too thin but still attractive. She asks me, "Would you mind turning around while I get dressed?" And then before I can answer throws the sheets aside and stands up, totally naked. "Excuse me," I say, turning around and blushing. "Do you like my body, Dr. Jackson?" she replies.

Saying nothing I stand there, trying to figure out what just happened. I had already seen her nude yesterday, during her physical. And why was I embarrassed when she was the one who was nude? I say to myself over and over, she's the sick one, try to understand your reaction in light of that. If you feel a certain way, remember that there are two people in the room. And that means, first, admitting that she has maneuvered you into an uncomfortable situation. Right now she has the upper hand. Anyway, we're not here for gazing, but for talking. So deal with the pathology.

"Body image seems very important to you."

"I'm an actress, you know. You can turn around now."

She has put on a sweater and skirt that showed just enough of her to be provocative while still covering all vital regions. She tries to look seductive and sits back down.

"What are you feeling now?" I ask.

"I think I look great. You doctors tend to think alike. You have no understanding of what it takes to be beautiful and succeed."

"Perhaps not. Do you feel you've succeeded?"

"Is that a joke?" Her voice drops an octave and she growls, "Well, screw you!" She extends her hand as if there were claws on each finger. "Just let me out of here, you asshole. I don't want to kill myself and now I want out! I signed in voluntarily. Now I want out of here!"

"You're not feeling suicidal?"

"Not in the least. Although I might if you keep me locked up here any longer. Just give my things and let me out!" She is standing and screaming at me and I just don't have the energy to fight it. "Fine," I say. "Do you want to see me as an outpatient?"

"What the hell for? I can look up my old psychiatrist if I need any help. I'll see him if I need anyone. He wouldn't ever treat me like you do."

"I thought you couldn't afford him."

"Don't worry, you bastard. I'll find a way."

Frankly, he's welcome to have you back. "Okay, Ecaterina, you're on your way."

"Sandra, I'm going to let Ecaterina go home."

"Fine by me, Max," she says. "As long as she isn't suicidal anymore."

"She says she's not."

"Can you trust her?"

"I don't see that I have much choice. She's not crazy. I can't keep her locked up."

"That's not what I asked, Max. All I wanted to know was could you trust her. Borderlines tend to not be the most consistent group. They say one thing to one person and something quite different to another and who knows what's real?"

"You're right. It's amazing. She told Irwin that Irwin was the only person in the whole hospital she could confide in. Then Ecaterina told him she would kill herself. I see Ecaterina an hour later and she tells me she wants out and is okay. Then, when I discuss it with Irwin, I get my head ripped off."

"That's called splitting, Max. Ecaterina is working to split the staff apart and cause arguments. How did you handle it?"

"I told Irwin to go to hell. That it was my decision."

"Very diplomatic, Max. You played right into her hands."

"But why would she do that? Why would Ecaterina want the staff to argue among themselves?"

"Heaven only knows, Max. But it would be nice if you could remember what is the patient's pathology and what is yours." Sandra sighs and walks away.

And then there are the days when I don't care what my patients think. Perhaps this is when I am more sure of myself, more certain that I am doing what I want. Then there are days when I feel like I'm moving backward, trying to grasp what has been happening. Wandering the floors, I look for someone who can help me figure it all out. Except everyone is too busy right now. Everyone is doing their job. We all have roles to play, functions to fill. AAAAArrrgh! If I can't know my coworkers as people, how will I ever know my patients?

Denise at our residents' meeting says I tend to dichotomize too much and feel too little. Denise knows how to recognize feelings better than just about anyone. She reminds me of a big sister, warm and kind, but won't let me get away with anything. Which is okay but I feel weird when I'm told that I have problems with my feelings. Denise thinks that is part of my problem.

Unless it's just a dream I'm watching. As I sit up in bed I remember. I'm on a stage with five beautiful women. We're all involved in some sort of bizarre show. It is interrupted when one of them, who is the oldest, gets stabbed in the back. The most beautiful is accused. All the while, a pro basketball game is going on in the background. I watch the scenes but do not participate. Zoe nudges me as I groan and says, "What's wrong?" Her hair is in her eyes as she tries to stifle a yawn, then gives up and opens wide. Seeing my chance I dive right in. She giggles after we kiss and tells me, "You were having another psychiatric nightmare. Go back to sleep." She turns over before I can protest and settles into a gentle, easy breathing.

As I lie awake, wishing that my brain would stop so that I could go to sleep too, I remember the new psychiatric facility invented by the residents that day. We wanted to call it "Mom's."

"You see, we could staff it with all these real Moms. No schizophrenic or crazy Moms."

"Great! It could be like a lunch counter, except all we'd serve is milk and cookies."

"Mom would probably yell at you a lot."

"That's true. But she'd always let you know how much she really loves you. You'd always get a little smile."

"Give you a gold star for being in the clean plate club?"

"The possibilities are endless. Do you think they already have these in California?"

Simon comes down to day hospital today. Day hospital is the goal of all patients and their doctors. It's the first step in transition out of the hospital. It's an open ward, with groups and lunch break and activities and a staff that has time to do more than just make sure no one is getting killed. It's one of the solid advances of community psychiatry. Unfortunately for Simon, it is also the end of limits and becomes a hellish experience. "It's all so hopeless here. No one will ever recognize my greatness." With his arms waving wildly overhead, he sticks his tongue out and screams, "There's no health here!" Eyes bulging, hair flying, fat wobbling, shaking his fists at me, he shouts, "I don't want to die! How could you do this to me!? What will you do next?"

Send you back to the ICU, of course. Sandra told me this would happen but I wanted to try it my own way. I thought he was doing better. After all, we had half a discussion this morning. Showing me a string quartet he had written, he stated, "You know, Dr.

Jackson, I'm doing alright now. I want to get out of here. Can you help me?" His voice was almost sweet. It was certainly music to my ears.

"Well sure, Simon," I smile, "that's what I'm here for. How can I help you?" Now I'm the one who is fidgeting.

"For one," he screams, "you can stop being such a murdering swine!"

Frankly, psychotic state or no, this phrase is starting to wear a bit thin. I'm glad he can make logic out of chaos, but I would prefer a different nickname. Something like Slim. I respond, "I'm only here to help you."

And the anger turns to depression. "But you'll never understand how sad I am."

"Can you help me understand?"

"I want to. I really do. Only it seems so pointless. I'm such a wonderful person but I'll never be better."

"You can never tell, Simon. Let's keep trying."

But the day hospital was not a rousing success.

On Monday, Simon and I meet for our session. As he talks to me I start to feel a large weight on my back. What does he want from me? I think, and then, why do I assume he wants something? I wonder how I got the power to give people what they want. Or to think that that is the goal of my patients. But it seems that every second I have to make a decision about what to say, or not to say, what will help or hurt. And every moment of decision commands a moment of indecision. And I think, why am I having all these thoughts? Who am I? What is going on here? Why do I spend so much time thinking about who I am when I sit with my patients?

After the debacle in the day hospital, he's back in the ICU full time. He has stopped and started his medications several times and now begins again, on the same promise that this will get him out of the hospital faster. A band is forming which needs a sax player and he wants to be there. And although he is not much calmer with me, I'm no longer called "you swine." At least not for now.

He looks down at the floor and tries to control every word he says. Each syllable is enunciated as if at a spelling bee as he says, "Hello Doctor. I wanted to talk with you today. Things are much better. I'd like to return to practice next week. My friends need me."

"Well," I say, playing for time. I'm standing by the door of his room, which I always leave open. No sense in tempting an attack. "You know I like to move slowly. Why don't we try to work something out?"

"Yes. I'd like that. I'm feeling much better. You don't have to be afraid of me. I know that I'm not Mozart. But I'm not crazy. I don't have an illness. I've got to get out of this place!" He stands and begins to screech. "Are you afraid of me? Do you want to keep me from my friends? Is that why you keep me here?"

By now, I know this scene and edge out the door. One thing I've promised myself is to stay out of this argument. I say to myself: "You are not crazy. You are his doctor. You are not his friend. He didn't come to the mental hospital to make friends or have arguments. He came here to get well. And he is doing better. Be his doctor." But why is it so hard to remember what I am doing when he starts to scream at me? Sam says, "You've got to be firm. Limit setting is what is required here. Firm limits help manics get out of the hospital."

"Yeah, Sam. But that's harder than it looks. Things get pretty intense sometimes."

"That's what you're here for. I'll talk to him if you want."

As the three of us sit around the table I begin to fidget. Why isn't anyone saying anything? Simon hasn't exploded and Sam hasn't cured him. So I can't figure out whether I'm hoping Simon will prove me out by being impossible or if I really want to learn something here. Finally, Simon turns to Sam and says, "So, your mother wanted you to be a doctor." Sam turns purple and I start to giggle, my beeper goes off, and that's about it for this interview.

When I answer the page it's Sandra, who gives me the good news/bad news riff.

"Good news first," I beg.

"Okay, Max." She smiles. "I have a healthy outpatient for you. A law student. I think he'll be a good therapy patient."

Naturally, I am suspicious. "Are you sure this isn't a schizophrenic dressed as a lawyer? You wouldn't try to fool me, would you?"

She laughs. "Max, don't be paranoid. This is a good patient." She pauses. "And the bad news is that there's an admission for you. An elderly man from a nursing home."

"Rats!" I explode. "I hate this! I'm gonna go nuts from the work."

Sandra looks at me questioningly, but I spin on my heel and walk down the hall.

So I begin my night being on call with the pleasure of admitting Hymie, an eighty-five-year-old man who looks older and talks younger. He's the definition of crotchety and it seems he broke another patient's wheelchair in his nursing home. So they have "dumped" him into the mental hospital. Dumping is a time-honored medical tradition that holds that if you can find some other institution to take care of a patient who you either don't like or don't want, all you have to do is put them in an ambulance, no matter what the patient wants. This usually happens to old people in nursing homes, which is unfortunate, since we are all going to be in one someday.

"Hymie, why are you here?"

"Hey, Commodore. We can get those Nazis now. Where have you been? I've had to fight alone!"

"Hymie, do you know where you are?"

"Oh." He begins to whisper. "I get you, Captain. Not safe to talk here. Okay. Mum's the word."

"Hymie. Do you know who the President is?"

"Thank God for Roosevelt. He got us out of the Depression and now he'll get us out of the war."

Hey, Hymie was too old to even be in the war.

I had supervision with Molly yesterday and while talking about how depressed Simon seemed to be, I realized how depressed I was sounding. When people ask me, "How are you doing?" I respond, "Well . . . you know." Somewhere inside me there are an awful lot of feelings about what's going on. Molly says, "It's okay. Let yourself be depressed. This can be a horrible year."

"Yeah," I say, "but it has its good side too. I really like being a psychiatrist. Hell. I like my patients. Most of the time. Although I've had some pretty horrible dreams."

"It's good you're letting it out somewhere. Are you in therapy?"

"Uh no. I've thought about it, but I don't really know why I would want to go."

"Well, it's your decision, but I went into analysis as a resident and it was very important to me. This is the time to deal with your feelings. While you are having them."

"I promise to think about it. Thanks." Jesus. How sick do I look? Why am I afraid to see a therapist? After all, I am one. Could the issues of my discomforts at work and my lack of desire to be in therapy be related? Zoe says, "Of course they are. They're both you."

I lay down to sleep after my phone call to Zoe, wondering if these issues will ever be resolved.

It's hard to relax in a mental hospital. There is a certain something in the air that makes it very unlikely that any form of sitting back and putting your feet up is going to take place. Your beeper is always going off. It's a hideous noise and like the telephone, it always sounds at the worst possible moment. Like when you're in the bathroom, and you hear this beeping from around your feet. Or just after a patient has told you they plan to kill themselves because no one has the time to give them. Today, my beeper sounded the maximum danger signal as I walked in the front door. It was Sam. "Uh, Max, can you come down to my office?"

Sam has a nice office. At least it has an air conditioner. And a few chairs that won't break your back. Although no room at Asylum is exactly what I would call pleasant. Mental illness may not be contagious, but there is surely an odor a building takes on after one hundred years as an institution. Especially when the building is early high school to start with. Sam wants me to know that this is "face the facts" day. Sam being tough is a little like being pelted with marshmallows. His voice stays soft, but he gives it his heart.

"Max, what are we going to do about Simon? I surely expected he would be out of the intensive care unit by now. I see him still begging for limits and needing our help to get back to his outside life."

The use of the word "we" is ominous. "Well, Sam, I think he is getting better. He's not as crazy as Hymie. He's not a basket case. On some levels, Simon is very healthy."

"We both agree on that. Right now we've got to get him out of the hospital and the ICU. Now, why won't you give him meds? I thought we had this all straightened out." He sighs.

"He does take them sometimes," I protest. Actually, he stopped them this time after two doses. "I'd like him to, but he really doesn't want them." I pause, then go on. "Anyway, he's not as manic. Really, now he's mostly depressed."

"Nonetheless, you don't do him any favors by letting him stay in the ICU."

"Now wait a minute, Sam. If he's changing, how do we know he's not getting better? Maybe the treatment plan is working." This is a desperation ploy.

"Max, I thought we had this all worked out. If he stayed crazy, it was either meds or out the door. What happened?"

"I really don't know. I just didn't feel comfortable with it."

"I know it's hard. But you've got no choice. Simon gave up some control when he came here. If he was competent to decide for himself he wouldn't be in the hospital. You're halfway there but you're abrogating responsibility to him by not treating him fully with all the tools at your disposal."

"I don't know, Sam. I know the meds would help him, but I don't think it's right. I wouldn't want them."

"But you're not psychotic. Would you like to be as Simon is now?"

This is a good point, one that often occurs to me. "No, I

wouldn't. But I don't like the role of forcing anything on someone. All he needs is a little more time."

"Max, you're not here to have your patients like you. You are a doctor. You don't refuse treatment to a patient for personal reasons. If he needs meds, then you give them. If that's hard for you, then we can try to work that out. But not at Simon's expense."

"Well, then what should I do?" I know what to do, of course. But it's such an adult thing to do.

"You've got the guardianship, Max. Use it. Afterward, we can talk all you want about your feelings. But you knew it would come to this weeks ago."

"I guess so. But I dread telling Simon."

As well I should have.

"Why do you want to turn me into a machine?! Why do you want me to go crazy?! Are you crazy!? I can't stand you! They won't work. I'm too manic. Nothing will ever work."

"Simon," I say, as calmly as I'm able, "we discussed all this before. I told you there were a limited number of choices. If you don't want to leave the hospital, this is the treatment plan we'll use. This is a final decision."

Simon remains unfazed by my calmness. "Go to hell and stay there, you murderer!" Then he turns and walks away.

But he didn't hit me and he didn't say he would leave the hospital and he didn't say that meds won't help him. He turns back and yells to me, "All I want is a little constancy around here. I want to know what the hell is going on!" Does that mean limits?

Zoe meets me at the hospital door to take me home. We talk about how she feels with the patients she has seen in the women's clinic and then we talk about how I feel and how our days are going. I tell her how tired I am at the end of each session, and she responds, "Isn't that why they call it work?"

"It really is work. Somehow, in my fantasy, I thought I'd just sit there and smile and the therapy would happen all around me. Instead I get exhausted."

Which I am tonight. I'm so sleepy I can barely make it through dinner. I remember how exhausting internship was, with the one-hundred-hour workweeks and nodding off while talking to patients. But this really takes it out of me in a different way. The hours are not as long, but there are those eternal minutes when you sit there confronting yourself through your actions toward your patients and your mind begins to spin.

Simon is screaming at me about his depression and trust and drugs and I feel myself nodding off. I shut my eyes and see my body turn to bones and watch the bones dissolve. In the dream I shout, "No, no, stop the hallucinations, make them stop!" but it doesn't work. They weave in and out of my sleep like a holy terror waiting to pounce. I guard my mind against the onslaught and wake up. Simon is still crying at me as I excuse myself and walk away.

So I can't sleep at night and I doze during the day and I'm exhausted. It affects everything I do and every interaction I have. When I'm tired I'm angry and even I don't like myself that way. So what do others think? Who cares? Not a great way to get along, especially somewhere like Asylum, where every move is interpreted ad nauseam. But sleepless nights and crazy days make Max not only dull but a bit out of touch with what we in the business call "successful life strategies." The nurses get angry at me. Social workers think I'm a yo-yo. Sandra says, "Max, these people are your friends. Don't drive them away."

"Forget it, Sandra," say I.

Molly is kind to me. Our weekly sessions are pulling me through. I suppose the angst is written on my face as she opens with, "So, how are things at the hospital?" She's using her most empathic voice, the one she saves for a patient who is about to jump out the window, which would be very bad for the therapist, indeed.

"Molly, I don't think I'm going to make it. I'm so incredibly tired and I'm having nightmares."

"What are you dreaming about?"

"This place. All my patients. And going crazy myself."

She smiles and waits a few seconds before answering. "Welcome to the club."

"Oh, great. Does this go on forever?" Terrific, just terrific. Welcome to the club, she says. Somehow I am not reassured.

"No, it doesn't go on forever. But there is rarely an easy day. You get your satisfactions but the pain never stops. There is no job that makes you more yourself."

Or as Dr. Seuss says, "Today there is no one who's you-er than you." "So what do I do with my pain?" I ask, while thinking, oh God, don't tell me to go into therapy.

"You remember the good moments"—"Thanks, God"—"and savor them. Your work with some of your patients has been fine. You have Simon back on the right track. And you got Ecaterina out in record time. You can be proud of that. It wasn't painless, but look what you've done, and you needed your patients to get there. And they needed you."

All this makes me feel better by the time I get home. Maybe it's new easiness about my job. Perhaps it's the weight off my shoulders. Most likely it's because it's Friday. *Après le deluge,* or something like that. Zoe and I are going to New York this weekend for a little vacation, the first since this all began. Which seems a mere lifetime ago.

Zoe has finished her medical school interviews, so all we can do is hope and wait. I'm not sure what I'm hoping for. Neither is she. After nine years of medical education I'm still not sure what I want. Of course, that's part of the attraction of psychiatry for me in the first place. No clear-cut answers there. Other than that, I guess I would have been a surgeon. But denial has never been my best defense. Zoe, she'll be a great doctor. As for psychiatry, she says, "No way." She thinks one shrink per family is plenty.

Mom and Dad are very happy I'm going to be a psychiatrist. After all, there is hardly a profession imaginable that is more right for a boy from Cleveland. And it sure beats some of my alternate plans. Such as becoming a juggler or a writer. As the neon signs blinked through the night, we sat with Dusty and Angel in the naked city.

"We've been on the road for three months now," Dusty tells us, as he braids his hair down his back. "But we're doing a lot of performing and getting great reviews. I think NYC may be ready for vaudeville."

Zoe and I are lying on the bed playing with the cat. "Wow," Zoe says, "it's great to see you. Don't give us details, let us soak you in."

"No, no," I interrupt. "Give us details." There's a minor note of desperation in my voice, I suppose. But traveling through the States performing to great reviews with ten of your best friends has a pretty nice ring to it. But what was life for Dusty and Angel is only vacation for me and I want to know more. "I'll tell you the truth, kids. I'm pretty envious. I like what I'm doing, but it can get painful. There are many days I'd rather be with you."

Angel grins and says, "Thanks a lot. You mean you'd rather be with us than work?"

"Really Max," Dusty continues for her, "that's the nicest thing we've heard all day."

"Hey, now. Don't give me crap. I'm serious."

Zoe chimes in. "My poor bear doesn't know what he wants to be when he grows up."

Dusty asks, "Hey, Max. Why don't you be a doctor?"

"I am one."

"I thought you were a psychiatrist."

"I am a psychiatrist."

"So you went to graduate school?"

"No, medical school."

"Why didn't you want to stay a doctor?"

"I am one. This is a specialty."

"Oh." Angel picks it up. "Did you have to go to school?"

What is this, career counseling? "I'm in residency now."

"Is that fun?"

"It's okay. I kinda like being a shrink." Why are these people asking me all these questions? Don't they know I'm trying to find out about their lives?

Dusty asks, "What do you like about it?"

"I don't know yet. I'm trying to be at peace with myself."

Zoe starts giggling uncontrollably. "If you're at peace now, then what has been going on in your head for the past few months?"

But it's starting to make sense to me. "I'm talking about all those things because I'm clearing them out of my head. I feel relaxed now, sitting here, at least on the inside. Of course, that may be different come Monday." Zoe continues to laugh at this.

Dusty has finished with his hair and is pinning stars on his hat. "Sounds to me like you've got a pretty good job. You don't want any of this traveling stuff. Don't you read the *Enquirer?* Success and fame breed trouble."

"You always seem to have a good time."

"That's because you only see us when we're with you. Even being a vaudevillian is hard work in the eighties."

Are therapists like good friends? Mine keep me on the straight and narrow. Why not start a friendship society for mental patients? Oh yeah. That's part of day hospital. Six hours a day to hang out together and then it's off to the real world. Except if you happen to be a mental patient, then your real world is likely to be a small ghetto of other mental patients. I'd rather be in NYC with Dusty and Angel.

But after a mere twenty-four hours it's time to go back home. On the way home Zoe asks, "I wonder why they want to be our friends?"

"I guess it's because we're such wonderful people."

"No! Now I'm serious," she replies.

"Well, so am I. I'll testify to your greatness if you'll testify to mine."

"Fine, Max. But I still want to know. What makes people like each other? It seems so important."

"Being around others is a comfortable way to be. I think the most valuable thing in a person's life is the happiness they create with other people. Maybe we're good at that with each other."

Zoe takes off her shoes and sticks her toes in my face. "You know you're the most important thing in my life," she says as I swerve to avoid an oncoming car and park by the side of the road.

"I couldn't be me without you, you know."

"That's alright," Zoe responds. "You don't have to be."

I have never had a patient who did not describe feeling alone. They talk of standing naked in the world, with no one to hide behind. I myself might rather be mad.

Rubbing my eyes, I sit in my office on Monday morning. I've been in the hospital for an hour already and no disasters have struck. Yet. Hymie has gone back to the nursing home, my chronic patients are quiet as can be, there are no new admissions waiting for me, and Simon is still taking his meds. And crying. I close the door and take a deep breath, fantasizing about being over the hump, and the phone rings. "Hello?"

"Dr. Jackson. Do you know who this is?" It's a rough feminine voice and I know it.

"Hello, Magda. What can I do for you?"

"I just wanted to say hi."

"Well, hi."

"You got some time? I got some problems."

I look at my watch and think of the thirteen phone calls and twelve patients and who knows how many meetings I have to go to and say, "Actually, Magda, I don't. Why don't you make an appointment to see me?"

"Just a minute, Doc?"

"I can't right now."

And the voice starts to get louder. "Well, that's okay you ass-hole. You're like that, I know. Never have time for me. Well, up yours!" And the smashing of the phone reverberates in my head. I've got to do better with these calls.

Except the phone rings again. Ready for Magda, I hear the silky sweet voice of Ecaterina ooze over the phone. "Dr. Jackson," she purrs, "I'd like to come in and see you."

"That's fine," I say. "I thought you had a psychiatrist."

"Can't we talk about that later?" I feel like she's trying to melt my brain with sound waves.

"Sure, Ecaterina. How about next week?"

"Why not now, Dr. Jackson?"

"Can't it wait?"

"Okay. See you then." And gently cradles the receiver.

Whew. Well, I got one out of two to come in. And now for the best call. I get to contact Jerry Smith, the great outpatient Sandra has found for me.

"Hello, is this Jerry Smith? This is Dr. Max Jackson at Asylum calling. I understand you wanted to set up an appointment."

"That's right. I'm sort of depressed."

"How about next Monday at four?"

"I'll be there. How will I know where you are?"

"I'll find you. Meet me in the lobby."

Don't want to freak out now. Have to keep things in perspective. Too many patients and too much to do. But don't want to forget the important things, like Zoe and preventing nuclear war. Must concentrate on positive fantasies. "Fairy tales can come true . . ."

Shirley certainly believes this. Schizophrenia is not going to keep her from fantasizing that she can have anything she wants. She's so wrapped up in her delusions about the Russians and the electrodes in her head and how obeying the commands is the only way she'll ever get what she wants that it's only a tiny step to her believing anything else a person could say. Skinny as a rail, her dreams are bigger than can be imagined by me. And she won't accept reality until it all comes true. She's reading books upside down and talking in giggles and snorts. She varies from silly to sad and is angry at me today because I went away this weekend and took a day off.

Simon is on his way to being better. He still has nothing good to say to me, but what the heck. No more screaming, no more "You murderer," no more disasters in day hospital. He is getting even fatter, which I would not have thought was possible. But I'll take it. It's strange how he has my hopes so high. Maybe those medications do something.

Neither Shirley nor Simon wants to juggle, so I have to make up my group from other patients. I walk into the dayroom and shout out, "Who wants to juggle?" No one moves. "Come on. It's a great activity. Anyone can do it." Still no movement, so I start to implore. "Just come and watch. I'll show you a few tricks." A few people stir so I throw out the key line, "Maybe we can plan a field trip." The offer of an activity that will get them out of the hospital for a day is a mighty big incentive and three brave souls get up to join me. As we go off together I inform them, "You're going to have a great time. You'll be juggling in a week." Even if they don't, I'll have a good time. Anyway, this is a potential for a success experience, which can't be a bad thing.

Unless only the doctor feels like a success, since all the three of them want to do is watch me. So at least I can hope my act is better than reading *Time* magazine. And it makes me feel good.

I'm through almost a quarter of the year. At home I curl up by the wood stove. I've just finished stoking the thing and can feel the heat, as well as a fine smell pouring out. And the fire provides a soothing antidote to the stimulation of the day. I wonder if I hate my job. It's ugly. It's horrible, it's stupid. But I'm not sure if any of that is relevant. I dream of Oregon, of cool breezes and hot sun, but my mind sails back to a cool autumn and where I am. The future seems more real. I'm not sure why this is, but it is difficult to discount the job. Now if I only knew what it was about the job that drew me to it. The pain and the nightmares are real enough. But there is more to the landscape than that.

"You know, Zoe," I murmur as we lay down to sleep, "I'm pretty confused about my work. It has so many bizarre twists and turns to it."

"You could use a day off."

"I really could. But I don't have vacation for a while. No rest for the weary."

"Will this be a good week coming up?"

"I hope so. We always have our resident group. I can blow off some steam there. Hopefully someone else will take most of the heat."

"I'm glad," she says, closing her eyes. "You need a few more good days."

In our resident meeting I bring up the issue of difficulties in telling doctor-patient relationships from person-person relationships. Denise asks, "How do you know what your patients are getting out of relationships with you? That seems a bit presumptuous." She is angry and disgusted. "You're the one who gave them the label of patient."

"Now wait a second," I respond. "I didn't give them the label, I'm trying to get past it."

"Well, you'll never get there by assuming you know what kind of relationship they want."

"I don't understand."

"You've got to be you. If you act like a doctor then your patient has to choose a role to take. If they want to be a patient, then it's you who seems to feel the pressure."

"But I just want to act like a person and have them act like a person, too."

"But all people are different," Eric chimes in. He seems frustrated by my inability to understand. Leaning forward in his seat he says, "You want them to act like your friends, but that's as artificial as doctor-patient. You just have another role in mind." He leans back.

Nancy, who rarely speaks, leans forward now. She is so quiet that we all have to strain to hear her. "If you can be yourself," she whispers, "the patients will be themselves. If that's not happening, then you have to look within yourself."

"You mean all this suffering is my fault?" I raise my voice in anger. "How dare I presume? Is that the question?"

Denise is furious by now. "Why do you always have to be such an extremist? Why don't you just find the medium that makes you happy?" She lowers her voice. "Just be yourself and accept yourself for who you are. Both your patients and your friends will benefit."

What, pray tell is happening here? All I wanted was a little help and I'm getting attacked. This really stinks. Maybe I have some problems, but who wants to hear about it all the time?

Luckily, my beeper goes off which takes my mind off the current hassles as I swear to myself and leave the room.

Bobby finds me later, tall, dark and handsome Bobby, a fellow resident and someone I barely know. Rounds have ended and we're talking about things. He asks me, "Max, how have things been with Simon lately? Have the meds helped?"

"What do you mean?" I can feel myself getting defensive.

"You just waited so long to start them. Are they doing any good?"

And the anger in me, anger I didn't know was there, comes to a boil. "Damn, Bobby! What the hell is this? Why won't you leave me alone. He's my patient! I'll do whatever I want to!"

"Whoa, Max. Slow it down. I'm just asking."

Hanging my head, I mumble an apology thinking, "What just happened?"

"You got pissed off."

"I know that," I say with a snap, and then catch Bobby smiling at me.

"What's so funny?" I ask.

"Calm down, Max. We're all having lots of problems here. You don't have to suffer all alone."

We stand there in silence for a moment and he turns to me and says, "You want a ride home?" I gladly agree. And I realize again how little I know him, although we've been working together for months.

All the way home he talks about wanting to get to spend time together, of carpooling and mostly of being friends.

"Bobby," I said, sitting in the front seat of his car. We had been stopped in front of my house for fifteen minutes, enjoying a quiet moment. "This is very important to me. I like the people at work, but I don't feel very close to them. It seems too dangerous to get close."

"I know what you mean. We're all working hard and we all want many of the same things and it's an awfully tough year. But I'd like to give it a try. I need some help, too."

"What is it about that place that makes us so isolated from one another?"

"I've got a lot of theories," he says, "but I'm really not sure. We value our work and we're all competitive and we've been pushing so long to get it. But it sure would be more fun to share the experience."

"Did Sandra set you up to this?" I ask.

"No, of course not. Why?"

"It's not important. She thinks I cut myself off from others too easily. That I don't allow myself the friendship that's available." I reach for the door handle and start to leave. "Thanks, Bobby."

"I'll see you tomorrow."

As I walk in the front door I grab Zoe and give her a big hug and a kiss. "I think I made a new friend today."

She kisses me back. "That's great Max. Who is it?"

I sit her down on my lap. "Bobby. One of the residents. He's a nice guy. He gave me a lot of help today." I described the horror show that had occurred in group and the pleasant aftermath.

"It sounds like you did okay."

"I still felt pretty bad." I've got my jacket off and kick my shoes in the corner.

She rubs my temples and holds me close and says, "So what if it's all true? Maybe you are competitive and angry, but I love you the way you are."

"I know, Zoe. But you're different."

"Oh, yeah. I have two heads? I bet most people have similar feelings to you in this process. And I bet one of the most common is that you have to do it all alone. Except you don't. Anyway, you're going to be a great psychiatrist."

"Thanks, love." We collapse together on the sofa and I put my head in her lap. "I really want that."

In my dream that night I am at a party, dancing with Zoe. She takes me by the hand and we get into a canoe and start paddling down a river. The river slowly fills up with canoes and soon becomes so crowded that we can no longer move. And the boat in front of us catches fire and the fire starts leaping from boat to boat and there is no way to get out except to jump in the water and I don't remember if I can swim. Zoe leaps in and laughingly calls out to me as screams start to rise from the canoes all around me. I stand up and leap and awake holding on to Zoe, vaguely at ease.

"Love," I nudge her.

"Yes, sweetheart?"

"I think I'm starting to get the hang of this stuff now."

"That's nice," she says. And drifts back to sleep.

3

Acting Out

Jerry Smith is quite easy to pick out in the lobby. For one, his sense of unease just standing amidst the madness made it quite apparent that this is his first trip. If there had been a riot going on it is unlikely his semiglazed look would have changed. This was a seriously frightened man. Indeed, given his sport coat, tie, horn-rimmed glasses and penny loafers, he had good reason to be afraid. After all, one goes into law school for the express purpose of not having to deal with people like those found at Asylum. However, he hadn't made it yet, so I was all too happy to welcome him to the state system. Where we provide good care for less. But not cheap.

"Hi. Jerry Smith?"

"Oh! Good!" He moves close to me and looks relieved. "You must be Dr. Jackson."

"Right. Glad to meet you." We shake hands and I suggest, "Let's go up to my office."

He still seems tense so I decide to give him some good news. "It's away from all the madness."

Having regained his composure, he responds, "That's not necessary. I don't mind this."

"I do. I'm glad we'll have a quieter place to talk."

We've started to do a weird sort of dance that is new to me. Generally, when a patient is admitted to the hospital and to me, we're stuck together whether we like it or not. Now, we both get to choose. So I want him to like me and my hospital or, at least, understand, and he wants to impress me, too. None of this, "I can be as crazy as I want to." Quite the opposite. A real covering over of any anxiety. Except, as always, it doesn't really work.

As we sit in my office, I say, "I hope you weren't waiting too long for me."

He smooths his hair back and fidgets a bit. "No. Not too long. That's sort of a strange lobby. When you told me to wait there . . ." He trails off.

"Not what you expected?"

"This place is a madhouse!" he blurts out.

I laugh a little, then catch myself as this seems to make him more nervous. "Was it frightening?"

"Well," he says, "is that what I'll look like if I come to see you?" He pulls out a cigarette and taps it on my desk.

"That all depends. Why did you come?"

"I'm not sure. Things haven't been going too well for me lately. I've been sort of unhappy." He puts the cigarette back in the pack and sits on his hands.

"Tell me about it."

"I've been thinking about my feelings all week. I guess I'm feeling lonely, although I'm not really sure. I mean I guess I'm always lonely and I don't want to be. It's just that it's so hard." He stops and looks up at me. I nod and smile and respond, "It's so hard?"

"I just don't understand why I don't meet more people. I'm so tired of leading an isolated life. I don't know how to get to know anybody. I've been this way my whole life."

"Why don't we try to focus in on what is so bad right now. You seem to be in a lot of pain."

"Well, all I ever do is just go to school and go to the library and then I go out jogging and then I go to sleep."

"And this is worse now?"

"It's not worse, it just won't get better." He starts to sniffle and reaches for the tissues. His face twists as he tries to hold back the tears but they start to leak out, first a trickle and then he is crying buckets of tears. After a few minutes he slows down and looks imploringly. "I'm just so unhappy."

"That's an awful feeling to have."

"I sit alone at night and read or else take a walk but I can't ever seem to get my mind off how sad I am." He starts to cry again and reaches for the whole tissue box. He is actually an attractive man, with a pleasant face and nice hands. There is certainly nothing about him physically that would keep him from other people. He is even able to smile after his tears as he pulls himself together.

"You know," he says, "I haven't cried in years. My father always told me not to cry. He was really a very good father, but he didn't like to see me cry. Is this the sort of thing I'm supposed to talk about in therapy? My father and stuff?"

"It sure sounds important."

"It is important. I owe everything to him." And he starts crying again. I may not get a lot of information this session, but at least the emotion is honest. And he's talking. Anyway, I'd love to have a patient who can tell me about his father and stuff. Although I don't think I'll tell Jerry that right off.

"Tell me about him."

And on we go into the session as Jerry tells me about his father, a lawyer, and his mother, a nurse, and his three siblings and his relationships with them when he was young and the bout his mother had with drugs and how driven he has felt to succeed and on and on. And while I still don't know why he's depressed and sad I at least know a lot about his past and his present and figure we got something to work on here.

I notice that our time is up and mention so. Jerry wipes his eyes again and says, "Thanks. Will I see you next week?"

"I'll be here. We can talk about setting up a regular schedule then, if you want to."

"Oh. I want to continue. I'll see you next week."

Whooppee!

I look up over my desk so I can see Herr Freud, Sigmund the Great, First Ruler of the Kingdom of the Unconscious. All Hail, King Sigmund, conqueror of the mighty mind, explainer of the impulses, ruler of the primitive drives! All Hail, King Sigmund, master of ego, master of id! The picture of Herr Freud adorning my office wall is an etching that has many little Sigmunds imbedded in a larger one. Sort of like the picture of a person holding a picture of the person holding a picture and so on. Except the good doctor doesn't need hands to hold his picture. Besides, if he's really looking down all he's going to see is a huge mess, the accumulated paperwork of four months of undone charts and letters and process notes on sessions with patients and so on. But oh, what a wonderful session that was with Jerry. Therapy. Real live therapy.

"Zoe? I had to call you. I just had a great session with my new patient."

"Terrific, Max. Did you cure him?"

"Not yet. But I'm getting close."

"Wonderful. I bet you're the best therapist that ever lived."

"Aw shucks. Maybe the second best," I say, looking up at Siggy.

"Oh no. You're number one. And I love you. Don't forget to get dinner on the way home."

"Shouldn't we go out and celebrate?"

"You're mad," she says, and blowing kisses, signs off.

And oh how I'd like to just sit there, but duty calls. Simon is waiting for me in day hospital, just outside my door.

He looks better, Simon does. His massive girth is covered in clothes instead of rags. His hair has been cut neatly and the wild-eyed look is a thing of the past. Of course, it's been replaced by a face covered in sadness. But finally, we can have a real conversation. All it took was months.

"Hi, Dr. Jackson."

"Hello, Simon, how are you?"

He sits in the office, throws his sax and music on the desk, adjusts his bulk to get into the seat and puts his head in his hands. "I'm incredibly busy. The band awaits me. There's so much to do. And I get so depressed that I eat all day sometimes."

"It sounds like things have been pretty hard." How brilliant. He starts to cry and looks around my office for a tissue, which unfortunately Jerry has finished off. I never thought that therapy would move this quickly. I expected much more time before patients got all teary on me. But as an experienced outpatient therapist, I need to deal with this now. Simon had started to take his meds regularly and within a week was out of the intensive care unit and back down in day hospital. Pretty soon he may be an outpatient, too. How about that?

"Zoe," I ask, "what do you think love is?"

She looks totally dynamite as we sit on the sofa, our feet in each other's lap, our conversation diverted from the day's activities. "I think it's when one person tries to fill up all the holes in another."

"You mean I can fix you and you can fix me? That sounds magical."

"Well, that's what love is. It's magic."

"Sometimes I think my patients want me to fill up all the holes in their lives. Is that love?"

"Are you going to do it?"

"I don't think I can. All I can do is help them do it themselves."

"Then you are showing them how to love themselves. That's a form of love."

"I guess so. I like this kind an awful lot."

"You can have both, you know." She wiggles her toes and stretches out. We yawn together and she smiles. "Teach your patients that."

I could tell by the way the phone rang that it had to be Sandra, about to ruin a good day. And it was. I was about to meet Tam Luck. Tam Luck, a little Vietnamese refugee. Tam, who had been living in a refugee camp in Thailand for seven years, finally came to America, oh America yearning to be free, and then went crazy. He had come with his brother, hoping to bring his family over later, but instead it is his brother Ho, who is bringing Tam to us. Sandra says, "Max, I've got an admission for you. Could be an interesting case." This is a code phrase in the medical profession that means, "You're in trouble." I tense, then sigh, then ask Sandra to, "Tell me about it."

"Well," she says, "do you speak Vietnamese?" This is a pretty silly question, but I can see where we're headed. "Of course not. I went to medical school. Do I look like an Asian studies major?" I tap my pen a few times on the desk. I hate getting admissions. I despise them. And this one only speaks Vietnamese? "Well, Max, I'm sorry. He does speak a little French, too. At least when he speaks." Sandra manages to get a little sympathy in her voice as she presents this to me. But there is also an undercurrent of, "Don't give me any backtalk, I hate this part of it, too."

So off I go to meet my new wunderkind. He looks like a character from a horror movie, only forty years too young. He's the crazy old uncle who sits in the back room and cackles anytime someone goes in there. Thin as a rail, his eyes empty, standing rigidly in the hall, he is twelve going on sixty-two. But I know that he is twenty-eight and has been like this for almost a year. When he speaks it is babble. Babble in any language. So here I am. Lourdes sprung to life. It's great to see the confidence he has in me.

To be totally truthful, I wasn't Tam's first choice. After months of searching for private hospitals, he has already discovered one of the American medical truths. It costs a lot of money and if you don't have it you end up in a state hospital. Which I don't think is so bad if what you want is good care. But it is rarely the dream of a foreign visitor to spend their time there. Nonetheless, he is here and so am I so all three of us sit down with a friend of theirs to talk together.

For hours Tam just sat there and didn't say a word. Just giggled uncontrollably and ran around some. Otherwise his brother shouted at me in Vietnamese and French while his brother's friend tried to put it into English which he had learned from a few soldiers and I tried to sort out four voices at once, with the English one being only marginally more understandable to me. I felt like I was on Ellis Island. At long last I had enough information and history to admit Tam, but no idea what to do about him. He looked like a destitute homeless man, totally out of touch with me and the world. Sam says that a chronic, long-term psychosis is a bad sign but we have to try our best. Nonetheless, I suspect this will not be the most satisfying case of my short career. Oh well, as long as Tam is mute, who cares what language he isn't speaking.

And then it's up to day hospital for him. Like the rest of the hospital, it looks like time has passed it by. The couches are WWII surplus and the patients remain so deep in personal tragedy that it might as well be a prison camp as well as look like one. Everyone complains all the time about how it looks here, but if it was the Taj Mahal it wouldn't make any difference. The air of despair is just too heavy. Maybe one in three of these folks will make it out of here with their lives intact. The rest are looking at a long-term disaster. Imagine yourself, or myself in that position.

"Hi there, Mr. Jackson. I'm afraid that you have a lifelong debilitating illness that won't kill you but will make it impossible for you to work, turn you into a social outcast and a pauper, and everyone you know will pretend you have died. Oh yes. And by the way, you will be in pain every moment of your life. Now, do you have any questions?"

The first thing that anyone in a mental hospital does is deny that there is any reason for them to be there. And who can blame them? If you walked onto the ward and saw Tam on his first day, here's what you'd get.

Speaking no English would normally be considered a nasty drawback to psychotherapy in America, but these are not normal times. After about five minutes on the ward Tam decides he's had enough. So he tries to leave. Unfortunately, since his brother is sure that Tam will die without supervision, I suspect that his leaving may not be such a good plan. So we grab him. And on and on the day goes, with Tam running around and all the chickens trying to catch him. Somehow, this didn't fit into my idea of what psychotherapy should be. Only one thing to do at this point. I called up Sam and said, "You better get up here fast. My patient is really acting up. You've got to do something soon." To which he said, "Tam is your patient. Do whatever you have to. Just don't cause any problems." Damn! So Tam goes to the ICU. Another therapeutic success.

But if I'm going to be a therapist, I've got to feel a little more empowered. That's the word for now—empowerment. Of course, I could ask, "Empowered to do what?" Change things, I suppose. Find a new mantra. "Do what works."

Some mantra, eh? This, of course, doesn't really work. But it does make me feel a little more in control. So I go to exercise tonight. Nautilus will clear the body and soul, if not the mind. Everyone at Nautilus looks so healthy. Look at those muscles bulge. Look at everyone lifting huge weights and tossing them around. The men have that macho look so favored in magazines and who knows where else. The *GQ* look without clothes. The women are pretty tough, too. People converse there. Mostly they talk about running marathons or taking large doses of steroids or of drinking too much over the weekend. Real life. Real people. I find it hard to start a conversation. "Hi. I couldn't help noticing that you're three times my size. Is this to compensate for a deep feeling of insecurity that can only be mastered by an external display of masculine prowess?" Do I really want to get punched in the head? But it can be hard to turn off the interpretation model.

As when I turn to Zoe and say, "Maybe you're angry due to your anxiety over your application to medical school." This comment is offered in the most soothing voice that I've got.

Zoe looks like she's been struck in the face. Recoiling in anger she fixes a baleful glare at me. "Well, thank you, friend." She takes a deep breath and spits the words out at me. "Maybe I'm angry because the only thing you talk about is the loony bin." She walks away from me and then whirls back. "Maybe I am having my own issues now and am sick and tired of hearing about Asylum." She starts to sniffle and I realize that I've messed up but can't quite figure where. Zoe never gets that angry unless I've punched the same button too many times. I try again.

"Wait, Zoe. It's my life, and I'm just getting used to it and it's important to me." I've tried the empathic approach. Let's see if it works.

"Stop it! Don't try any of your psychiatric mind games on me. I'm not one of your damn patients! How dare you interpret my anger!" Her eyes are dancing in the light and I want to say how beautiful you look when you're angry. Somehow I hold back. "You better leave the job at the nuthouse and treat me like your wife and lover and friend. If I want a psychiatrist I'll go find one. What I want from you is your respect and understanding."

Lying in bed at night I roll over to make spoons. "You were pretty sore at me tonight," I say, showing all the intuition that has made me a great therapist.

The anger gone now, Zoe is able to grin and murmurs in my ear, "I'm worried that you'll like psychiatry so much that you'll try to change your personality to be a better psychiatrist. I like you the way you are."

I snuggle in a little closer and say, "It's just so hard to turn off." I sigh. "I don't want to be a therapist in the house, either."

"I have a suggestion then," Zoe tells me. "Stop talking about psychiatry in bed." She turns into a fork and goes to sleep.

In my dream I am in a car riding in the country. Zoe is next to me and we are looking at new homes on the block. We go into one and it is filled with new furniture. I look around to ask Zoe a question but she isn't there. A salesman appears and tries to talk me into buying the whole place. The room starts to fill up with things and then it all starts to melt. I grab a brass hourglass but all the sand falls to the floor and the hourglass melts in my hand. My hand starts to burn and I am back in the car with Zoe riding toward the woods.

At work today I got another admission. Does this go on forever? So now I have Benny as a patient. Actually, he should be referred to as nothing less than, "the incredible Benny." Possessor of the best delusional system in town. Benny thinks he's George Washington and is dressed in full Revolutionary War garb. When Benny reads, "George Washington slept here," he wonders when. Right now he's particularly upset because Benedict Arnold seems to have disappeared with the war budget and the British are attacking. Now this wouldn't be so terrible for anyone except for one minor problem. Benny is pretty sure that his mother has seduced old Benedict into this plot. And this makes Benny awfully angry at his mama. Now I don't know what General Arnold would want with Mom and the money, but I do know one thing about Benny. He's nobody's fool. He's been trying to get away from his family for years and threatening his mother as a spy certainly has gotten him out of the house. Although he could have just asked. After all, he is the father of our country. As he tells me over and over.

I've started to like crazy people. I don't know if I should be worried about that or be glad. Wanda is a case in point. Wanda is the last of the hippies. Long straggly hair, granny glasses, ratty blue jeans, a big woman, always flashing the peace sign or giving you the raised fist. Wanda hears voices. Lots of them. By last count she's got at least eight friends who share her head with her. Mostly Wanda works as a janitor and has a little apartment and does okay. But when the world gets a bit too much, Wanda flips out. And moves into her own private world of friends. It's not such a bad way to go. She came in to visit us this week after a man made a pass at her, which was a lot of stimulation for such a quiet lady.

I walk on over. "Hey, Wanda. How are things?" She turns toward me and gazes toward space. "Ah, that's right, yes, the department will get right on that, yes, I'll have all the cars moved, ah, I'm fine. How are you?" She flashes me a gigantic grin, terribly pleased that she figured out which question came from me, and which from the others.

"Well," I tell her, "it sounds like things are okay." How the hell would I know?

She looks over my shoulder and starts muttering. Then she stares right at me and asks, "Can you refer me to the governor?"

This is a new one. "What's that, Wanda?" She smiles again and motions to a chair with her foot. "The mayor will get the chief . . ." She breaks off suddenly and shouts over my shoulder, "I've told you a million times, not while I'm having a conversation!"

She turns back to me and says, "Move that car. I'll be seeing you." And she walks away muttering.

"Dr. Jackson! Call Security STAT! Dr. Jackson!" Like a nagging mother reminding me it's time for school, the paging system jars me from a quite beautiful sleep. I had been dreaming of Hawaii and luaus and such and was about to have a big dish of poi when BOOM! "Dr. Jackson! Dr. Jackson!" What a bummer. I'm out of bed snarling furious when I can't get enough sleep and you never get enough sleep when you're on call. So I snarl. No one better get in my way, or I'll try to eat them alive. Angry? Who me? Just a healthy reaction to stress and being awoken to the awful feeling that something terrible is about to happen. I look like a mess, right out of bed. Oh well at least it's an excuse not to shave today. What's awaiting me of such crucial importance is Tam Luck, who has just punched out the lights of another patient. Not bad for a tiny little man. But rather than admire his boxing prowess, I have been called to deal with this act of aggression. I grab Tam by the arm, trying hard not to ruffle his feelings or clothes, and sit him on a chair.

"Tam," I say, "what is going on here?" He looks at me with an idiot's grin and vacant eyes. I try again. "Why . . . did . . . you . . . punch . . . her?" This is my idiot's trick. If they can't speak English, talk slower. That would surely work if someone was explaining Greek to me. So I try a different tack. "Tam," I say, "no hit. No hit!" And I mimic hitting myself in the head. Tam Luck is no dummy. Insane, perhaps, but no dummy. So he kicks me in the shins and runs away. I call in some shock troops and off we all go running down the hall after him. Imagine.

A skinny little man in black pajamas is being chased through the halls of the world's oldest living hospital by an unshaven man in his white pajamas and two huge men who look like they just got cut by the Green Bay Packers. My first thought is, "Who would I help in this picture?" My second thought is, "Why am I involved in this chase?" So I yell to my cohorts, "Go get him," and I return to my office to sit down. I make a muscle in order to prove to myself that all those weeks of Nautilus haven't been in vain and collapse in my chair. What a way to start a morning. My leg hurts. But at least I have missed rounds. Now I can get some breakfast and shave and then maybe half the morning will have gone by.

"Dr. Jackson! Dr. Jackson! Call the operator STAT!" My feet come down off the desk as my hand goes to the phone. At this point the only thought in my head is, "What is it this time?" I know that it can't be good news. So I call the operator. Tilly answers. She's a great operator who tries her best to help me avoid the craziness, sitting as she does in one of the hospital command seats. She's got a real nice voice, which is good, cause I never get to see what she looks like.

"Max, honey," she drawls out in a transplanted Georgia accent. "You better get down to the clinic right away. All sort of hell is breaking loose there."

"Thanks, Tilly," I mumble and head off down the hall. I reach up to scratch my face and confirm that I still look like I just woke up and that my current appearance will convey to all concerned just what a hard worker I am. Maybe I should grow a beard.

Ecaterina stands before me. Being held by two policemen. She's a mess. She looks like she's been dragged through a giant mud puddle and left to dry on a hot plate. Her dress is ripped, her earrings gone. Her eye is black, although I can't tell if it's dirt or injury. She hasn't lost her voice.

"Dr. Jackson! Make them let go of me! They tore my clothes!" She gestures to herself in case I haven't noticed. "Now they're hurting me!"

I turn to the officers and ask, "What happened?"

Like police officers in general, they are a bit unnerved at being around mental patients. (Mental patients know this, too.) "Well," one replies, "we found her by the docks, a knife poised above her heart, screaming that she was gonna kill herself."

He stares up at the ceiling, then continues. "She looked like this when we found her. She won't tell us where she's been. She keeps shouting about her rights." The whole tale out, the police look at each other, then their eyes start to wander over the other patients. Coming back to me, he asks, "Can we get out of here, now?"

Ty, the Asylum policeman has arrived. "Hey, Max," he booms, "what have we here? Looks like you let one of them get away."

"Thanks, Ty. I need a hard time. Can we let these guys go now?" The police look pleadingly at Ty. He's got the build of a wide receiver and a nightstick as long as my arm and a smile that borders on diabolical. No question about it. Ty has the right job. "Sure, Max. Let 'em go. We can handle it."

Ecaterina doesn't like this plan. "They can't go. I'm going to sue them. Look at what they did to me! I'm an important person!" And so on. I tell them they can go.

Ty also takes off and Ecaterina and I go to my office. We look like two bums fresh off a park bench. "Can you believe this, Dr. Jackson? Look at what they did to me! I'm a mess."

"What happened, Ecaterina? You do look like a mess."

"I'm hungry. Look at my dress. They ripped it."

"Ecaterina! What is going on!? We were supposed to meet for an outpatient session today. This isn't how I expected you to show up."

"I told you what happened!"

"Tell me again."

"They hurt me. Look at what those officers did to my clothes. My wrists hurt, too. I should sue them. I can, you know."

"What happened?"

"Dr. Jackson, I was suicidal! Are you stupid? Can't you understand anything?"

"You were suicidal?"

"I'm not now, I'm upset. Wouldn't you be? Look at what those two men did to me. I'm bleeding." She looks down at her knee and notices that she is in fact bleeding and starts to cry. I give her a tissue from my recently purchased box and sigh.

"Ecaterina," I start, "do you think you better stay in the hospital tonight?" It's more a suggestion than a question.

"Why should I? I'm okay. Except that those policemen beat me up. I have important friends. They're in a lot of trouble." She starts sniffling again.

"Why don't you stay here tonight, Ecaterina? It'll be safer that way. No one can hurt you here." She nods her head and I hope that I'll find out some other day what the hell is going on here.

It's lunchtime now and a chance to sneak away from all this mess and grab a bite. As I turn toward the coffee shop, I feel a tap on my shoulder that I, unfortunately, recognize. And I know without turning around that Sandra has bad news for me. "Max," she starts out in her soft voice, "let's talk in my office." Shades of the bad boy at the principal's office flash through my head, but when we arrive Sandra looks as helpless as I feel. "It's about Benny," she begins.

"Benny who?" I interrupt. I plop down in a chair and put my feet up on her desk. She's got some little candies and I start sucking them down. Any port in a storm.

"Your new chronic patient, Benny," she begins again. Now I remember. Valley Forge and all that. "I've got bad news, Max. Do you know where Benny is?"

The suspense is killing me. "Of course not. I barely know who Benny is."

"Well . . ." she starts. I can see this is going to take all day. "Tell me Sandra!" I shout.

She takes a breath and says in one gulp, "Benny's in jail. He shot his mother in the legs."

I spit my candy on the floor. "Sandra, I just can't take it anymore. This is too crazy. What the hell did he do that for?"

"He said his mother was a countersubversive trying to prevent the victory of the American forces and needed to be stopped." She starts to smile when the words come out.

"He kneecapped his mother to prevent the British from winning the Revolutionary War?" I can't help smiling a little, too.

She breaks into a big grin at this point and between half-formed giggles and snickers says, "The worst thing is," and by now she is laughing, "he shot up his life-size bust of GW by mistake! It's ruined!" Both of us convulse in laughter and tears on the floor of Sandra's office like a pair of baboons and all the while I'm thinking, "What the hell is so funny about Benny being in jail while his mother is in the hospital?" Then I give it up and laugh some more. If there is one thing I've learned this year it's that there is no way to understand another person's human condition.

And that certainly would be a full day for anyone except at 3:54 P.M., six minutes before the cutoff point, I am again to hear, "Dr. Jackson, call the clinic, STAT!" Yes, it's another admission for yours truly. It's Hymie again, calling himself "an American patriot." I bring him to the ICU and he's swearing all the way. "You goddam young whippersnappers. I've got a good mind to throw you all in the brig and do away with the lot of you." He starts kicking the side of the elevator and screaming some more about those fascist bastards when he suddenly spins on me and asks, "When do you plan to kill me, you shit?"

"Not to worry," I reply. "I'll take you somewhere where you'll be safe. You're with the underground now. Everything is fine."

Hymie eyes me, letting his gaze wander around the elevator, then makes up his mind. "Are you an American?"

"You bet I am, Hymie. And no dirty fascists are going to get me either."

"That's what I told them at the nursing home," he reveals.

Yes, Hymie, I know. Right before you set fire to it.

I know what psychiatry is now. It's a process where disaster management keeps people out of jail and worse. Today I had to seclude Tam. We caught him drinking out of a punch bowl. And when we tried to pull him out, he pushed his head under and tried to drown. Then he ran through the unit naked, yelling God only knows what in Vietnamese and then punched another patient. Isn't American medicine wonderful? Boy, his brother must be real glad he brought him here.

Bitch, bitch, bitch. When does it end? I thought I was going to be an adult now and put all this in the past.

"Zoe," I say, as I collapse on the couch, "this was the worst day of my life." She doesn't respond and I look her way. She's sitting motionless, her face dragging on the floor, eyes wide open, but nothing seems to be going in. "Helloooo in there," I try, but still no response. Once again, "Hi, Zoe. What's going on?"

With a tense smile she responds, "Ace, I'm pretty tired of hearing about how terrible your days are. I'm scared to death about medical school and I haven't been able to tell you about it."

"Well, tell me."

"Fred called today. He got in." Fred is a friend from way back who is also applying to medical school. Or I should say, who just got into medical school. "When will I ever get in?"

"Don't worry, sweetie, it'll be soon. Someday you'll be able to have all this fun, too."

"That's just it. I don't want to have fun just like you. Somedays I think you love being a doctor and other days you seem to hate it."

"Well," I start, and then stop to think. "That's mostly true. I do like being a shrink. It's interesting and fascinating and I get to help people and all that. But sometimes I get so tired."

She makes a sniffling noise and asks, "But why? What's so good about it?"

"What's good about it is that it's good for me."

"But what makes psychiatry so different from medicine? You used to hate that all the time."

"It's different because what you do with your day is different. I spend my days with patients, not looking at lab tests. I spend my conferences discussing the meaning of life and reality, not the meaning of nasal polyps. Psychiatry is like medicine for philosophers. Sort of the doctor equivalent of "Rocks for Jocks.""

Looking puzzled, Zoe inquires, "Then why do you say you hate it so often?"

"Well, it's not easy. The pain you deal with is so great that you turn to despair or humor. Trying to confront how horrible it must be to be so sick is almost inconceivable. And all you do all day long is try to help people confront how sick they are. Everyone you work with is under the same pressures you are and there seems to be no one to turn to to express the frustration of wanting so much to help people and finding that so often the disease is beyond your control. That's one reason I like Simon so much: he's getting better."

"That's all bullshit, Max."

"What is?" I'm outraged.

"It's all intellectual stuff. What's really going on?"

"I don't know," I sigh. "It just feels right. Even with the pain, I sort of like it."

Zoe ponders this. "I don't want to be a doctor if it's going to be so much agony. I remember when you were an intern that I thought you were going to die half the days."

"Psychiatry is nothing like that. Not only did I abhor internal medicine, but the hours made it ungodly. Or maybe it was the combination of the two. But whatever it was it was awful. This is nothing like that. This stinks only when I let it get to me. And sometimes I have to let it get to me because I realize that these are people who are in so much pain. And that makes me sad. But the nice part is that I get to feel."

"Then why do you always come home shouting that you want to tear someone's lungs out or smash beer bottles on your head? It really doesn't sound like too much fun."

"Well . . . it's not much fun. But I like myself when I do this and that counts an awful lot."

"Only to ten. I like you all the time. You don't need some dumb old job to like yourself. Do you think I'll get into medical school?"

"Of course you will." I take her in my arms. "How else will I ever be able to have you understand this if you don't live it yourself?"

"No way, Max. This is enough of living it for me. I want to take care of people's bodies and give them herbs and things. And deal with the physical as well as the mental."

"Is that a hint?" She reaches up and takes my face in both hands.

"Let's see if we can squeeze some feelings into that head of yours. Too much intellectualizing spoils your health."

Every morning we all meet in the ICU for the morning report. This is a time when we go over all the patients and their ills. It is also the time when staff gets to interact with one another. We sit there in a circle. The room is as bleak as the rest of the hospital and the walls are decorated with crayon drawings by the patients. Crayon. I guess you can't stab yourself with a crayon. Everyone wants to talk about Tam, who is now in a locked seclusion room after kicking three patients. Irwin opens it up.

"You know, we work very hard up here." It's easy to tell that this will not be a totally factual account. Irwin is not a very factual person. Straight out of the 1950s high school yearbook picture, his main technique for accomplishment is to bore in first and then apply thumbscrews. He sways in his seat with excitement as the charge of battle rushes through his system.

"I certainly believe that," I counter, as my first move.

Irwin parries. "It's horrible to work in a place where you are in danger all the time."

I counter and thrust. "This must be a very difficult place to be when it fills you with torment."

The attack is recognized and he falls back to regroup. "It's hard because of the patients and all the torment they are in."

"I certainly agree." And I smile. Perhaps the exchange is now over. But no luck.

"If we got a little more support up here from the doctors and social workers, things might go a little bit more smoothly for everyone."

"What exactly is the specific problem we're talking about?" I try to shift the field of action.

"Tam is unmanageable. He runs away when we approach him and needs to be secluded all the time."

"It must be frustrating to work with someone who doesn't understand you. Makes the whole process of setting limits so much harder." I sort of wish that Sandra or Sam would step in soon and deflect a bit of this conversation. It's rapidly escalating and I have to work with these people for a long time. But again, no luck.

Irwin thrusts. "What we are lacking is a cohesive treatment plan for this patient. No one seems to know why he is here or what we are doing." Actually, not a bad point. Although I'm in too much of a fighting mood to pay much attention to anything besides affect.

"And," I say, "when we don't know what we're doing, we seclude the patient?" Oops. That was below the belt. But, dammit! I feel it. At least it hits home.

Irwin becomes furious. He looks over at the head nurse for support and, when none is forthcoming, stands up and yells, "We seclude him because there is nothing else to do with him!" He flushes and sits.

Continuing to disobey the first rule of psychiatry, I reply, "And I guess it's easy to seclude a tiny little man who won't fight back." Never, but never, interpret the affect.

Luckily, Irwin is being literal and replies, "It takes three strong men to do it!"

Sandra finally steps in and says, "Why don't we talk this over later on. Maybe in team."

The whole room gives a collective sigh and we move on. But it won't leave my mind and as I seethe around the hospital Sam taps me on the shoulder and says, "Why don't we go to my office for a moment?"

Sam is wearing a three-piece gray suit. He's dressed for success. He looks at his watch, gold, and tells me, "I've got ten minutes." How he can figure this out is beyond me, since his watch is always set fifteen minutes fast. Must drive his patients bananas. Maybe it's a stress test. In a quiet voice, Sam says, "You seemed pretty angry today." Oh yeah? What a surprise to hear that.

"Please, Sam! Don't analyze or interpret me! What do you have to say to me?" I look up at the clock, but there is no way to tell how much more time I have to sit there.

Sam can't help himself. Always answer a question with a question. "What's going on between you and the ICU staff? I've heard some angry reports and this morning's interaction with Irwin was very unpleasant."

"Hell, Sam. He's tough. I can't deal with his passive-aggressive bullshit. They treat Tam like a dog 'cause he's easier to push around than the murderers on the unit and they claim that I'm sabotaging their great therapeutic effort." Having said my piece it sounds a bit more hollow than I had hoped.

"Well, Max, the staff may have some problems, but it seems to me that your feelings are overtaking your ability to work well with the rest of the team." Sam leans back, looks at his watch and waits for me.

"Look, Sam. I'm tired and overworked and I want to be a good psychiatrist but I don't have the energy to cope with a staff that won't work with me. I get along just fine with staff members who want to be part of a team. But if Irwin or anyone else doesn't, then I just don't give a damn." I start thinking to myself about all that I went through when Simon was in the ICU. I could never get a good limits plan going because no one up there would work with me on it. I would set the limit, and when I left, someone would let him get away with something. Or maybe I was never clear about what I was doing. As Simon put it, "No constancy."

Having given Sam the opening he's been waiting for, he knows what to do. "Max, I know you have some problems dealing with being in a position of authority. But that's your job. You have to be a leader. It's not enough to be able to work as part of a team. You have to lead the team. And that means everyone on it."

Doesn't Sam know I'm a team player at heart? But the ten minutes are conveniently up and I don't get to say my next piece. I try to explain my position to the other residents but am met with little sympathy.

Bobby wonders, "Is your conflict with trying to accept the world as it really is, rather than as part of your fantasies?" Eric says, "You want to be part of the system for your own ego, but deny the reality of the system." Denise tells me, "You've got so much repressed anger at the world and your inability to change it that it's hard for you to make realistic decisions about what you want from your life." Sandra chimes in with, "You have the ability to express yourself in very positive ways, but you often sabotage the message by letting your emotions rule your logic. You have to lead by being yourself, not by convincing others to be you."

In psychiatry this passes for support. At least you never have to worry if people are being honest with you.

Zoe says that I'm doing better than ever. I've noticed recently that whenever people at the hospital say that I'm doing my worst,

Zoe says that things are on the upswing. Maybe my anger is coming out where it should. When am I going to learn how to be a psychiatrist?

When I'm sitting with Zoe by the wood stove, while she knits and I read, all these questions seem so far away. She's been knitting me the same sweater for the last three years, but to preserve this scene and these feelings it could take three hundred years and I would be happy.

Tam Luck oh Tam Luck oh Tam Luck all I hear is oh Tam Luck from the morning that I wake up my heart is full of aching oh Tam oh and so on and so on. On Monday he's sick and he's crazy and it's my fault and if I only cared about him just a little bit more everything would be fine. And more magical thinking like that. Sam stops by to check on the progress and he is convinced that everything that has screwed up is my fault, so at least there is unanimity. All I want to scream out is, "Hey! Has anyone really looked at this patient? Taken a good look at the raw material we are working with here? The nicest thing we can do is send him back to Southeast Asia where at least he can talk to someone." Scientifically speaking, this patient is a lunatic. There is no way to reach him. Medications make no difference so far. Nothing works. He stares out the window and punches people and why haven't I found the cure yet? Schizophrenia comes in many forms. This is not one of the nicest. Listen:

"Diagnostic criteria for a schizophrenic disorder
At least one of the following during a phase of the illness:
  1. Bizarre delusion (content is patently absurd . . .)
  2. Somatic, grandiose, religious . . . or other delusions . . .
  3. delusions . . . accompanied by hallucinations of any type
  4. auditory hallucinations in which either a voice keeps up a running commentary on the individual's behavior or thoughts, or two or more voices converse with each other
  5. auditory hallucinations on several occasions . . .
  6. incoherence, marked loosening of associations, markedly illogical thinking."

Tam's form of the disease, called "disorganized type," also notes: frequent incoherence and blunted, inappropriate or silly affect.

Somehow, I don't think that even Berlitz Vietnamese will help me.

I spend the day talking to everyone about the Tam situation for the umpteenth time, still looking for that miracle cure. This man has been sick for years! Dr. Bently, the unit advisor, wants us to change his meds. Except that he won't take what we have to offer him anyway. (Dr. Bently pulls me aside and whispers, "He's a walking dead person anyway.") A typical Irwin comment is, "You know, Max, I don't understand how you can expect to make it as a psychiatrist when you can't handle a simple patient like this." He loves to set me up and then pull the rug out. No need to be paranoid here. It's real. Anyway, his idea is to keep Tam locked up in a little room forever. I veto this one. The social worker thinks I handle the brother badly. My inspiration at this point is to suggest the brother take matters into his own hands and take Tam home. Simple, n'est-ce pas?

Unfortunately, not so. I presented my plan to Sam, Sandra, Dr. Bently, Molly, and the team planning conference and they all thought that I was out of my mind. You don't deal with problems by sending them home, you know. Or so I now understand. But I managed to spend five hours trying to hear that. So he seems to be here to stay. Barring the sort of miracle that I, unlike the experts, have little hope for.

Command table, ICU. At three in the morning, everyone seems insane and I'm no exception. I just told a patient to, "Get the hell out of the room!" and the rest of the staff is staring at me. So alright already. I made a mistake. But it's been a pretty long night. Things began around eight o'clock in the hospital patients' dorm. We caught two patients getting drunk in the bathroom. Oooh.

Cindy, head of the dorm staff, is talking to me while I eat the crumbs of leftover cookies. She's at least twenty-two, just out of college, and is scared to death every moment at her job. Like the rest of us. "Dr. Jackson, what should we do?"

Speaking with my mouth full, I ask, "What are the patients doing now?"

"They're both asleep," she tells me.

"Aha!" I respond. "Why don't we let them sleep it off and deal with it in the morning?"

Amazed by my brilliant suggestion, I lean back in my chair and look around for items to juggle. Cindy, however, is not impressed. "Dr. Jackson, it's against the rules. They can't stay here." She tries to pout but is either too young or too old and looks a little silly.

"Well," I say, "I think we'll all breathe a little easier if we break this rule, just this once, rather than cause a fuss."

The hard line gets set. "I'll have to call my boss. I don't have the authority to let them stay."

"Oh. Well, do what you want."

She stands up. "I think they belong in the ICU."

"Tell me why."

But she is too frightened by now to do anything but just repeat, "They can't stay here."

"Well, who are they?" She points them out, explaining that one returned from a visit with a little "brew." The dorm staff wakes him up and marches him in to see me. Or sort of coaxes him in my general direction.

He's a bit woozy and staggers over to me. "What's your name?" I ask. He's a monster, at least six feet four inches and muscled. Luckily he's woozy.

"Well hey, Doc. I had me a little nip. Help me sleep."

"What's your name?" I repeat.

"Edgar, man, Edgar."

"You know drinking booze is against hospital rules. Why did you do it?"

"Hey, man, look, I'm sorry. Okay? I won't do it again." He smiles. He's got a great smile. With a very nasty edge. "Okay by me, Edgar. You can talk about it with your own doctor in the morning."

Cindy is incensed, but no way I'm gonna get into a struggle with a giant over a "few beers."

As I walk back to the ICU for rounds, however, I hear over the paging system, "Code 99 Dorm!" Code 99 means violence is brewing, so off I run.

Edgar is in the center of the room. There are seven men standing around him. Everytime one makes a move toward him he gives a threatening look and they back off. It's like a scene from a kung fu movie, except that Edgar does not look impassive. He looks angry.

"What is going on here?" I whisper to Cindy.

"I called my boss and he said to kick Edgar out. He went wild when we tried." Cindy is as white as a sheet. Edgar is screaming epithets around the room like, "You stupid asshole nutbrains! I'm gonna kill you so bad!" And so on.

I edge within earshot of him and say, "Hey, slow down, be cool. Everything will be okay."

He turns to me and snarls, "Screw you. You sic your big boys on me when you left? Not man enough to take me on your own?"

"Look Edgar. We just want you to sleep it off till the morning. Why not spend the night in the ICU?"

"Yeah? Lock me up like I was some crazy nut?"

I signal to the group that we should try to get him upstairs. This consists of a mouthed, "Do it," which fools Edgar not at all. Grown to about fifteen now, the circle moves a little tighter. "Ed, things are too intense right now. Let's go upstairs where we can sit and talk this out."

He starts to move toward the door with his circle of escorts remaining around him, then turns to me and shouts, "Forget the ICU, punk! Better watch it on the streets! I'll take your head off! We'll settle this one on one!"

Nice, eh? So now Edgar is asleep in the ICU and I'm awake and worried about whether I'll live through the year when a nurse calls me up to tell me that a pregnant patient says she's about to deliver.

Mrs. Myers says she has already had about seven pregnancies. But there are no babies. The pregnancies are all in her head. However, given the fact that she is totally alone in the world and has no one to talk to, babies seem like a good idea. So she keeps trying. Her projected father-to-be is a man who murdered his only child because he thought the kid was a vampire. Why did she choose him? I don't know. Mrs. Myers is straight from *Children of the Damned*, bloated face, strange, luminous eyes, and a look of fright to knock your socks off. She's fat but not pregnant, not in labor, and totally psychotic.

"I can feel it! It's coming!" she shouts at me. "I've got to get to a hospital!" We're in the ICU examining room, different from the rest of the hospital mainly in its 1940s examining table. Otherwise, just as bleak and dreary. Especially at 3 A.M. "Mrs. Myers," I try, "I don't think you're in labor yet." At last I get to use that medical training.

"What? Are you crazy, Doctor?" She sits up on the table and pulls her shirt off to show me her belly. She looks like a Biafran. "I can see the baby. Can't you?" She points between her legs and we stare together.

"No," I start, "I can't see a baby. I don't think it's time yet. You have to go into labor first."

"I am in labor! I can feel it!" I put my hand on her belly and we stand there in silence for ten minutes. I dream about my next day off. Mrs. Myers dreams about a baby. But there is no labor.

"I'm sorry," I say, "but you're not ready to have a baby yet. Here, let me help you put your shirt on."

"Forget it, Doctor. You're nuts. You're trying to kill my baby. I'm gonna have it now." She grabs her shirt and leaves the room.

Four in the morning in the ICU. I just secluded Larry for trying to strangle someone. Julie is tied to her bed after trying to jump out a window. Four different patients are freaking out in the dayroom in their own personal horror shows. They're all practicing their yells for *Return of the Banshees*. My beeper goes off and the operator tells me, "Sorry, honey, we got an admission for you."

It turns out to be a twenty-year-old guy who tried to rape his mother. Wanted to get the sins of the father out of her. Wanted to rape his mother! What am I supposed to say tonight? This guy tried to rape his mother! Talk about unresolved oedipal issues.

It's five o'clock and we're all bedded down. Tomorrow I learn how to be a psychiatrist.

At nine o'clock in the morning Simon comes into my office. I find myself missing him after all the craziness there's been in the hospital. It's just amazing what the passage of time will bring. As well as rites of passage. He's been on medication for a month now and is doing alright with it. He's back in his own home, eating his own food, sleeping in his own bed. He's playing in his band. He at times seems almost proud of how far he's come. Although he can't really get any pleasure out of his life. He seems to have a basic issue—an inner belief that everything he does will fail and that he is doomed to depression. It's another hard piece of psychiatry I have to learn. When you have your gallbladder taken out and go home, you get better. With manic depressive illness, when you stop being manic, you get depressed. And the healthier you get, the better able you are to understand how sick you are. Sort of like cancer. Except nobody wants to sympathize with you. Like the plague, mental illness is always treated like it's your fault. Actually, most illness is treated like it's your fault. Mental illness is the only place where people admit it.

Simon is no stranger to this information. He looks haggard, as if no amount of sleep could be too much. His three hundred pounds weigh heavily on him. Carrying half a dozen manila folders with sheet music falling out of all of them, he plops them on my desk and himself in a chair and starts right in. "Dr. Jackson. I'm at my wit's end. My parents came to visit with me this weekend. Was that alright?" he inquires. He looks hopeful that I'll give a direct answer, and when I don't he goes on. "I guess it was, maybe not. They left Sunday. We're getting a lot of words out at each other. There's a lot of tension between us." He blurts out these last few words and settles in. "Now," he seems to say, "we can begin."

I've seen a few movies like *Ordinary People*, by now, so I respond, "Tell me about that."

Simon takes off again. The mania may be gone but the pressure is there. "My father isn't coming to visit me anymore. He said so. I think he's distancing himself."

With my head propped up by my hand, I ask him, "Why does that seem so important?"

Simon seems startled to hear me speak and stares at me. "You mean to my father?" Of course not, I think, but stay silent. "It's all so cruel," he continues, "Dad needs the support. He's angry. I'm angry, you're angry, too."

He starts to tell me of the devastation of his family and then slips into the story of a dream. "I'm playing at the symphony and I see a great composer. I think it's Mozart. I start running to him and he keeps getting farther away. Suddenly I realize there is something behind me and I wheel around. My father is standing there laughing at me. I reach out to him and he disappears." He starts to sob and I offer him my handkerchief, having once again run out of tissues for the office. "That's a very sad dream," I say to him, feeling grief myself. Simon, however, has grief levels I know nothing about. He begins crying uncontrollably and then lifts up his head and shouts, "I hurt him! It's all my fault. I'll never get him back." Then his sorrow and anger and medication bring him back down to earth and he cries softly once more.

"It sounds like you feel guilty," I tell him. He nods his head and says, "I hid under the bed the day he left. Then I prayed."

"When who left?"

"My father."

"Why was that?"

"My father was my friend!" he shouts. "I blame myself. I called to him not to go but it was too late!" He cries again and we sit there in silence, while I try to understand what he is talking about. The anger and depression fill the room. Finally, after a minute that feels like hours, he looks at me and begs, "Will all of this make me a better person? Does it mean anything?"

I'm beyond clinical impassivity and respond, "I hope it will, Simon." And he brightens a tiny bit. At least I hope he does.

While wiping his eyes and brushing the hair from his face, Simon says, "I wake up depressed and go to bed depressed. I'm depressed all the time." He pauses and then tells me, "I stopped my meds."

Oh, marvelous. "Do you think that was a good idea?"

"I just can't stand them. I feel bad all the time."

"Worse than now?"

"Worse than anything. I'd rather be depressed than drugged."

Well, okay then. Throwing caution to the winds, and hope to the stars, I try honesty with him. "It's your decision now, Simon. You're able to decide for yourself what it's worth to you. I have some fears that you may get worse and end up back in here. But I'll see you whether you take meds or not. Let's just keep it an open topic."

He seems surprised by the lack of argument and unsure of what to say next. After a pause, he decides on, "Thank you."

Later on, Molly tells me that I might have responded, "Thank you for what?" and tried to explore the issues of dependency and independence, but instead Simon and I just sit quietly and let the air clear. Finally, Simon breaks the silence. "I'm just so sad. I need a relationship with someone. I'll take anything. I don't want to be lonely anymore. It's ridiculous to try anything in life. I'll just end up crazy. I'll just cry all the time. I cry about being sick, about taking meds, about having no father in my life. I've messed up every relationship I've been in." He sniffles and then the tears come again.

I try to empathize with his sadness and say, "It must be terribly hard."

He glowers. "You've got it all and I've got nothing. My life is degrading! What do you know about hardness?"

"I can see how much you hurt. You have to explain the rest of the pain to me."

"I need help!" he screams. "I wish I could be happy." And cries his way into the hall and out the building.

Molly thinks I did basically okay in this session. Not great, but okay. "You were able to share some of his depression with him. That's important. In time he will learn that he can trust you." There is no baby in the room today. Molly thinks I get too distracted. Rats.

"It felt alright. But it's awful having to sit in a room filled with so much sadness. I thought I was going to cry."

"Tell me, Max," Molly asks. "How do you feel about Simon?"

Caught off guard, I reply, "What do you mean?" Pretty witty, eh?

"He seems to like you. All that talk about wanting a relationship with a father. Do you feel that was directed toward you?"

"Well hell. I hadn't thought about it. I don't think I've done anything to give him the idea that he should think of me as something other than a therapist. He used to call me names, but that was when he was sicker."

"Max, do you know what transference is?"

"Well of course. That's when the patient acts toward you like you were someone else, even though there's no good reason for it." The little light bulb in my head goes off. "Oh. You mean he may treat me more as a friend than a therapist?"

"Who knows who he is treating you like? Transference means that you will receive feelings and affect that are meant for someone else, often someone from early on in the patient's life. The point is, for now, that he is thinking about you romantically or sexually and you are going to need to address it."

"Huh? What do you mean sexually?"

"That's often what people mean when they talk about longing for a relationship."

"Why would I want to address it? Why not just leave it alone and see if it goes away?"

"Because, one, it won't go away, and two, that's giving up the whole purpose of therapy. What goes on in the room between the two of you is the work of the therapy. That's where a patient gets to experience the full range of emotions they can have in a safe environment. And if one of the ways they feel is love or romance, then that's what you talk about. Didn't you say that with Magda?"

I shrug noncommittally and say, "Yeah, I suppose so. But that was different."

All month long people are smiling at me. Now it's Molly's turn. "The only difference now is that you don't want to talk about it. You're acting different. Not the patients. Why?"

"He's so sick. I'm happy just to get him out of the hospital. I don't want to push him now."

"That's a reasonable way to feel. And I suspect that the fact of his gender may not be meaningless. But remember, you're his therapist. And even if it makes him sad, you still need to do therapy. And that means things may get intense for a while."

Luckily for me, our time is up. Saved by the bell. But obviously, not for long. As my brain starts to churn I am struck by the awful knowledge that my patients need me to work on my feelings, too.

But before I go home today I must see Ecaterina and try to find out what is going on. And who the hell she is. After refusing to talk to me for the better part of a week, she has finally consented to an interview.

I find her sitting on a sofa in the corner of the unit, hair tied back, an austere look on her face. She is wearing no makeup, and the hollowness of her cheekbones is accentuated. In a simple white smock, she appears as a prisoner in a World War II film, awaiting the interrogation by her diabolical captors.

"Hello, Ecaterina."

She looks me up and down and then turns her head away.

I sit there silently with her, having played this game once before. After a minute of silence she responds. "When will I get out of here, Dr. Jackson?"

"There are some things we ought to talk about."

"I don't know if I care to."

"Well," I say, "let's give it a try."

"I'll try."

"Great. Now why did the police bring you here?"

"The police are stupid morons."

"I can understand that opinion. But it doesn't help my question."

"They are idiots."

"They may be. Why, out of everyone in the whole world, did they choose to grab you?"

"Who can guess the motivations of such fools?"

Growing frustrated now, I answer, "I could make a guess. You were probably trying to kill yourself."

She makes a sound that is something of a snorting noise. "If I was trying to kill myself, then why would I have called them?"

"You called them?"

"Of course. I needed to be brought here."

"Why was that?"

"I was feeling suicidal."

Oh. How about that. "What was making you feel that way?"

"My therapist has abandoned me. That fool."

"Is that why you made an appointment to see me?"

"Brilliant deduction, Dr. Jackson."

"Thanks. But I still don't get why you were suicidal."

Sighing, she replies, "Do I have to tell you everything? My life is horrible, my lover left me, I had no one, and you want to know why I tried to kill myself? Don't you understand the pain I am in?"

"I'm trying. Why weren't you able to call or come in to see me before you called the police or tried to hurt yourself?"

"I was out of my mind with grief."

"Are you still?"

"Am I still what?"

"Out of your mind with grief?"

"No. I'm better."

"How come? What has changed?"

"Just seeing you," she responds, and I can't tell if it's sarcasm or not that I'm hearing.

"Are you suicidal?" I ask.

"No. Of course not. So let me out of here."

"Will you contract with me not to hurt yourself without calling or coming in first?"

"Why should I do that?"

"So that we can have an agreement."

"I don't want one."

"I think it will make it easier for us to work together if we can make agreements to work this way."

"Well, Doctor . . ." She pauses, thinking. "If it means so much to you, I'll agree. Now, can I get the hell out of here?"

"Will you come back and see me as an outpatient?"

"Do I have to in order to get out?"

"No."

"I will. Thank you for all your help, Dr. Jackson." Again I hear a slight sneer in her voice. "Now may I go?"

"Okay. See you next week."

"Zoe, I think I may really be losing my mind. I know that I say that every day is as bad as it gets, but lately it really feels that way. I am just at my wit's end. Everybody I deal with is nuts and I don't seem to be able to control it at all."

Zoe rolls over to me in bed and wraps her arms around me. "So what are you going to do about it? There's no point in your feeling so insane."

"I don't know. Sometimes I wonder if I'm going to survive. I'm not sure where to find the strength."

"Max, don't worry about the strength. Worry about what's happening to you."

"But I don't know what's happening to me. I don't seem to be able to spend enough time with my therapy patients because the crises are so common, but when I do sit with them, I feel such grief and agony and confusion that I don't know what it all means."

She hugs me tight and dissolves some of the anger and asks again, "What do you want?"

"Shoot, Zoe, I don't know. What else could happen?"

"Anything can happen, Max. And you'll survive. And your patients will survive, too."

"I hope so. I really need a break."

I'm sitting under a tree by a small river in the South of France. I smell the water lilies. The river makes a gentle, rustling sound. I look up and see Zoe, standing beside me in a long blue gown. She has on a red hat. Reaching down she takes my hand and we walk down the river, toward an open field. Her gown vanishes and we stand alone. I lie down in the field and go to sleep.

"Zoe," I say. "I feel like I'm in therapy ten hours a day."

"You are," she replies, quite correctly.

4

Anger

"How do you feel, Max?" Sam looks sad and concerned, a little like a coach wondering if his halfback will be able to return to the game. Hunched over in his chair, fingers gripping a pencil too loosely, he taps the desk nervously. What must I look like?

"How the hell do you think I feel? How the hell am I supposed to feel? I feel like garbage!" I scream the last one at him and put my face in my hands. Tears won't come. I feel in a daze, a daze punctuated only by an urge to blow up in rage.

"Look, Max. It's not your fault. You can't take responsibility for someone else's life." Sam's eyes seem to plead for the right answer. But I will not give it. Or cannot.

"Not my fault?" My voice rises in pitch and volume. "She's in a coma and I could have prevented it and it's not my fault!? Who the hell's fault is it? Do you want to take the rap? Give me a break!"

"Max, it's okay to be angry. Let it out."

"Don't patronize me! How the hell do you know how I feel?"

"At least she's still alive, Max. And they're pretty sure she'll pull through. Don't blame yourself."

"Yeah? Well, maybe I just don't want to hear about it right now. I gave her the medication, I let her out, and she overdosed on the pills. Jesus, Sam. What happened?" And still the tears won't come, even though the sadness is overwhelming.

"Go home, Max. Get yourself some space. It's not your fault. She has an illness. She's sick. Understand? If she had had a heart attack and you were a medical intern it would be no different. It's sad when our patients get worse. A GP feels it and so do you. But you didn't try and kill her. She did that herself."

"It's not the same thing as a heart attack. I knew this woman. I talked to her two hours before she left." I start to sob. "She told me she wasn't suicidal. Help me, Sam," I beseech him through my tears. "What else could I have done? What could I have done?"

"Go home, Max. You've done all you can."

Sandra has been sitting silently next to me and begins to speak very quietly. "I don't want you to feel all alone with this, Max. If there is any blame, then I share it and so does Sam. Our job is to make sure that this can be prevented whenever possible. Don't try to shoulder this alone. It's not all yours and you don't have to."

My rage bubbles over again, even though I know that Sandra's comment is meant to soothe. "I feel all alone! I wish I had listened better, if only I wasn't some puny first year resident who didn't know his ass from his elbow, then Ecaterina would be sitting in the ICU at Asylum, instead of in a coma at Boston General. I'll let you have all the blame you want. I still have mine." I start to sniffle and want to touch someone, to be held, to make it all better again. But Sandra keeps talking to me.

"Max, at least she's not dead. You can be guilty and angry and sad and anything else, but be thankful for that. I don't have any blame to give you, and I certainly didn't hear Sam blaming you. So if you feel it, it's coming from you."

"I know that Sandra." Wiping my eyes, I try again to clear my head. "But I feel so bad. She was my patient. I blew it."

Sam comes in again. "Max, she still is your patient. This isn't the end of the world. Listen to yourself. You sound like Ecaterina now. These are exactly the sort of things she would say. Looking for someone to blame, crying then screaming, feeling persecuted."

"Please, Sam. Don't analyze me now." But I know there's more than a grain of truth in this.

"Max, try and listen." Sandra does reach out and hold my arm. "You did a good job with a difficult patient. About 10 percent of depressed and suicidal patients kill themselves. It's a fatal disease. You are not as powerful as you think. At least you get to try again with her."

"Go home, Max," Sam repeats. "Give yourself some time to think."

Sitting motionless on the bus, eyes glazed, head tilted at an odd angle, I'm looking nowhere. Thoughts go back and forth until there is no place left to search. There is no answer in my head, no exit from the feelings, no escape from the knowledge that a piece of me has died today. I couldn't do anything to help. Damn! There was nothing I could do about it. Damn! Medicine is an inexact science. Damn! What am I doing? Why bother?

At exercise nothing is any different. Work my legs, work my arms, feel those pectorals bulge. Turn off the mind, concentrate on the body. Feel who you are, don't think about who you should be. Or were.

Zoe tells me, as I lie in bed at five in the afternoon, "They were right, Ace. You're not omnipotent. It's her life. You don't control her."

"You should have seen her note," I sob. "She said that if only someone had understood her, it would have been alright."

"Great, Max. So she's a manipulative bitch. You're acting guilty when you should be mad as hell at her. Instead you're angry at yourself and the rest of the world. That's her trip and her illness."

"I don't get it. Why should I be angry at her?"

"Because she hurt you. God, everyone who ever met this woman has probably felt guilty."

"You're right, but it doesn't do me too much good now.

Whether they're reasonable or not, I've got some pretty mixed-up feelings."

"Drink the beer and go to sleep. You'll feel better. I'll be here."

Simon misses our appointment the next morning, so I have plenty of time to sit and think. I don't want to have to be here and worry whether one of my patients will live out the week. In desperation I seek my peers. "Tough luck," says Eric. "It could have happened to any of us." "Yeah, but it didn't," I think. Bobby tells me, "I know you must feel horrible and so do I. I'm scared that one of my patients will kill themselves. If you want, let's get together for lunch and talk." Oh God, I want to, but I feel contagious and refuse. Everyone feels sorry for me and everyone seeks me out. "Look! It's the man with leprosy! Pay him some sympathy and you can touch." Mental illness may not be contagious, but it has infected me.

Hiding in my office, waiting for a patient to come in, I pick up the phone and call one. "Simon, you're missing your session."

"Oh, Dr. Jackson." He sounds as if he's been crying, too. "I wanted to see you but I was too depressed. I don't know if I'm going to make it." Please, don't say that to me.

"It's okay, Simon. Come on into the hospital to talk. Things are not as hopeless as you think."

"Are you sure?"

"I'm sure, Simon. Believe me, things could be worse."

Molly sits with me in silence as I describe my turmoil over Ecaterina. And then says, "What you feel is normal. Let it run its course and then let go of it. From what you've told me it sounds as if she'll pull through. You'll still be her therapist and you need to have worked through these feelings of responsibility to be useful to her. You won't get the support you need at the hospital, because you have your individual needs. Everything Sandra and Sam said is true. But you need to come to it on your own." Then she gives me a hug.

Denise tells me, "Ecaterina really is a pain in the neck. If you're pissed off at her, that's your right. Just be careful not to take it out on your other patients."

"Dammit, Zoe! I feel like I'm doing my best. And people are dying to get away from me."

"You're not God, you know. Just because you do your best, doesn't mean the right thing will always happen."

She turns up the thermostat on the sauna. Sweat makes her shiny and bright and I can finally think of something else. It's nice to watch her body glisten.

"Don't withdraw from me, too" she continues. "I don't care if you can't function at the hospital, but I need you to be here with me. I'm in turmoil myself. Med school worries are no small thing. So get your anger out, but stay with me." Her glow looks more and more appealing.

"Alright. So I won't be so depressed. I refuse to be depressed! How's that?"

"I don't know if I can believe you. Please try and be honest with me about the way you're feeling."

"If I can figure it out, you'll be the first one to know."

Eight years in medicine. And for what? Pain and depression? At least Simon comes in to see me. Still depressed, he has reacquired a slightly wild look in his eyes. Toting his sheet music, he drags himself, literally pulls his bulk into my office. Crawling to a chair he melts into it.

"Dr. Jackson, I am absolutely terrified of music. I can't do anything. I can't get anything done! Everytime I start composing I feel so miserable I can't function." The tears come now. "Everything is a struggle. I've been seeing you for months and nothing is better. Wouldn't you want to die?"

"It sounds awful Simon." Please don't kill yourself.

"I feel like I beat on myself."

"Can you stop it?"

"I play my music. But it's so intense. Everyone will think it's crazy. Don't you see? I sabotage everything!"

"How do you do that?"

"I can't let well enough alone. I build myself up in my mind.

That way I get all the love that I need. But it's all so sad. I've let everyone down. All the unhappiness. I want to scream."

"Does that help?"

"I don't know. But it happens."

I shift in my seat as I get ready to make an interpretation. I definitely will grow a beard this month. I need something to stroke. "It must be hard not to feel at ease in the world."

His voice tightens as he says, "All I want is a normal life. I'm so afraid. I'm so alone."

"What are you so afraid of?"

"I'm afraid of my rage. I'm afraid of the rage of my father. I'm afraid he'll want to kill me! I need protection from my disappointment!" He starts to get very excited. The man who dragged himself into my office is now on the verge of explosion. "When will I have happiness? Who will be mine!?" And he collapses.

We sit and wait and my mind drifts to Ecaterina. "Come back," I call but I don't know who I'm talking to. And Simon stops crying and confesses, "All I want is to enjoy myself. Will it ever happen?"

"You don't have to be hopeless. Depression and hopelessness don't have to be the same thing." I hope.

Luckily, Jerry comes in to see me and prove the point. Depressed, yes. Hopeless, not yet.

"Hello, Dr. Jackson." He says the words so softly I can barely hear.

"Hi, Jerry." Thank God you're here.

"This was an okay week. Really okay. I got a lot done. I know I have a lot of responsibilities and everything, but I think I'm gonna be able to get things done."

"That's good to hear."

"Of course I can't do everything. I know better. I'm gonna take it easy and straighten things out, like you suggested."

"Like I suggested?"

"You know, you told me to think about things."

"Oh?"

"Do you think it's okay if I give up some projects?"

"Sounds like you're not sure."

"Well, I don't really know what I want to do." He looks around the office, looking inward I suppose, and then says, "Did I tell you my roommate at school died in an accident, a car accident?"

"I don't think so." I know so. "When was that?"

"Just about a month ago. It was pretty awful. It's been taking up most of my thoughts."

"I wonder why you didn't bring it up before."

"I guess I didn't think it was so big a deal. But it made me pretty worried. He was a good guy."

"A good friend?"

"I didn't know him too well. We just started living together this year. But I liked him. I miss him."

"You came here," I note.

"Yeah, I guess I was a little depressed. I don't want to die." He giggles and then stifles it. "It's not funny, I know, just . . . I don't know, sad."

"It made you feel depressed?"

"Yeah. It made it hard to go on. I started pushing pretty hard."

"If you push hard enough you won't notice you're depressed?"

"I don't want that. Definitely not that. It sounds like a huge treadmill. That's what happened to my father. He got on this stupid legal treadmill and never got off. I don't want to go so fast that I can't find a way to stop it."

"Good plan. How will you do it?"

"I don't know. I have to figure out what I want. I hoped that going to law school would help. You know, get another degree." He looks around at the diplomas on the wall and continues, "You must know what that's like."

"What's it like for you?"

"It's not helping much." He looks down. "I'm still pretty depressed."

"Depressed?"

"Yeah. I just sit around and I can't get anything done and it's an effort to eat or work or even just get up in the morning. Hell, I don't know why I bother sometimes."

"Why you bother to come here?"

"It's an effort. Believe me. I'm not sure what I'm doing here. I don't know what to say. I feel very uncomfortable. What is all this about anyway?"

I don't answer and he goes on. "I know, I have to figure it out. That's just the sort of thing I expected you to say. I guess I should have done this sooner but I couldn't get up the courage. I know, I know, I'm supposed to say what I feel but I don't know how. I don't even know what I feel so how am I supposed to say it?"

"Sounds like you're under a lot of pressure."

"Well I am. I'm feeling something and I don't even know where it's coming from."

"What's that like?"

"It's sort of like being drowned, held underwater. It's a very unpleasant feeling."

"Where's it coming from?"

"I don't know."

"There's only two of us here," I say.

"Well maybe," he answers, "it's from you. I don't usually feel this way."

"What is the feeling?"

"It's like you're going to punish me, you're the grand inquisitor waiting to find my faults and decide I'm no good. That's stupid, I know, but that's what it feels like."

"I'm going to punish you?"

"Look, it's very awful and painful and it hurts to be here. I don't like admitting I'm sick. Do you think I'm sick?"

I recognize the dodge and duck. "What makes it so painful?"

"Huh? Oh, I don't know. You just seem so powerful and I'm a nobody."

"Sounds scary."

"Oh, it is. It's a terrible way to live." He seems to shudder and pulls back into the chair. His eyes begin to puff up, but he holds the tears back. Silently, I wait for a movement or a motion from him and when none is forthcoming I ask, "What is the sad thought you are holding onto?"

Sniffling, each word softer than the one before it he stammers, "It's not a memory. It's just, just, that I'm lonely. I can't relax."

"Try it now," I suggest.

"Try what?"

"Just relax."

He takes a deep breath and sighs, then again breathes deeply, dropping his shoulders. On the third breath he shudders and starts to cry, tears flowing silently down his cheeks, an endless stream without a sound.

"That's a lot of sadness," I say, as the tears slow down.

"I don't know what it is," he mutters.

"You seem to use a lot of energy keeping your sad feelings away from the surface."

"I do. I do." He takes a few more deep breaths, but seems to expand rather than contract this time.

"What am I going to do, Dr. Jackson?"

"About what?"

"About my depression?"

"Do you really want me to tell you the answer?"

He smiles. "I don't know. I guess not."

"What do you think you're going to do?"

"Try to go out. Have a little more fun. Maybe I'll try not to worry so much. I'm always worrying about something or other."

"Does it make you less depressed?"

"What do you mean?"

"Does worrying make you less depressed?"

"Of course not. I can't ever figure out what I'm feeling when I worry." He stops himself and grimaces as he hears what he has said. I check the clock and see that our time is up.

"Sounds like we have a lot to talk about next week."

"I guess so. Thanks, Dr. Jackson."

"For what?"

"I don't know."

"You don't? Well, you're welcome." He leaves the office and I am so relieved.

Ed and Patty, friends from the pre-shrink days, run a retreat in New Hampshire, so Zoe and I have decided to spend the weekend there in a desperate attempt to cool out. Between her med school worries and my psychiatry woes, we need it. For a winter day, it's quite warm, and the wind that blows through the now empty trees has only the vaguest hint of chill. As every year at this time I imagine, "Perhaps winter will not come."

"Ed," I say, "I love it here. You can't imagine how peaceful this seems to me." We're sitting in the cupola atop the main building, drinking tea and eating biscuits. There isn't a house to be seen in any direction and not a human voice other than our own. The White Mountains rise in the distance, covered by fog, a few solitary peaks showing snow-capped images. The air is still, the earth is brown and there is a faint scent of decaying leaves. With a deep breath I can feel the natural rhythms. "I can't believe all the madness exists when I'm here with you folks."

"What's it like, Max?" Ed and I used to live together during the Cape Cod years, before he plunged farther into the country and I took my detour into insanity.

"Basically, it's crazy." I laugh a little and take a sip of my tea. "I don't think I can talk about it. All I want to do now is withdraw and process. It's been too much too fast."

"If you want to relax, why not try the isolation tank?"

"The what?"

"It's a sensory deprivation tank. You lie floating in Epsom salts and it's dark and noiseless. It's a very good place to withdraw when you need to." Ed walks me through the main rooms of the house to the relaxation areas and shows me the tank.

"Ed, I'm a psychiatrist. A therapist. This is crazy California stuff."

"Don't be so conservative, Max. Try something different."

"But Ed," I protest, "if this works, then I'm out of a job."

"Best thing for you if half of what you say is true."

So I'm lying there in the tank, trying to relax and get away from it all and all I can think about is if lack of sensory stimulation will drive me insane. I think I saw a movie about this at one point. The salts get into my eyes which makes them sting so I close them, which changes the experience not at all. Now I can feel the tension in my eyeballs. Is this how it starts? Will the relaxation now begin? I think about the hospital, how I learn from my patients, how I seem to adopt their diseases and so on. This makes my arms hurt and I get a headache. I think about Ecaterina and how she almost died and how it wasn't my fault but it sure was a bummer and my stomach tenses. I remember that she is off the critical list and is returning to Asylum this week. And my back aches. Isn't this fun? And slowly my thoughts turn to Zoe and finally I can relax and then after a sauna I can sleep for the next sixteen hours.

"Zoe," I say as I awake, "I don't feel so rested. Let's not go back. Let's run away."

"I'd love to, Max. Anywhere you want to go?"

"Anywhere," I say, "but we're too damn busy and we've got too much to do."

"Ace, it's not so bad." She stands in the middle of the room and spins around. "After all, you've got me no matter where we are."

"I just want more of you."

"Don't give up, Max. You're growing up this year. Stay with psychiatry. You'll make it."

"So much has happened. All the insanity. Simon. Shirley. Ecaterina. Tam. When will I get to figure it out?"

"First figure you out. Insight into yourself will make the job more real."

"I'm feeling filled with anger and confusion right now. Even a sauna and a good night's sleep can't change that."

"Be angry if you have to, Ace. I guess that's part of learning how to be a shrink. I guess you have to learn how to deal with your anger. You'll probably have to deal with depression and obsessiveness and all the other defenses. I just hope you can figure out what's you and what's the hospital."

"I know what you mean. It's hard to help people when you feel infected by their madness. But I still want to help them."

"Then that's your job for the year." And she runs off to breakfast as I struggle out of bed.

In the middle of my juggling act at the Asylum talent show my beeper goes off. This admission is Gertrude, a forty-year-old woman with an IQ in the 40s. She's standing in the center of the room with her arms raised to the sky, tears pouring from her eyes, shouting, "I want my mommy. I want my mommy!" She further informs me that Daddy is in heaven and that God is after her. To feed her poison and make her go crazy. Perhaps she'll be a good playmate for Tam, who I'm now experiencing in sheer wonder. No communication exists, no treatment helps, nothing happens. Tam has sort of blended into the ICU scene at this point, just another chronic patient who doesn't talk, doesn't get any better and gets secluded a lot. Just beautiful, what kind of attitude is that? Aren't I supposed to help him?

"Sam, we've got to get Tam out of this place. We're doing nothing for him."

"Did you get the consults, Max?"

"Sure, Sam. The psychopharmacology people say there isn't a drug on earth that could help him. But they suggest we try them all just in case. The electroshock people say that he's inappropriate for high voltage treatment. They wouldn't touch him. He won't cooperate with endocrinology, kicked the neurologist and bit the X-ray technician. So far, nobody has anything to offer. Maybe we can find him a hospital in Thailand where he'll be able to speak to his doctor."

"Max, why are you in such a hurry to get rid of this patient?"

"What are you talking about?"

"It seems like you want him out of the hospital more than you want to treat him."

"Sam! I can't treat him! He's untreatable! Why can't you buy that? First you tell me not to act so omnipotent, and then you give me the message that I should cure anyone who walks in the door."

"Calm down, Max. You seem really stressed by this case. It sounds like you are feeling powerless."

"Powerless to cope with this stupid discussion!"

Zoe thinks that calling Sam's comments "stupid" was probably the major mistake. But why can't I communicate any better what I think is right? These patients are so incredibly sick. It truly amazes me. The healthiest of them knows more pain than I can imagine (Molly says that this is wrong, that everyone stands all the pain they can all the time), and no one is going anywhere. I came to psychiatry because I love the mind, its convolutions and its motions. I love the games it plays, the doors it opens, the amazement it causes. It's the greatest mystery in the world and it's right there in my head all the time. Yet at work, when I look at the mind, all I get is the agony of a mind gone mad. And while this impresses me with the potential of thought to shape reality, it is frightening and overwhelming. How do you fix a mind?

"Dr. Jackson, I've been sleeping all day. And eating. All I do is sleep and eat. I feel so depressed and I can't get anything done. All these depressing thoughts are going through my brain. I need more activities. I can't stand to eat anymore." He looks like a blimp.

"Well, Simon, I think it might be useful for you to restart your medication." He looks too depressed to believe. If the chair wasn't underneath him, Simon would merge into the floor.

"No way, Doctor." He emphasizes the first syllable, to make sure I understand the point. "I won't. I can't. They'll never work for me. I'll just get worse and worse."

"It might help. You never know. It seems like you've been putting up with this pain for a long time."

"Please, Dr. Jackson. Nothing will ever help me. It's all over."

"Can you tell me why?"

"I have nothing left in my life. I've destroyed everything. I have no family. All I have is my band."

"How can I help you?"

"This place is full of sad people, of crazy people. And you want me to take meds. Do you think that I'm crazy?"

"What do you think?"

"I have a lot of sadness. But I have my fantasies. Do my friends truly like me?" He reaches for the tissues. "It's all hopeless. No one could really care for me."

"You mean, why do I?"

"This is just your job," he weeps. "You don't like me. You

never will. You'll never be in love with me. You'll never be my
father. It will never change."

"When we talk you feel things for me?" I'll never be in love
with you?

"I find you attractive. It's true. I am so hungry for true love.
You're affectionate now. When will you leave me, too?"

Molly avoids saying, "I told you so." She does allow that, "It
seems that Simon's feelings for you didn't just go away."

"I don't believe it, Molly. He spends all his weekends thinking
about me. He dreams of me. He fantasizes about me. While I
spend my weekend trying to get away from it all, Simon is totally
wrapped up in me."

"It's an important lesson, Max." She puts down her knitting, a
tiny sweater, fit for a one year old. "The perception a patient has
of your relationship will not be the same as the one you have. You
are obviously one of the most important people in Simon's life.
Additionally, he thinks of you romantically. Finding out how and
why is a key to the therapy."

"It makes me a bit uncomfortable."

"Why is that?"

"Well, I'm not used to talking about another person's attraction to me."

"You better get used to it. It happens all the time in therapy.
After all, you were able to discuss the fact that Simon hated you
and thought you were a killer. That gave us lots of important
information. Why should this be any less important?"

"I guess it's not less valuable, it simply seems strange. I feel like
such a voyeur."

"Do you think there's something about the whole issue of
attraction that's uncomfortable to you? Perhaps attraction by a
man?"

"God, Molly. I don't know. It sort of reminds me of being in
high school. I still don't know what to do when someone tells me
they like me. Usually, in real life, you either pull away or try to get
close. Neither seems right here."

"Well, you do have to get close. That is, you have to let him
know that you're not going to reject him. But at the same time,

you need to set limits. It's not so different than when he was in the ICU. You can support his feelings, but let him know where your limits are and what the boundaries of therapy are."

Oh God. Limits. If I can only make it to Christmas and have a little vacation and get myself some long-term breathing space maybe I'll be able to set some limits. Right now there is a continuously dreadful feeling of waiting for the other shoe to drop. Who will it be? Tam going wild? Magda attacking me? Simon readmitted? Or perhaps Ecaterina, returned to Asylum.

She looks like an abused infant, head lolling to the side as she rolls onto the unit in a wheelchair. She holds her arms up at me and wails, "Look at what I did, Dr. Jackson. It's because you wouldn't treat me. This is all your fault."

"I don't get it, Ecaterina. How is it my fault?"

"You don't like me. You never liked me. Why didn't you help me when I needed it?"

"What was the help you needed?"

"I was depressed," she shouts, tiring herself out and falling back into her chair. "My psychiatrist had left me and then you kicked me out of the hospital."

"You wanted to leave. You said you weren't suicidal."

"I was sick!" she shouts. "Look at me! What kind of psychiatrist are you?"

A burned-out one if you must know, but let's not talk about that now. "You seem pretty angry."

"Well, wouldn't you be?" The color has begun to return to her face, but she has a long way to go to recover her previous elegance.

"I don't know. You seem to feel I let you down."

"You did let me down, Dr. Jackson. I tried to kill myself." There is almost a smug tone to her voice.

"I don't see how that was my fault," I respond, not knowing why I am bothering to have this discussion.

"You were supposed to help me!" she screams. "And this happened."

"This happened?" I ask.

"Yes."

"What do you mean, 'happened'?"

"I almost died."

"But that didn't just happen. It was something you did."

She looks at me with a start, then goes on as if I have said nothing. "How could you let this happen?"

"Are you still suicidal?" I ask.

"What's it to you?"

Exhausted, I answer, "I think you'll stay in the locked unit tonight, Ecaterina."

"Why?" she wails.

"That's my decision," I respond.

"Ah screw you. You don't care about me."

"Should we talk about that?"

"Why? If you really cared about me . . ." She leaves it hanging so I pick it up.

"I'd what?"

"Screw you."

"Is this related to your suicide attempt?"

She sits there silently, refusing to even acknowledge the question. "Should we stop now?" I ask.

"I'll do it," she answers. "If not with pills, I'll slash my wrists or jump off a bridge and you'll get sued. But I'll do it." She wheels her way down the hall. And I flee to Sandra's office.

"Have you got a minute, Sandra? I'm desperate."

I explain the previous interaction and then ask her, "What the hell happened? If she goes out and kills herself, I'm gonna fall apart."

"How do you see the interaction, Max?"

"I don't know. I felt like she was threatening me."

"Maybe she was. How did you deal with it?"

"I don't know. I was getting pretty angry. She's put me through hell and now is blaming me for her problems. Damn! I barely know her."

"So you fought back?"

"What do you mean?"

"You fought with her."

"I did not!"

"What would you call that session?"

"I was trying to help her."

"Well, you don't do that by challenging such an obviously ill woman just out of the hospital after a suicide attempt. When she says crazy things, you listen, don't argue."

"But she's not crazy."

"You mean she's not psychotic. She is definitely ill. My goodness, look at what she's done."

"Yeah, I know. I guess I'm pissed off at her. But what am I supposed to do?"

I walk over to the window to stare at the courtyard. The first snowfall of the year has begun and there's a light covering on the ground. Two patients are trying to play basketball, but the snow keeps covering the court and the ball. Nonetheless, they keep throwing the ball at the hoop and watching it sail by.

Turning back to Sandra, I say, "I do feel angry. I feel angry all the time. And sometimes I blow up at staff and sometimes I blow up at patients. What am I going to do?"

"Do you know why you're angry?"

Sitting back down, I scratch my head and wonder. "I guess I feel like I'm not accomplishing what I want to here. I thought I'd be able to save these people, to cure them. Instead I feel like a custodian, a prison guard, a priest, or an emotional dartboard. Shouldn't I be angry?"

"I don't know Max. Those are your preconceptions. It sounds to me as if you're learning all the ways to be a psychiatrist. Which in the long run will be very helpful to your patients."

"But why does it have to hurt so much?"

Sandra gets philosophical. "So you'll remember, Max."

My father called me on the phone tonight. He wanted to know how "work" was going. "You know, son, how proud your mother and I are of you."

"I know Dad. I think I made the right choice for myself, too. This is a pretty hard time, though."

"Why's that, Max?"

"It's all getting to me pretty bad. I'm either depressed or angry most of the time."

"Well don't forget, Max, the most important thing you'll ever do in your life is get married. So don't take Zoe for granted."

"I won't Dad. See ya."

Zoe rolls over in bed and asks, "Who was it?"

"That was my father. He told me not to take you for granted."

"Your father is a very smart man. I wish you'd leave your anger at the office and bring the rest of you home to me."

"Don't you think I'm getting any better? I'm really trying. I don't think I've said that this was the worst day of my life for a month."

"You are doing better with that, Max. It's just that you seem so distant sometimes. Last night I wanted to make love and you were just staring off into space. I didn't feel like you were in the same room as me."

"I know, Zoe. But it takes me two hours just to wind down from work. I'm afraid that if I open my mouth all sorts of weird feelings will come out."

"Just stay with me, now. Okay? I do need you. Even more than your patients. Don't take that for granted either."

When does it end, I wonder. Layers upon layers are exposed and no solution is yet in sight. Every day at the hospital more and more of me is dragged into the open. How dare it impose? When does a job stop being work and become an exercise in personal transformation?

Brriinnnggg! The phone starts ringing, jarring me awake from an all too dreadful sleep. "This is Dr. Jackson," I respond without thinking.

"Dr. Jackson. This is Dr. Miller. That's a pretty formal way to answer your phone."

"John! What are you doing, calling me at the hospital?"

"What are you talking about, Max? I called you at home. It's Saturday morning."

I check around the room. Zoe is lying next to me in bed. The air smells clean. No beeper to be seen. I am home.

"Sorry about that John. I get all confused sometimes. What are you calling me for? Where are you?"

"I'm in Boston. Just got in this morning. I'm on my way to the Far East for a year of travel. Want to come along?"

"Of course I do. But how did you get out of your residency?"

"I just quit. Come pick me up, guy. I'm at the train station. Let's talk face-to-face."

Poking Zoe in the side I tell her that I'm going to get John at the train. I wonder what he looks like now. He's going to Asia! But he made it through med school and is on his way to radiology. Another professional success story. Zoe offers one insight, "He still sounds crazy."

"Crazy! Are you kidding? Tam is crazy. John is not."

And my mind starts working on the possibilities. Maybe I can get a month off and travel. Maybe I can flap my arms and fly to the moon. Rats. I'm never getting out of that place.

John looks mostly like a doctor when I pick him up. "Well hey, Ace," he calls out. "How's the shrink business?"

"God, Johnny, I don't know. Right now I feel that I'm being ground to dust. People are either crazy or dying and I can't do anything about it and all everyone wants to do is analyze my anger. I know why I'm angry. It's because it's all too much."

John punches me on the arm. He pulls out a big map of Burma to show me the exciting places he's going. "Yeah, but forget all that. How is it being a shrink?"

"Small, very small. I do like it, I guess. It's an okay path. Right now, however, the path is taking a short detour through hell." We pull up by the house and go in. Zoe hasn't got out of bed yet, so I quietly make us a cup of coffee.

"Well, hey. No one ever said that everything in life would be a pleasure. It's got to beat treating acne."

"I guess so. But I'm in misery there now. All I want to do is withdraw whenever possible. Which isn't often enough. I was drawn to psychiatry by the philosophy of it. You know, thinking about what is reality and what makes people think and why do I obsess about sex all the time. Instead, I spend my time watching the sick get sicker and locking up nice people in small rooms."

I try to tell him about Shirley. Although her diagnosis, schizophrenia, is the same as Tam's, they are such different people. I wonder about these diagnoses. Shirley likes to sit in the dayroom and smile, smile, smile. Never angry, never cross, what goes on in her mind is just amazing. She believes that her reward must come someday. The government will see to it. It's all in those electrodes. I had found her cutting a hole in her dress yesterday.

"Shirley, what are you doing?"

"Cutting a hole in my dress," she smiles.

"That's it, huh?"

"Yes. Do you think it's unusual?"

"Do you?" I retort, smartly.

"Why? Why is it unusual? Why is it any more unusual than what you do? What does anything mean? I've been thinking about many things. Why is there up? Am I a human? How do I know that the control from without isn't really God?"

"Those are important questions, Shirley. But I guess I'm being more concrete. I suppose I wonder what makes it seem like an important activity to you, when there are other things that might get you out of the hospital sooner."

"But I'm only in the hospital because the Russians wanted to put me here. It has nothing to do with me. They did this to me. What if they're the crazy ones? How do I know that you're not crazy?"

"I suppose you don't. But we both know that at the end of the day I'm going home and you're staying here. So whatever I'm doing is more successful right now."

"But I can't be like you. You're a man."

She starts to make a low, growling noise. All at once she leaps up, looks behind her chair, then sits. She looks me in the eye and says, "You know, the Russians won't like this."

"What do you mean, Shirley?"

"I mean they may have to retaliate."

"I don't understand why you say that."

"Do you want me to call in the bombers?"

"No. Are you feeling angry?"

"You're such a man. I think you're crazy."

Right. "So what are we gonna do to help you get out of here?"

"I'm not leaving, Dr. Jackson."

"No?"

"I can't. No one will let me."

"You're a voluntary patient. You can leave whenever you want to."

"Oh no. I can't leave. Only higher forces can release me."

"Higher forces."

"You know, upstairs."

"You mean in Heaven?" I ask.

She eyes me warily and whispers, "Whatever you say, Doc." And then she grins. And I shake my head in amazement.

"So what do you think, John? Is this a job for me? Or should I quit and go traveling?"

Having finished the coffee and started into a bottle of Aquavit kept specially frozen for just these occasions, we sit down to a serious planning session. Zoe, freshly scrubbed, strolls into the room. She sits on my lap and asks John, "Has he been boring you with tales of the loony bin?"

Johnny gives her a hug. "He does seem a little stressed out. Maybe he needs medication."

"Quit it, you guys. It's not me, it's the hospital from which there is no exit."

"But Max," Zoe begins, "I thought that the only reality was the internal reality. You know, if you're crazy, then it's because you can't handle the scene. The problem isn't the world. That's just projection."

"Projection nothing! Sometimes you go wild trying to deal with all the madness in the world. That's a problem that most of my patients share with me."

"Well Max," John pulls at his beard. "Then why do you give them drugs and then send them back into the outside world? Surely the drugs haven't changed the problems that drove them into the hospital in the first place."

"Of course not. But maybe they'll be able to cope better if they are on medication or in therapy."

"Come on, Max. Do you really believe that?" Zoe lifts her left eyebrow and gazes at me with incredulity.

"I don't know. That's what everybody else says. Who knows what's true anymore?"

"Well that's great." John finishes off his Aquavit and starts in on another glass. "So this great job has you so confused that you can't tell what's true anymore. Why not just be an alcoholic?"

Grabbing my glass I nod in agreement. "Although sometimes I feel that this confusion is just what I need. Sort of a testing ground for all my feelings." And down goes the first drink as the second is poured.

"Let me get this straight now, Max. If you find out that everything you believe is wrong and you still believe something, then you're okay."

"Not exactly. If anything I believe in seems to be true at the end of this crazy year, then maybe it is true."

"But what if nothing is true? Then you're in trouble."

"Something has to work. Maybe it's all external reality. Maybe the fact that these people's world stinks explains why their life stinks. And I need another drink."

"But what does that have to do with medications and the outside world?"

"Well, maybe the internal reality is all that matters. Maybe the drugs do work. The only way to find out is to try them."

"Yeah. But the external reality counts, too."

"I know it does. But I haven't figured out a way to deal with it yet. And I don't know if wanting to is trying to take too much responsibility and control of someone else's life. Maybe helping with the internal reality is all I can do. I'm not omnipotent, you know."

"You seem pretty confused," John says.

"Well I am. There are a lot of competing ideologies here. I mean, how are you supposed to decide anyway?" The liquor has started to affect my speech.

"Decide what?"

"I mean, is it better for a patient to be mad and locked up and have their rights observed, or is it better to force meds and get them out of the hospital fast? Which takes away more freedom? Is there another alternative?"

"God, Max. Why not do whatever works? You don't have to force anything on them. Just let 'em go."

"But they're sick!" I fairly shout and almost fall from my chair. "They could die!"

"Well, that's up to them," John answers. "Nobody should stop another person from dying if they want to."

"Aha! If they want to. But if someone is psychotic, how do you know what they want? If someone says to you, 'I want to die to avoid those little green men who have eaten my mother,' what do you do? Do you let them go? It's highly complex!"

John looks at Zoe and says, "He's raving, you know."

She smiles and says, "He's just drunk and happy to see you."

Zoe has been patiently drinking her coffee while this little debate goes on. Her hair is braided straight down her back, she's got on a touch of purple mascara and her high cheekbones show off her eyes to magnificent advantage. Lunging at her I miss and fall on the floor. "Well, Ace. What's your internal experience of that? Or does the harsh reality of the floor make a difference."

"You don't like my theory," I shout up.

"I don't think you've got one. I think you like psychiatry but you don't know why and you get angry at it when you feel bad. But you like it. You're not comfortable with it yet, though."

"I'm comfortable with you, Zoe," I slur.

She and John pick me up off the floor and put me in bed. "I know, Ace. And I'm comfortable with you. And the difference between what happens inside your head and what happens outside may not be as large as you think."

And in the dream I am in an empty house. Every door I open leads nowhere. And then I stop dreaming.

My head hurts only a wee tad on Monday morning and I can walk without wobbling at all. John has left for parts unknown with the admonition, "Don't screw up," and Zoe is back at the med school waiting game. So it looks like I'm on my own again. There's a light snow falling and it looks as if we may have a white

Christmas. But as I shake my coat off and hang my hat on its hook, the phone rings and I know it's going to be hard to make it to the holidays without trouble. "Dr. Jackson? This is Irwin. Get up to the intensive care unit quick. Your patient is messing up." Oh, no, not Ecaterina. What has she done?

But as I walk in the door I see Tam, naked, a sheet wound around his head, howling like a dog in heat. Irwin turns to me and says, "What are you going to do about this?"

"How long has it been going on?"

"Hours."

"Hours?"

"I don't know," he says. "Too long."

"Well, it is pretty awful." I call over two attendants and ask them to lift up Tam and take him to his room. They accomplish that with no problem and I turn to follow when Irwin asks, "Don't you want to give him a tranquilizer?"

"Not yet. I don't even know what's wrong."

He glares at me and leaves. Terrific. Where is the support? I want to cry. Eight o'clock in the morning and I'm already locking up people and shooting them full of drugs and I don't want to be a jailer and I'm really so tired and I'm on call tonight and oh shit! I take a deep breath, let it out, and sigh. Tears are waiting to flow and I don't really know why and I thought I was angry and another deep breath and I'm okay I really am and I go in to see Tam.

He's sitting on his bed, and the screaming has dropped in volume so that I try to talk above it. "Tam. Be quiet."

He stops and looks at me. Then extends his hand and we shake. We remain in silence and he appears ready to yell again. I raise my hands and say, "No," very loudly and he seems to understand. I motion for him to lie down on the bed and he does so. Turning, I slip out of the room. My little boy has gone to sleep.

Irwin is waiting for me. "Shall we give the meds now?"

"Irwin. He's asleep. Let's let him rest." Me, too.

As the day goes on it gets colder and colder with the chill in the air gone, replaced by the freeze of winter. My beard freezes as I walk to lunch, my eyeglasses fog up as I enter the building. Like a disabled veteran I trudge into my office, looking for refuge. And finding it since most of my patients fail to show, given the intense cold they're dealing with. Simon, however, manages to make it in and that gives me some cause to hope.

"Dr. Jackson, I'm sorry I'm late." As always, he looks in disarray. Now, however, he has at least noticed the time and coped with it. "I've been sitting at home feeling jealous. I'll never be Mozart. I'll never have my father." He starts to cry.

"You've had many losses."

"I lost my family. I lost the girl next door. I'll lose you."

"Can you tell me more about that?"

"There is no way to keep people. I tried not to lose my father. But he went to New York. Maybe it was to get away from me. Why would he leave me like that? Why?"

"What are you feeling now, Simon?"

"I don't know. All this pain. I feel so hurt inside. I feel that my insides are being ripped apart. I can feel all that anger in me, screaming to get out, but not finding a way. It scares me! How will it get out?"

"Try to let it go now."

"I can't," he screams. "I am overwhelmed with hate!"

"And who is the hate for?"

"For everybody!" Then so softly I can barely hear, "Maybe for me."

"You can be angry without being bad."

"No I can't! I hate myself for being angry!" He puts his head in his hands and runs his fingers through his hair, over and over again. He grabs a handful of tissues to wipe his eyes. He blows his nose and sighs, then begins a gentle rocking motion in the chair. He looks like a very sad hippo.

"It's okay to be angry," I repeat. "If you hold on to it, then how will you ever let it go?" Right. Brilliant.

"I get guilty when I get angry," he wails. And then mumbles under his breath, "I can't, I can't."

"So is it the guilt or the anger that feels so bad?"

"The anger feels bad, but I get relief when it's gone. The guilt feels bad forever. I feel guilty now over things that happened years ago."

I think to myself that he probably is also angry about things that happened years ago, but repress the instinct to say so. Instead, I respond, "So why not stop the guilt, rather than the anger? Getting angry sounds productive."

"But I'm angry at everyone. I'm angry at my mother and my brother and my father and you and the hospital. None of you care about me enough." He starts to cry. "No one cares for me."

"Who does? Who cares about Simon enough?"

"I don't know. Do you mean I don't?"

Exactly. "Well, what do you think of that idea?"

"I don't know. Why would anyone want to love me? I was sure you'd be angry at me for missing our session last week. I thought . . ." and starts crying again.

After a minute I ask, "What did you think?"

"That you would stop being my doctor."

"No, Simon. I'll be your doctor. If I'm angry at you I'll tell you."

"Thank you," he sniffles. "Christmas is going to be horrible. I hope everyone doesn't hate me."

"Give them a chance, Simon. Give yourself a chance."

At the end of the day, Shirley is prowling the hall in front of me. She takes two steps forward, then one to the right, then one back again. She repeats this procedure till she hits the right wall, then starts the whole process backward. Every time she takes a step she says, "Oh wow!" then sighs heavily. Her hands move to her lips periodically as she walks backward toward me, but I can't make out her actions. Finally, I call out, just as she is about to bump into me, "Shirley, what's going on?"

She turns around and gives me a tremendous grin. Then holding up a huge red cup she shouts, "No water!" Then she laughs hysterically and strolls away. Two steps forward, one left and one back.

I try out the hall myself and discover no immediate reason not to proceed at my normal pace. Bobby meets up with me and we fall in step. "Bobby," I ask. "Are you upset?"

"Hmm, Max. I don't know. I always get angry at authority. You know that. I'm no more pissed off than usual. Why do you ask?"

"Cause I'm at my wit's end. I feel like I'm going to explode. I've been mouthing off to everybody, can't get my act straight, and even Zoe thinks that I'm totally confused about what's going on. Then I feel depressed and don't know why."

Bobby slows down so I can catch up with his long stride. As we turn the corner into the library, he tells me, "I don't think you're any worse off than me, or anyone else, for that matter. This is a tough time."

Denise and Eric meet us there for an end of the day cooling-off session. The last thing I need now is more teaching. Now I need angry empathy. "Look," I say. "Why don't we put all the patients on a bus and send them to Florida for the winter. They'll thank us for it."

"Not Florida," says Denise. "That's where my parents live. How about Alabama?"

"Fine with me. But what will they do there?"

Eric has an idea. "Why not set up summer camps for them? They can play volleyball and run races and have a great time. And no one will have to worry since they'll be out of the way of danger. And the patients won't feel bad since they'll just be on summer vacation."

"Great idea," I say, "and listen to this: it'll be cheaper than mental hospitals, so we can probably sell it to the state."

Bobby is concerned, however. "What will we do for a living if all the patients are gone?"

"Uh huh. That's a very good point." Eric scratches his head. He pulls on his handlebar mustache and seems to ponder. He's very suave in a suit, but I can't help wondering if it's all just an act, and he'd rather be in jeans. "Well, we would have to offer to fly down there as consultants. Or maybe we would just fly the patients down there in weekly shifts."

Denise is still feeling serious. "But that just perpetuates the notion that our patients have of life being somehow unreal. You know, they often act like their illness is all a big bad dream that's going to go away."

"Well, wouldn't you? How much pain would you want to believe is real?"

"I understand that Max, but it doesn't change the issue. It seems to me that until they accept their illness as real, that they will never move on. We can't help them escape."

"Well, Denise, I don't know. Even mental patients deserve a little vacation from their pain. Maybe all hospitals do is keep them in a constantly painful position."

Eric is still smiling over the concept of mental patient summer camps, but chimes in with, "It's all a question of figuring out if we're doing anything at all as doctors. If we're not, then we might as well help our patients escape. But if all this," and he gestures to the hospital buildings outside the window, as well as to the three of us, "means anything, then we have to help them deal with the pain."

Well. I don't know anymore. Who's getting better? Who have I helped? Some patients have got better and gone away. Many have stayed. One has nearly died. Patients come and go and I stay and watch them come back over and over. Is it enough to give someone insight into being crazy? Do medications stop the madness and the pain? How does anybody, including me, get what they want? How do you get your mind to let you be who you want to be? And now I sit with my patients and ask them to believe me, to take the meds, to come to the sessions, to (most of all) trust me to help them get better.

Zoe is waiting for me in the lobby and greets me with, "You're late."

"I'm sorry, Zoe. We were having a meeting to deal with our feelings."

"Great. And how about my feelings?" She is wearing a tight leather jacket and blue jeans. Her hair is in a fury about her head and the chill in the air has put a rose on her rosy cheeks. "You're so sexy, I could scream."

"Well, no touching," she says as we walk onto the street. "You can't get out of it so easy."

"Why not? Anyway, the meeting was fun. I needed a release."

"Oh. That's great, Ace. Now you can bring your anger home to me."

"Jeepers, love. It's not that way. It's just hard to communicate to anyone at this place."

"Well, for someone who is supposed to like it, you've got a weird way of showing it. I think you need a break."

"Before I'm broken."

Jerry is punctual and sane and I'm glad to see him. He's still drooping as he enters the office. As a matter of fact, he looks sadder than the first time I saw him. Maybe that means the therapy is working.

"Hullo, Dr. Jackson."

"Hi, Jerry."

"I had a pretty good week."

"Want to tell me about it?"

"I don't know. I mean, sure. Nothing much happened. I thought a lot about what we talked about."

"What was that?"

"About things, I guess. I don't know."

"You don't?"

"Dr. Jackson?" He lowers his voice and changes the tone to sound as serious as possible. "Can we talk about my girlfriend today?"

"Sure. What did you want to say?"

"I don't know. She's not really a girlfriend. I've only gone out with her a few times. We've never slept together or anything. But I like her."

"Uh huh."

"I don't know. She makes me nervous."

"Tell me about that."

"She's pretty forward. She sort of has a lot of excitement and she makes me uncomfortable." He picks up speed. "I was really attracted to her when I first saw her. She was beautiful and really got me going."

"What was so appealing?"

"She was nice to me. She was a good friend. We could just sit and talk and hang out together and have a nice time. I felt so relaxed."

"And then?"

"Well, I don't know."

"You don't know?"

"Well, I guess I started to get more and more worried. She wanted to get closer and started to neck a lot and I just wasn't ready for that. I'm not used to that. It was too much stimulation."

"How did it make you feel?"

"I guess it seemed like a threat."

"A threat?"

"A sexual threat. She would put her arms around me and I wouldn't know what to do."

"How would you feel then?"

"Angry, surprised and angry. I always feel that way when this happens. I think to myself why is this happening, why can't we leave things the way they are? Why do we have to have sex?"

"What do you make of all that?"

"Well, you must think it's pretty weird."

"I must?"

"Well, I think it's pretty weird. Jesus, I'd like to have sex. I fantasize about it enough, that's for sure. And I've heard other people talk about it forever. But I just can't seem to handle it when it comes my way. Even though I really want it."

"What might happen?"

"I don't know." Even he smiles when he hears himself say that. "Maybe I'd get stuck. Maybe things wouldn't work out. Maybe they'd get all messed up."

"Maybe. What would be so bad?"

"You mean with sex?" I nod. "I guess, that I couldn't do it, or something like that."

"Have you ever had a problem with sex?"

"I've never had a satisfying experience. I wonder what it would

be like. I wonder all the time. I wonder what it would be like to
have a girlfriend and spend a lot of time with her and sleep
together and have great sex and have breakfast together in bed
and go on dates and all that stuff. But all I can do is wonder about
it, since the reality never happens. And it's not that I don't have
offers. Things just don't seem to work out."

"Because you get scared?"

"Yes." He frowns and shuffles his feet. "You can't imagine how
strange it is. I'm sitting there with a girl and then she moves a
little closer and I get all panicked and flustered and I can barely
keep myself from fleeing the room. And then she'll leave and I'll
be all alone and I'll be angry at myself but mostly I'll be relieved."

"Relieved that she's no longer close?"

"Yeah. I guess so. I don't want anyone to find out too much
about me."

"What are they going to find out?"

"I don't know. I'm not really as good as most people think I
am. My parents think I'm some sort of perfect creature."

"How do they let you know that?"

"Well, they put enough demands on me to drive a nonperfect
person crazy."

"That's too bad."

He looks down and tears up. "It sure is. Jesus. I don't need that
pressure."

"And you don't need any more from some woman who wants
to get close to you."

"I sure don't. Hell, I've got enough demands on my life already. I don't need any more. Who knows what my girlfriend
wants from me? I don't want to have to take care of her. I have
enough trouble taking care of myself."

"So you push her away?"

"I guess so. Anyway, I don't know if I can perform in bed."

"You might not be perfect?"

He smiles. "Yeah, that's right. I might not be perfect."

"Maybe she doesn't want you to be. That sounds like your
standard, not hers."

"What do you mean?"

"You're the one who wants to be perfect."

"I'm pretty tired of it. I can't really be perfect, you know."

"Yup."

"What should I do?"

"About what?"

"About women and the way I feel. I want a girlfriend and I want to have sex and I want to relax more."

"Sounds like you need to relax more first."

"Yeah. I guess I don't have to be perfect." He tenses as he says this. "But I worry all the time that I'm all screwed up."

"You're not. You just have things to work on."

"I suppose. Are you sure? I can handle that."

"Good. Let's talk more about it next week."

At eight at night the hospital lobby is deserted. Tonight will be a different night of call. I grab Zoe's hand and we run up to my office. "The coast is clear," I whisper and softly close the door. She gives out a long, giggling laugh and inquires, "Do you know how much I love you, Max?" Her tongue makes a circle, licking her lips and then sliding back inside her mouth. Her eyes stay fixed on mine, growing bigger and brighter as I watch. The sparkle in her face comes from an inner warmth as well as the outer cold.

"Oh, Zoe," I sigh. "How much do you love me?" I imagine the same glow rising to my cheeks.

"I love you as big as this, Max." She stretches her arms out as far as they'll go, then runs over to me and throws her arms around my neck. "I've brought all the love that I save up while you're sleeping at the hospital."

I hold her close and feel the warmth of her body pass through mine. As we stand there under the watchful eye of Sigmund the First, I whisper in her ear, "I am so glad you're here, Zoe. My night would be awful without you." I hold her at arms' length and look her up and down. "Why don't you take off your coat and stay a spell?"

She giggles at me and says, "Okay, but don't laugh at what I'm wearing."

"Come on, show me. What's so funny." I grab for her jacket, but she backs away.

"Just be real gentle, cause," and she breaks into a huge grin, "I don't have anything underneath." She throws off her parka to reveal a half-naked beauty, a delight, so inviting, her belly smooth and clean, her hands hooked in her pants.

"Holy cow, Zoe. I wouldn't call that nothing." I move a little closer and she backs off with the admonition, "Warm your hands first."

Then she beckons with her finger, as I rub my hands together. "Come on over here, and I'll show you how to get a little mental health." Slowly I move forward as she calls out to me, "Come here, my love. I'll make you all better." Then I rush to her and squeeze her until we try to get inside one skin.

"Oh, baby," I moan, as she pulls my head to her chest. "You are something else. Something wonderful."

"Yes, my love? What else am I?" She grabs my hands and puts them in hers and then, BEEP BEEP BEEP BEEP BEEP BEEP BEEP BEEP . . .

"Damn Zoe! Where the hell is my beeper? Goddamit!" I find the stupid thing tossed in a corner with my shirt and turn it off.

"Very sexy, Ace." Zoe sits on my lap, as I call the page operator, and starts to lick my ear.

"Hi, Tillie? What is it? Good. Say, can you hold my calls for a few minutes? I'm real busy." I hang up and turn my head, moving Zoe's tongue from my ear to my mouth. I can feel my own body growing taut under hers and grab her round the waist and lower her to the floor.

"Well alright, Max. Why don't you take it all off and let me see those muscles bulge? Let's have a little physical therapy in this office of yours." She tilts her head back and offers me the whole lovely curve of her body as it slopes down to meet mine.

My mouth goes to hers and then separates. "Whew, Zoe. I love you. I feel healthier already." I get my hands on her pants when BRRIIINNNGGG! BBRRIINNGG!

"HELL!" I start to pray that the phone will stop ringing of its own accord but on and on it goes. Disengaging myself from Zoe, I get up to answer it. "Dr. Jackson? This is security. You better come to the acute unit. Ecaterina is throwing a fit."

"Sure, Ty. I'll be there as soon as I can."

"Shit!" I yell as I turn around, then notice that Zoe is now naked, standing silently in the center of my office. Her finger in her mouth, other hand dangling in front of her, legs at a distance to give her good balance, and I am overwhelmed by desire as I start to fantasize about making love with her. Back and forth the images shift in my mind, till she comes to me and wraps her body and mind around us. We settle back on the carpet as she slowly undresses me and begins to rub me with her hands and her body. She reaches up and unplugs the phone, then pulls me down on her. "Ace, just stay with me for a moment. Hold me tight."

"I will Zoe. I'll always hold you. I'll . . ." BEEP BEEP BEEP BEEP BEEP BEEP BEEP BEEP BEEP BEEP!!!!!!!!!

"AAARRRGGGGHHHH! Where is that goddam thing? I'll kill it! I'll throw it out the window! I'll kill whoever called me!" Then Ty is yelling at me through the door. "Hey, Max! Move it! Ecaterina is gonna kill herself or somebody else and you better get there fast!"

Throwing my clothes on my body I leave Zoe on the floor with my heart and run off to the ICU. I am confronted there with Ecaterina, holding a razor blade, alternately trying to stick it in her own wrist or into the faces of the two men grabbing at her arms. There is a circle of others watching, patients and staff. "Look," I shout. "Somebody get all the patients out of this room." This accomplished, I turn to Ecaterina and say, "You seem angry."

"These bastards are trying to hurt me."

"I think they're worried about you."

"Then tell them to leave me alone." She starts swinging wildly with her blade as the attendants fall back.

"Sure, Ecaterina. They're afraid that you're going to hurt yourself. So am I."

"You're afraid. I bet."

"I really am. I want to talk to you about your depression. I won't get that chance if you kill yourself."

"You just want to use me like all the others." She is whining, but weakening.

"No, Ecaterina, you're here so that we can help you. Put down the razor blade."

She has stopped threatening the attendants with the blade and now looks at it in her hands as if it is some foreign object with a life of its own that she has no idea how it arrived on her person. Without comment, she drops it on the floor and then collapses in a heap next to it.

"Crap. Will somebody get her into bed? This is too much." The formerly threatened mental health assistants step back into a caretakers' role and lift her off the floor and into her room. "Put her on suicide precautions and we'll start over in the morning. Shit, Ty. Sometimes this place sucks."

"You ain't kidding, Doc. Least you got an office."

The staircase seems darker than usual while I trudge up to my sanctuary. The bare light bulbs on the wall are either broken or flickering with the last remnants of since spent energy and one has to look down to avoid unseen hazards left by patients or staff. Turning the corner to my office, I try to cheer myself up with the knowledge of the pleasure that waits within. At least true love will save the day.

"Oh Zoe," I call heading back inside. "I'm here. All hot and bothered and ready for you."

But the note on my desk said, "Love you, Ace. It works better at home. Yum." And Freud may be right about sexual frustration. I think I'm going crazy.

5

Dissociation

Groping around the sand with my hand I find the number eight suntan oil and start to spread it on my body. Not only does this keep the flies away, but it also prevents my skin from totally roasting. We urban types often have a hard time at the beach. And this is quite a beach. The sun is hot. The sand is hot. The air is warm. The ocean is delightful. And this dead tired psychiatric resident who has escaped for a solitary week of relaxation and fun in the sun is immobilized with wonder.

The ganja man, wearing heavy duty shades that he has obtained in a trade for the national product of Jamaica comes by. "Hey, mon. Want anything?" But I've already got what I need. I look down at my arms again to check out the tan. Zoe is sleeping next to me, and after the ganja man has gone, we are the only moving creatures in sight. If we were moving. "Hey, love," I yell. "Throw me a beer."

Zoe barely stirs and mumbles, "I think they're all gone." I pick up my head to answer and just stare at her. With her clothes off she is even more beautiful. Her skin is nice and brown. Her body shines with oil reflecting the sun. She lies there in an elegant relaxation, then moves to turn over, muscles rippling through her stomach and legs, then down her back as she rolls. I drop my head back down. Too much excitement might overload my circuits.

Lethargy has set in and I'm in no mood to change it. After five days of lying in one place, wearing one bathing suit and moving only to flip the other side into the sunlight, there seems to be a light emerging from the peak beyond the waves. Who knows what it is. All that counts is that it's there.

I'm halfway done with this year. Great. And I'm on vacation. Terrific. Now, if I could only get myself to stop obsessing about all the work I'm not doing. I'm still dreaming about the place.

"Help me, Zoe! How am I ever gonna get out of that mess?"

"What are you talking about, Max?"

"Asylum."

"You crazy loon. The only way to get out is to take your medication and follow the rules. If you can't deal with the limits that the place sets, then you have to stay until you've got it right."

"Thank you, Doctor." But I get the point. Now everything is perfectly clear. She was behind it from the first. She wanted me to do this in order to facilitate her own med school admission process. No wait a second. What am I saying? That's paranoid drivel. Whoa. Maybe I need to stay another week.

Anyway, what makes my job so bad? Why do doctors complain about their jobs so often? Why do I? What's my beef? "Zoe? Are you sure there's no more beer?" She shakes her head and I get up to buy some from the beer lady. Who for some reason looks like she's enjoying herself at work.

But wait. I enjoy myself at my work. If you break it down second by second and minute by minute (or more likely, fifty minutes by fifty minutes) it's a pretty good deal. But there's something about the entire package that makes you wonder.

Dick and Jane, our new beautiful people jet set friends on the beach, walk on over. They are an enviable pair. Dick is a banker. Tall, dark, and handsome and all that, he can sway people to his side just by grinning. He's the sort of person that I tried to become good friends with in high school so that no one would beat me up. This was on the theory that the only good defense against a bully was to have a bigger bully on your side. Sort of parallels the defense programs of most nations. This technique had a limited benefit in high school, since most of the bullies didn't know the meaning of friendship. As is also true in world affairs. Dick, however, is not a bully. He's a charmer.

"Hey, Max," he calls out, laying his towel down on the beach. He's got a body that would put most of Nautilus to shame, and I am tempted to cover my eyes, as a reflex maneuver, to prevent an avalanche of sand being kicked in them. Dick, however, is either oblivious to it all or trained to take it in stride and acts like a normal human being. "Do you have a minute?"

"Sure. Have a seat in my office." I look down at my legs which are starting to fry in spite of all my precautions and cover myself with a towel. Dick is bronzed, of course.

"I wonder if you have a few minutes to talk to me about a problem."

"As long as it doesn't have to do with sunburn."

"Nothing like that. It's just that I'm very depressed and don't know what to do about it."

Since I can't respond, "Take a vacation to Jamaica," I go with, "Tell me about it." Now I don't know if this is a mistake or not. Do I really want to take on new work at the beach? On the other hand, this is a much healthier person to talk to than I normally get. To say the least. Anyway, he sure looks like everything is going well in his life. What could be going on? "It's like this. My mother just died and I'm having trouble sleeping at night. Shit. That's not it. I can't concentrate and my mother died two years ago. I don't know what's going on. I can't seem to get happy."

"Let's start over, Dick. You're unhappy, and it has something to do with your mother?"

"I don't know. I can't get through a day without having terrible thoughts about myself and my life. I'm driving Jane nuts and I'm afraid she's going to leave me."

"Have you considered seeing a therapist?" Obviously, this is not a little vacation problem.

"Yeah. But how do I know when it's time?"

"It's time when it bothers you enough so that you can't enjoy your vacation."

"I guess so. You look so relaxed here. What makes your life so happy?"

Huh? Everyone certainly has their own point of view. "I don't know. I guess I do like vacation." Jane joins our conversation, having finished talking with Zoe. She's about five foot ten, a scant four inches shorter than Dick, and lovely. Also tanned to perfection, she sways gracefully when she walks, her long blond hair turned into a mass of curls and waves by the salt and sun. She sits next to Dick and arches her back, then asks, "Has he been telling you about his problems?" She's a bit of a tart.

Tearing my eyes away from her body I focus on her face, which is no less distracting. But I manage to answer, "Why don't you ask him?"

"Well, Dick?" she inquires, lying back on the sand and stretching out her hands.

Dick lies down next to her and pulls his sunglasses over his eyes. "A little. I don't want to talk about it now." They both stop talking and I crawl over to Zoe.

"Hey, Zoe. Want to take a walk?"

"Sure, Ace. Let's do it."

We get up to take our daily trip around the cove. As I stand I can feel the tension slip from my head, roll down my back and out the base of my spine. I feel lighter and cleaner and more relaxed than I can remember. "Zoe, I feel great."

"That's nice to hear. You're looking pretty good, too."

"Thanks. It's nice to be taking care of myself instead of everyone else."

"That's for sure. But that's a problem that all you doctors have."

"What's that?"

"You spend so much time saving the world that you forget that you're people, too. And then everything in your body and your mind messes up and you don't know why. It takes a full week of vacation to remember that it's an important thing to take care of yourself."

"I'm not the only one, you know. Dick was telling me before
how unhappy he is. And he and Jane don't look so pleased with
each other."

"So maybe you should give yourself a break. What do you say?
Maybe it's okay to have a lot of self-doubts and stuff and still be a
good psychiatrist. Maybe you can even make a mistake or two.
Nobody's perfect."

"Except you sweetheart."

Zoe smiles her biggest grin and replies, "It's true, you know."

In my dream I have missed a therapy group and return to find a
new member there. I leave the group angrily and am contacted by
people who want the group destroyed. We set off to find them but
the group retaliates and comes after us. I am alone in a carnival
and fall into a well, but am caught by the bucket. I look up to see a
sea of angry faces. My own face contorts and I wake up.

"You know, Zoe. You can't ever really get away. No matter how
far you go."

"Yes, Max. Dorothy said that."

And indeed, before you know it it is time to go back. Watching
our last sunset on the beach, sitting in deck chairs, sipping daiqui-
ris, we listen to the waves. Sunsets seem to go on forever here,
with colors brightening the sky long after the sun has slipped
below the horizon. With the gentle rocking motion of the ocean
providing the back beat and the palm trees and sand the back-
drop, the aura of everything being okay is reinforced until even
thinking about all the craziness that awaits on return seems fool-
ish. The main topic of conversation among the tourists and idlers
is the state of their tans. Perhaps people obsess about their tans
on the beach because there is very little else to obsess about. And
no matter how hard you try, you still bring your defenses to the
beach. Dick and Jane want me to be a psychiatrist here and my
main issue is trying to set limits around my time. So what else is
new? And my journal is filled not only with thoughts of peace and
comfort, but with schemes about work and life. On and on.

The crickets come out as the sun goes down and add their

noises to the sounds of the sea. Turning to Zoe I say, "That was a nice sunset tonight." Hardly the sort of conversation I ever have in the mental hospital. And again it is difficult to put together the reality of the craziness of the world with the moments of peace in my life. And if the feelings aren't guilt they are something else, like not knowing what the rules of the world are and what part I play. I want to remember all I ever learned about diversity and variety and spice of life and all that, but what extremes there are. If I moved all my patients down to Jamaica would they all still be ill? Would the change in climate make a difference? Would they want to be here? And how do I reconcile the reality I work in with that that I find myself in? Ten years ago I knew it would all be easier. The world would be changed by now. We would have peace on earth, justice for all, equality for everyone. The sick would be cared for and the reality of hard choices would be changed. But it didn't happen to the world. And all I see in my work is pain. The point of becoming a doctor was to work to build a better people for a better planet. And instead I'm trying to hold together a few lives, including my own, while we watch the world try to hold itself together amid a tidal wave of death and poverty and horror. So you can take a vacation to Jamaica, but there is no way to forget what has been left behind.

My parents used to ask me every week what I wanted to be when I grew up. And after a while I took to telling them that I would be a doctor. It seemed so clean, so pure. But if you want to treat sick people then you better be ready to treat all your own symptoms, too. Because if the world has problems, then they are only the larger reflection of all the troubles we have as individuals.

"Hey, Max! We're landing. Back to Boston!"

"Great, Zoe. Back to the old mill."

"You've been lost in thought for hours. What's on your mind?"

"Nothing much. Just wondering what it all means anyway."

"Give it up, Max. It doesn't mean anything."

Brrriiinnnggg! I roll over to grab the phone and hear, "Hi ho, Max. Nice to have you back."

"Oh hi, Bobby. How have things been?"

"Okay, except for Ecaterina. Have you got a minute? I didn't want this to wait till tomorrow."

"Sure. I figured she'd do okay. The last thing she said to me before my vacation was, 'Hey, man. Go away for three years. I don't give a damn.' "

"In that case, Max, she was pulling your leg. On the first day you were gone she said she was going to kill anyone who tried to talk to her. So we wanted to send her to the ICU, but she freaked out and tried to stab herself. She bit someone on the nose. We finally got her up there and then she just fell to pieces."

"Sounds terrific. How is she now?"

"Well, after that she calmed down and then started complaining that, 'The only reason I'm sick is that my therapist won't give me regular sessions,' and other things like that. I think that she missed you."

"Well son of a bitch. She has a very bizarre way of showing it."

"Actually, Max, none of your patients took your vacation too well. Wait till you see Simon."

"Can it wait till tomorrow? I want to spend my last day of vacation in peace."

"No problem. Welcome home."

Zoe curls around me in bed. "Let's go back to sleep, Ace. I love you."

The new mantra as I head into the hospital has something to do with staying calm. I want to remember Jamaica, remember the feeling of lying in the sand, listening to the ocean, drinking sparkling rum beverages under the palms. I want to remember how relaxation feels. Perhaps remembering is the key to mental health. If I could remember back to the womb I'm sure it would be a nice relaxing time. Maybe that should be the new trick in psychotherapy. Prebirth remembering. I'm sure they have it already in California.

I try to sneak into my office without any of the patients seeing me and am of course unsuccessful. Ecaterina is standing by the door. She has left the acute unit over my vacation, apparently no longer suicidal, and is now in the day hospital. She gives me a long, hard stare and walks through my door after me.

"Welcome back, Dr. Jackson," she drawls out, barely moving her lips. "I'm so glad to see you." This, ladies and gents, is sarcasm.

"Hello, Ecaterina. It's nice to see you, too. I'm glad you're out of the ICU."

"You're glad?"

"Yes."

"Well, that's pretty hard to believe, seeing as you are the one who locked me up there. Luckily, Dr. Watson had the sense to let me out."

I am not going to get into this today. "I'm glad. Now, how can I help you?"

"I need my privileges changed. Dr. Watson said you'd take care of it when you got back."

"Uh huh. What do you want?"

"I want to be able to come and go as I please."

"Are you going to kill yourself?"

She looks startled. Such outspokenness certainly is not expected. By either of us I suppose. "That's a very nice tan you have, Dr. Jackson." This is from an expert.

"Thank you, Ecaterina. You didn't answer my question."

"No, Doctor, I'm not going to kill myself."

"Great." Got my fingers crossed. "I'll make the changes."

She tosses her head and walks away, and a nice little walk it is, without even a thank you.

Closing the door I look around my sanctuary and notice that all the plants have died. Seems the temperature in my office fell to about thirty while I was away. As I start cleaning them up and throwing them away, there's a knock on the door. Simon opens it and peers in. "Come on in," I wave and sit down.

"You scum!" he screams.

I smile at him, knowing in my heart that he's just missing me. Anyway, I like Simon. There's something about the freedom of his mind and the willingness to question that is very appealing.

Besides, he's interesting. As a group, there are few that can match mental patients for fresh views on the world. "Hello, Simon."

"I hate you!"

My smile continues, as I think about the fact that I have a job where things are varied and wild, ever changing and fun. And knowing that no matter how hard the struggle, there is the joy of being a healer and working with people you care about. "You seem angry."

"When I look at you I see the blood of terror, the hopelessness of the world laid bare at my feet!"

I will not let my vacation glow be sucked into the vortex of horror. After all, I am a participant here, but not a passive one. "Tell me about the terror."

"You are the killer of my hopes. When I enter life all music begins! I am the majesty of sound! But I am so bad. They will all see how bad it is. I am fear surrounded by love. I am love surrounded by fear. There is nothing for me. It is all gone. All gone." Simon hasn't left his chair yet, but his spirit seems to be soaring. His eyes are as wide open as a pair can be and his mouth is moving constantly, spewing out words as they come to his mind without a moment's hesitation about their logic.

"I feel overwhelmed by your anger and sadness, Simon. What are you feeling now?" Remember, this is a patient. What he's saying is real, albeit weird. Even though it looks like a show, this is actual life. Which unfortunately is what makes it so painful.

"I will always be so alone. Alone at home. Like a stone. There is nothing to live for. There is no hope for me." He starts to cry and I make a guess.

"I am back from my vacation, Simon. I'm going to stay your therapist."

"Oh God!" He lifts his head and looks around as if confused about what to do next. Seeming to decide, he looks at me and says, "Oh, thank you. I'm glad. Thank you."

He sniffles. "But I hate you."

"It's okay. I'll still be your doctor."

Amazingly, he nods and leaves the office with a half smile and somewhat of a lift in his step. I put my feet on the desk and wait for another disaster to solve.

Bobby, however, is the next visitor to my office. After greetings and welcome backs and such, he tells me, "I admitted a new patient for you while you were gone. Let me introduce you to him."

My new patient's name is Elroy. Elroy says, "Everyone in my world is trying to kill me. Even I am trying to kill myself. I have an idea that all the chemicals were put there for a reason. But I don't know what it is. But people are making it and it's killing me. Everyone in my world hates me. They start wars where I die or people I love die and I am left all alone. Everyone in my world loves me. Everything they do is for me. They just don't understand what I want."

All I can do is look at Elroy. Why is he in the hospital?

"I'm here because I need a place to get away from all the killing. It's such an ugly world. How can a sane person go on?"

Is Elroy going to kill himself?

"All I do all day long is try and kill myself. I make shit and throw it in the ocean. I drive my car and destroy the air. I pay my taxes and people turn it into nuclear weapons. You're killing yourself too. Or maybe I'm killing you."

Elroy is depressed. So depressed that he tried to hang himself. "I was just looking for a more efficient method."

On and on.

Ecaterina turns up at my door and Elroy shuffles away. She sits down by my desk and starts to mumble. I ask her to speak up and she puts her hands on the desk. "Look, Doctor. What am I going to do with my life! I don't have much help. Screw it! Why do I tell you? Just forget it."

The phone rings and it's Sam. Ecaterina takes off down the hall before I can say excuse me and Sam, after a brief welcome back, brings up the subject of Tam. "Have you been to see him yet, Max?"

"Hell no, Sam. I just got back. Nothing too bad, I hope."

"Why don't I meet you in the ICU and we can see him together?"

Tam is mute. Totally. And also naked. Totally. And covered with dirt. And sitting in the corner of a seclusion room with a very stupid expression on his face.

"Well, Sam," I said, "it looks as if you've cured his assaultiveness."

"He's been like this for three days. Won't move for anyone or anything. We were trying to wash him in the room but it just seemed to get worse. What do you think we should do?"

"Wait a minute, Sam. You're the boss."

"C'mon, Max. He's your patient. This is what you're here for."

"Well, what in heaven's name have you done to him? He was fine when I left."

Sam smiles and leaves the unit, glad the problem is on someone else's hands. I turn to Bailey for an explanation, who after her first six months as a nurse at the hospital is an obvious ally in the fight against mental illness.

"So what happened?"

"I dunno, Max. For the past three days he's just been sitting there. We tried meds and water and talking to him and everything else, but he just sits. We tried English and Vietnamese and French and nothing works. His brother and friend are too frightened to come visit, so we seem to be stuck with him."

"Well, then, we must investigate." Just back from being a world traveler, I am now ready for detective work.

Tam is a mess and all attempts to communicate by voice prove fruitless. Even screaming doesn't get a reaction. I try making faces. This also gets me nowhere but brings on a feeling of intense silliness. Little lights, jumping up and down and loud noises also do not seem to be the answer, so I take Bailey by the arm and we exit the room. "Nice going, Max. You've got a real talent with patients."

"Thanks. You're very sweet. What do you think of my tan?"

My beeper goes off at this point and it's Sandra. Knowing that she rarely calls with good news, I steel myself. At least it's an excuse to leave the scene of this disaster. Moreover, she notices how relaxed I am from my vacation, although my patience is wearing a bit thin. "Max, nice to see you." She gives me a sort of half hug, half handshake, as if to say, "I'm on your side but I can't quite admit it."

"I had a great time. Although I don't mind being back. As long as you don't have an admission to tell me about."

"Bad news, Max. That's exactly what it is."

"Great. Just back from vacation and you're killing me already. Let me guess. It's an interesting case."

"Not quite interesting. More bizarre. Her name is Eve. She's a tattooed lady from a circus who beat up a cop at a bar. She came in while you were gone. She's on a court paper and is in jail now. But when she gets out of jail they're sending her here and she'll be all yours."

"Terrific. Is she crazy?"

"I don't know, Max. That's for you to figure out. But she sure is mean."

"Zoe," I moan, pulling the covers over my head. "I can't move. I don't want to get out of bed."

"Max, it's okay. Stop complaining. This is Saturday. Your horrible week has ended and it's the weekend. Relax. Now you can go back to enjoying being a psychiatrist."

"I don't know, Zoe. I'm at another point where liking talking to patients seems to have very little to do with getting along in my job."

"Tell me all about it, love."

"It's just so tense at the hospital. Everything is so high pressure and there's so much to do and all the patients are so dependent on me in order to stay alive."

"How do you know that's them and not you?"

"What does that mean?" I don't mean to snarl on a Saturday morning, but this has a heavy sound to it.

"What I mean," she snarls back, "is that you may encourage dependency in your patients and this makes them more dependent on you."

"Why would I do that?"

"I don't know. You're the psychiatrist. But I bet you would find your job and your life a bit less taxing if you could convince your patients they're on their own, than that they should depend on you."

"Well thanks a million."

"I depend on you. But I don't think you plan to take care of them the way you take care of me. No matter what anyone wants."

"Of course not. But they really are counting on me."

"Look, Max. If we're going to talk about this, you have to be reasonable. Your patients aren't the only ones who need to learn limits."

"Hey, that's nasty. I've had a tough week. Can I tell you about it?" I go on without stopping. "At least my fellow residents showed general relief that I had returned. But everyone, from patients to staff seemed sort of semihysterical about the state of health of my patients. Ecaterina was a barrel of laughs and I was sure she was going to kill herself. Then she sulked around and sent me strange notes, then said she could live without me and refused to come to our appointment. Simon showed up once, then kept missing appointments. I didn't put much weight on this at first, but later on it seemed to loom larger, since Molly feels that I haven't properly acknowledged how much he cares for me."

"None of that sounds so irregular. You work in a crazy place. At least you get supervision."

"But, Zoe, it just gets stranger by the second down there. Tam cured all his old regressive behaviors with catatonia. Sam and Sandra kept after me all day to tie up loose ends, but all ends seemed unconnected.

"Then Elroy was admitted to me. I wanted to keep him a day patient, but he wanted to be locked up, since the other alternative was to die. I tried to explain what a drag the hospital was, but I guess in his version of reality, a hospital could be a veritable paradise, so what the hell. By this point I am thinking about ways out of this reality myself. Now, I am told, I haven't helped them deal well with dependency issues, due to the fact that I'm messed up. Or something like that. But what I want is blue skies, nice ocean, hot sands, and total relaxation. Instead I have true madness, anger, and snow."

"Okay," Zoe allows, "but at least we had a good week together."

"That's true, my sweet. Wednesday, I drove in with you. But in ICU rounds there was another fight on whether to let Tam go back to Thailand. I kept saying yes and everyone kept yelling at me. At least he stopped being catatonic, although I don't know why. Magda began calling me on the phone after missing our appointment. Each time she had a new name for me, until she settled on peabrain, which seemed right to her so she stayed with it. My sin is unclear, but surely had something to do with not caring enough.

"Well then I have about sixty-three meetings with every social worker, supervisor, and administrator in the hospital for some fool reason or another and for heaven's sake Zoe, what is going on?"

She, who had fallen asleep and curled up around me, awakes with a start. "Are you alright, Max?"

"No. I'm not. What the hell is going on? My whole week sounds like a disaster report. Why aren't I having a better time of it?"

"Do you want some suggestions, Ace?"

"Sure. Just be kind."

"Basically, it seems that you enjoy yourself when you're with patients, but not when you have to cope with the hospital."

"Well. That's definitely true."

"But you're in a bind."

"Why's that?"

"Because the only way you get to be with patients is through the hospital. In fact, everything you've learned so far is because of the work and time you've put in there."

"So where does that leave me?"

"It seems to leave you in a tough place, since the bottom line is that it's going to continue to be painful to learn psychiatry."

"Shoot, love. How do you figure that?"

"Imagine you are one of your own patients. Now, as the therapy gets more intense, what is a patient likely to do?"

"Pull away. Only that happens not only when the therapy gets more intense, but also when feelings get intense. Like around my vacation."

"That's the whole point. So when you go on vacation your patients start to freak out because it makes them realize something about themselves and their relation to you. Well, the same is true for you and your job. When you return from vacation you realize how dependent you are on the hospital to provide you what you want. It's a teacher and a workplace and an authority figure and everything else. So you resent it and react as if it was an enemy. You want it to take care of you but you also want to be on your own. You struggle with it."

I start to sigh and really want to roll over and hear no more of this, but Zoe won't let me off that easy. "Hey, Max, you asked for this."

"I don't have to like it. And what's the point anyway? You seem to be saying that if I'm depressed it's my own fault."

"I am saying that. You want the goodies of being a doctor and a psychiatrist, but can't see that there is quite a process you're going to have to go through. Until you learn to cope with your own feelings about authority and dependency and all the rest, how can you expect to help your patients?" I start to feel like a fetal position is the only way to cope and Zoe notices my curling up into a little ball. "It's not so bad, Max. It's called live and learn. With the right mind-set, it can be the most exciting thing to do."

"So how do I survive the present, Miss Pollyanna?"

"By remembering who you are and what you want. If you can stay focused on that, then things will be alright. And then you'll be able to see your patients again as fascinating people, instead of burdens."

I open my mouth to protest but decide against it. Why hit my head on the wall again. "I want to go back to sleep, Zoe."

"Best idea you've had today, Max."

Sandra calls me on the phone and tells me that Eve, the tattooed lady, has left jail and is on her way to Asylum. And into my care. Sandra then fills me in on the details.

"Being in the circus is only one of her fantasies. The tattoos

really make no sense except as some sort of showpiece. I don't
know why she had them done. Although it does make her look
ferocious."

"Why was she in court?" I ask.

"She beat up a cop at a bar."

"Great. Just great. And why is she coming to a mental hospital
instead of going to jail?"

"Good question. I have no idea. But the judge is committing
her and we have to deal with it. You don't have to keep her here
forever, but you at least need to do a good evaluation before
letting her go. Have fun."

Have fun. What a novel idea. Trudging up the stairs to the
acute unit, all I can do is pray. That doesn't work either.

Eve is large. Not a tub like Simon, but six feet of muscle on
muscle that I have never seen this side of the East German track
team. "Hi," I say, warming up to the task.

"Who the fuck are you, buster?" She points her finger in my
chest as she sneers down at me. Her hands are covered with
pictures of skulls and things, but at least her face is clean.

"I'm your doctor. Dr. Jackson. Max Jackson." Your choice,
actually. Why argue?

"Then get me the hell out of here, idiot."

"I can't do that yet. We need to observe you for a few days."

"Observe me? You'll what? Back off, Jack, or else you'll regret
it."

This is terrific. "I'm sorry, Eve. I've got no choice. You're here
on a court paper and we have to follow its directions."

"Oh yeah? You already stole my life and my clothes when you
put me in jail and now you want to rip me off again? You screwing
bastard!"

I scan the room to make sure there are support personnel, a
few burly health workers around before I go on. Eve had threatened to kill her mother, so I need to give her a warning. "One
more thing, Eve. I need to call your mom and let her know where
you are."

"You'll what?!" She stands and starts yelling. "You leave my
mother out of this! You call her and I'll kill you!" She starts

pacing and I try to signal the mental health assistants. But they've heard the commotion and are on their way. "My momma doesn't have nothing to do with my life! You leave my momma out of this!"

I jump up, standing to try and gain an advantage in this conversation. "Look, Eve, we just call her because you threatened her. If she doesn't feel threatened, no problem. What are you so upset about?" Can it be this simple?

No way. Eve puts her face three inches from mine and screams, "I'm an adult! Do you understand? I'm an independent adult! My momma doesn't tell me what to do. You be careful, asshole, about what you say about my momma. I'm an adult!"

At this point the mental health assistants move between us and I beat a hasty retreat. Sam says I ought to be careful. Thanks, Sam.

Even when she's not screaming at me Eve is quite scary. So angry she looks ready to explode at any minute, so strong she can fight off a room of men, so bad-mouthed that motherfucker is a compliment from her. But she's smart and quick and funny. Sometimes. Just the sort of person that middle America is afraid might take over the world someday. Except that she can't take over her own life. Either the police or her mother are always after Eve. She ate the whole apple.

She has quieted down so I make another attempt to reach her. "Look, Doc. Everything's cool. I've been a little down but it's all okay now. Everything is roses for me. I've got a job and a car and a house and a mean old boyfriend so I don't need you anymore."

This is from a woman who was sleeping on a grate the night before she was arrested. "I don't get it, Eve. Why were you on the streets?"

She starts walking back and forth in the dayroom. "Look, you fuckhead. I don't need your shit! That was before. I don't need you now. You need me! I can do a lot for you. I . . ."

"Slow down, Eve." It's like skipping stones on a lake. I keep glancing off. She hears nothing I say and nothing she says gets across anything that she feels. All I hear is her anger against the world and her place in it. We are all, "Shitass moron pinheads," and she could, "Whip us anytime," she wants to. Except there is no house, no car, no family and no friends.

We call her an antisocial personality disorder, which includes:

Three or more of the following:
1. truancy
2. expulsion or suspension from school
3. delinquency
4. running away from home
5. persistent lying
6. repeated sexual intercourse in a casual relationship
7. repeated drunkenness or substance abuse
8. thefts
9. vandalism
10. school grades below expectations
11. chronic violation of rules
12. initiation of fights

At least four of the following since age eighteen:
1. inability to maintain work behavior with frequent job changes . . . significant unemployment . . . serious absenteeism . . . walking off several jobs
2. lack of ability to function as a responsible parent
3. failure to accept social norms with respect to lawful behavior
4. inability to maintain enduring contact to a sexual partner (ten or more partners in a year)
5. irritability and aggressiveness as indicated by repeated physical assaults or fights
6. failure to honor financial obligations
7. failure to plan ahead . . . impulsivity
8. disregard for truth, as indicated by repeated lying, conning others for personal profit
9. recklessness

And although this definition probably includes people that you know, as well as half the urban centers of America, what it fails to include is that she is depressed as hell, and all this comes after a childhood that was nothing short of disaster, from foster homes to sexual and physical abuse, with malnutrition and who knows what other injuries. And although Sam says, "There are plenty of people with that background who aren't in mental hospitals," I still find it hard to believe that environment is not a huge part of this picture. In the meantime, I've got to try and help this sad person who scares me half to death.

Arriving home, I am frightened and tired and definitely in need of strong medicine. "Zoe!" I call. "Honey, I'm home."

She's waiting for me in the bedroom with a tremendous grin on her face. There's a half-empty bottle of champagne on the floor and confetti everywhere. She dangles a letter in front of my nose and her smile splits her face like a ripe tomato.

"You got in!" I shout and she nods yes and smiles even larger. "Where, where? Tell me!"

"Right here."

"Here?"

"That's right. Right here. Boston. Yeah. I got in! I'm gonna be a doctor!"

It slowly starts to sink in. Zoe is going to be a doctor too! "Congratulations! How does it feel?"

"I'm excited. I'm scared. Max, will I be able to make it? What if I'm not a good doctor?"

"Don't be silly, my love. You'll be a great doctor. Anyway, isn't this a little early to worry about that?"

"It's just so strange. Now we'll both be doctors. And you'll have to listen to me complain about it all the time."

"Hey! That's not fair. I was just about to tell you what a wonderful day I had. How I took your advice and concentrated on my patients and everything was great." So I lied.

"Well you better start saying terrific things to me about being a doctor because now I'm gonna be one just like you."

"You're going to be a psychiatrist?"

She throws a pillow at me. "I mean a nice doctor. One who cares about my patients and all that."

"I know you will, gorgeous. You will be a wonderful doctor."

"Oh, Max. I'm so confused. This is great and terrific and marvelous but it looks so hard."

"It is hard. But don't worry, you'll do fabulous. And then you can take care of me."

"Have some champagne, Ace. That'll take care of you."

"Good deal, Zoe. Welcome to the club."

"What do you mean?"

"Well, medicine has the longest initiation process of any guild left in America. Face it, you'll be in training for the next ten years."

"Thanks, Max. That's cheery information. This is pretty heady stuff. I'm scared."

"You'll do fine."

We sink into the sofa together and put our arms around each other and start to talk at the same time. When we've run out of things to say we sit in silence, each lost in our own thoughts about the future.

"Can we go to bed now, Ace? I'm pretty tired." She starts to shiver and reaches out to me. "I just need to be held now. I can't really believe that it happened. Everything changes so fast."

"And if my life is any indication, it's gonna keep on changing. One thing is for sure in this field. Nothing's ever the same."

"What do you mean, Max?"

"It's like you were telling me yesterday. The process of getting what you want is so intense that you better be ready to know who you are and what it is that you're after or else."

"Don't scare me right now, okay?"

"I'm sorry, Zoe. It's great you're going to be a doctor. There are many days when it's the best thing in the world. And when it's not, that's okay too. At least you get to learn a lot about yourself."

"Hey, Sandra. Guess what?"

"Zoe got into medical school?"

"Shit yes! How did you know?"

"I could tell twenty yards away. You're beaming with a glow that goes beyond your tan. Something good must have happened and that's the best thing I could think of. Congratulations."

"Thanks, Sandra. Can we talk?"

"Sure, I've got a few minutes. What about?"

"About being married and in love and being a doctor and everything and keeping your life together."

"Which of your patients is getting married?"

"Not funny. With Zoe going to school and a very busy time ahead of us I'm a little worried. No. I'm a lot worried."

"Why's that?"

"Well. She's going to count on me to be behind her and I'm having trouble finding the energy to take care of myself this year. I'm not that worried about the relationship, at least I don't think so, but I am concerned about how the two of us will find the energy to keep each other going. I figured that since you'd been through this, you might have some words of wisdom."

"That's a nice request, Max. I wish I had an easy answer. When I was in medical school, my husband nearly went crazy waiting for me. It seemed like my life took up all the time we had together. But he didn't complain very often and we got through okay. Although I guess we changed."

"How was that?"

"Well, I took more charge of things in our life and I was more assertive. But I've always been pretty assertive."

"I'm not really sure what I'm worried about. Zoe and I are pretty tight."

"I know that. The two of you have seemed to be real close. I think you'll make it alright. What I suspect, though, is that your negative feelings about medicine are part of what's worrying you."

"I'm sure you're right. I've felt so co-opted by the system so many times that I do get worried about what it will do to Zoe."

"The best thing I can tell you about that is to let Zoe pick her own issues. She's not the same person as you."

"Yeah. But am I gonna have to live through the whole thing all over again?"

"Maybe you'll learn something new."

"That will be nice. I've always wanted to study anatomy again."

"And you can teach her a little humanities to go along with her science courses."

Right.

Dr. Knight is lecturing today on the psychotherapy of psychoses. "You don't need drugs to treat patients. You need to sit with them and to hear what they are saying. The main purpose of medications is to treat the anxiety of the psychiatrist, who doesn't want to confront his own psychotic potential."

What? Can I believe my ears? Where was this guy six months ago, before I learned anything?

Bobby sits up and takes notice. "Wait a second," he says. "That sounds nice in theory but it doesn't have much application to my life here."

Dr. Knight is nonplussed. He has the analyst's trick of turning things back to you like nobody's business. "Your life here?"

Bobby seems to be getting a bit angry. "My patients are in horrible pain. Medications help them to deal with it. We don't do them any favors by letting them sit around crazy."

Hey, I've heard this before. Sam must give his lecture to everyone. And, I finally get to respond to it. "I don't know about that. What the hell is so great about giving people meds so they can function in a world that has no place for them? Anyway, I'm not sure how much pain we're getting rid of."

"That's crap." Bobby hates getting this angry and starts to fidget in his chair, but goes on. "I don't think medications cure anybody. But things are a lot better since we started using them."

Dr. Knight asks him, "How are they better? What are the changes?"

"Well, there are no back wards full of incurables who spend their lives in straitjackets. There are a lot more people we can see by using medications and not having to devote five hours a week to each patient. And the patients are much better able to get a job or get out of the hospital and get on with their lives."

Dr. Knight responds by saying that the most important thing to remember about someone who is psychotic is that he lives his life the best way he knows how. "Psychosis is an acute emergency reaction to and chronic management technique for intolerable pain. It represents a sacrifice of perception to preserve psychological and physical life. The psychotic reaction shows the most massive disturbance of thinking, mood, and interpersonal relationships to be found in human beings." Dr. Knight then goes on to say that psychotics are at one end of a character spectrum, with normal people at the other, and that symptoms exist along a continuum of pathology.

This is more than Bobby can stand. "But these people are crazy. They're not a little bit worse than neurotics. They are very different."

"How are they different?" Dr. Knight gets all crinkly round his eyes and his mouth turns up just a fraction.

"They hear voices and they are delusional and they act in very self-destructive ways and they are totally unable to take care of themselves outside the hospital."

"And that somehow makes them different from anyone else in the world? We all hear voices. We all believe things that are not true. If these people are unable to leave the hospital, then they are like us, only more extreme."

"But you would want to treat them with psychotherapy when it doesn't work." Bobby is emphatic.

"How do you know that?"

"Because I've been trying."

"It's frustrating, isn't it?" And he really means it. There is no rancor in his voice, only understanding and something that, luckily, falls just short of pity. Bobby is put off balance.

"Yes, it's frustrating. I don't think it works."

"It takes a long time." Dr. Knight is really on a roll now. "But it's worth trying. Tell me how your medicines work."

"Well, the patients stop being so self-destructive and they do take away many of the symptoms of the disease."

"I agree with that, Bobby. But how does it help the patient?"

"It helps by making them feel better." He puts a heavy accent on feel.

Bobby has grown a bit more strident and I'm feeling left out, so I cover. "What confuses me is that I don't know what better is."

Having been fed another straight line, the good doctor asks, "What are the possibilities?"

"Well, it would be nice if the patients felt that their conflicts had been resolved and there was no longer any need for them to be psychotic. But it seems okay, often, just to have their symptoms go away."

"Why is that?"

"Well, they seem to be in a good deal less pain."

"Are they in less pain or are you?"

"I am glad when I no longer have to tie someone to a bed or worry about them killing themself. But I assume the patient derives some benefit also."

Dr. Knight frowns and pulls his beard. "I personally am not so sure about that assumption. Certainly medication and symptom relief can be seen as beneficial to society and the doctor in the short run. Especially with psychiatrists wanting to join the mainstream of medicine. But I seriously question if we are helping our patients or just relegating them to a chronic course without any real treatment."

Bobby and I both want to sit and talk after this lecture. He continues to be angry. "Damn! He misses the whole point."

"I guess I do too. What was wrong with what Dr. Knight said?"

"He's trying to find one solution to all psychiatric problems. He's no better than people who want to push drugs on patients. We've got patients here who are addicted to psychotherapy and have been getting it for twenty years."

"But that's also true in any field of medicine. Not everything works for everybody."

"That's why we have to use every technique we've got. We can use medicine and psychotherapy together, as well as family therapy and anything else we can think of. We can build new schools and new cities and everything new under the sun but we can't rely on any one technique. We don't have one that works well enough. I just get so frustrated when I hear dogma. If anything really worked, of course we'd all use it."

"I think his point about choosing our method of treatment based on the doctor's or society's issues and feelings is a good one."

"You're right, Max. It is a good point. I agree with Dr. Knight completely on that. But just because we like it best doesn't make it bad."

"But it does make it very hard to evaluate. We don't do enough thinking about whether we're trying to help the patient or ourselves, or some higher social goal."

Bobby stretches out all six feet of him and sighs. At least talking has defused some of his anger. He pushes the blond hair out of his face and asks me, "Do you know what you're doing? Because I sure don't. I want to help my patients. I love being a therapist. But it does seem a lot of my energy is spent keeping people off the streets or out of someone's hair. And they keep bouncing back in here, so I usually don't feel like I'm doing a very good job of it. Of course I like it when a medicine seems to help someone stay out of the hospital."

"I hear you, Bobby. At least Simon seems a bit better. Ecaterina almost died and you've seen Tam and I'd hardly call Eve a cure, so I really don't know. I'd hate to think that I spent all those years in med school just to be an agent of social control. I could have done that by going to police school."

"Yeah," he grins wickedly, "but this pays better."

And so, after three straight weeks of sleeping with Zoe I am on call again. I take deep whiffs of the strange hospital smell and realize, with finality, that I am no longer on vacation. No longer anywhere close to Jamaica. I put my hand in my pocket and find a small round object. Pulling out the marble, I puzzle for a second on its origin and then remember my session with Shirley.

She reacted to my vacation by stopping her medications. This was secretly fine with me, since I didn't think they did anything anyway, and after Dr. Knight's lecture, experimenting seemed a good idea. What the hell? She bowled into my office with her eyes flashing. I could almost hear her electrodes beeping. "Shirley," I inquired, "what's the problem?"

"Dr. Jackson. I am sad because I cannot cry."

"That's horrible." I can feel my face twist into a scowl as I say this, thinking about my tendency to ignore her noises, missing the point of her pain. Still, it is somewhat out of focus to have someone who is moaning hysterically, really belting it out, tell you they hurt so.

Shirley answers, "Yes it is horrible." And begins to growl.

"Do you want to stop it?"

"Of course, but I can't. I cannot cry."

"Would it help if you took your pills?"

She slows down to a soft sighing and then begins to beep madly. "How would I know? I'm sick. I'm crazy."

"I think it might help." Why did I say that? Am I that uncomfortable?

Shirley screws up her face and looks at me with a half-puzzled, half-disgusted expression. "Well, you'd say that."

"What do you mean?"

She starts to chortle and says, "I can only do what my electrodes say. You'll never understand the danger we're in." And then reaches into her pocket and pulls out a blue marble, with mottled pink and white spots, and gives it to me. "Merry Christmas," and then the beeping noise again.

"Thank you Shirley, but when you sound like that I guess you're telling me something painful, too."

With a strained voice she tells me, "You didn't have to go away."

"Why's that?"

"You're healthy. Your life is perfect. I'm the one who is sick."

"Did you miss me?"

She can no longer maintain even the simplest emotion and begins a hooting noise. Wiping her eyes, unable to speak, she stands and asks in the voice of a petulant teenager, "May I go now?"

"Of course, Shirley. And thank you for the present."

At moments like this I wish I had a dog. I could scratch its ears and it would wag its tail and that would be all we need.

Zoe is coming to join me for dinner tonight, so all must be kept quiet. Still exuberant after her med school acceptance, she has also added the anxiety of long-term commitment, intense debt, being a student again and coping with how stressed out we're both going to be. Or, "Who has the free time here, anyway?" We just need to relax.

Which is not what Zoe is up for now.

"Ace. I've got to talk about med school. I got in! I got in!"

"I know, love. It's terrific, fabulous."

"That's how I feel. I want to shout it from the rooftops."

"Someone will call the police and have you committed if you do that."

"They'd just bring me here and you'd have to deal with me."

"I'd have to lock you up overnight."

"Max! How can you say that?"

"I think it's the only way to get you to spend the evening with me here."

"You're damn right it is. I'll never put up with this place again."

"At least not until you're a resident yourself."

"When that happens, you better be ready to bring me dinner. And I'll see if you want to spend an extra night sleeping in a hospital."

"Don't count on it, sweetheart," I say. "I think I've had enough."

Molly says I'm in a normal stage. "You're starting to feel a little more comfortable in your job, but at the same time, you can no longer use denial as a defense. You have to start coping with what it really is that you do at work." She's pregnant, so we know that she found a way to cope.

"I don't use too much denial. Well yes I do. Oops. I don't want to believe it, much of the time."

"But now, Max, the time has come, where you have to move on to be a better therapist. There's more to therapy than listening. There is also believing."

"Well of course I believe what my patients say."

"Do you? Good. You must know that to believe your patients is to understand how much they believe what they are saying. They are not trying to make up something because it sounds good or puts the universe in order. They say it because they believe it. Even if it sounds crazy."

"So I shouldn't try to struggle with them?"

"You can struggle, but there's no point. They have to start believing otherwise. They can't be argued out of what they are saying. Who can?"

"What do you mean?"

"Max. You're an optimist. You think that everyone can and should have a wonderful life. That's fine. But when a patient is telling you that all they see is horror, as Simon does, he is serious. It's not an academic point for him."

"That's why I never tell my patients what to do."

"Wonderful!" She really seems pleased and I beam. Then she continues. "When I say you use denial, what I am saying is that you don't accept your patient's view of reality as valid for them. And you have to buy it to work with them. Now that's scary, because it means you have to be very secure in your own system to be able to handle exposure to theirs. When Simon is manic and psychotic, you have to accept that as real for him. It has nothing to do with medication. It has to do with being willing to believe. The whole issue of meds will disappear for you when it stops being an existential question and becomes a practical issue in relation to reality."

"Christ, Molly. That doesn't seem fair. What does all that have to do with being a doctor?"

She just smiles, which always gets me. I feel like a stupid second grader who is lucky that his teacher is so nice. "Try and think about it. Use your instincts. And all this will be easier when you relax. For instance, your work with Jerry seems pretty good."

"Do you think that's because I'm more relaxed?"

"Uh huh. He's not as scary and you can figure out what's going on. But beware, all the same issues will come up in their own way."

Great.

Elroy meets me in day hospital. He seems calm. In fact, he is almost motionless. Like a mechanical man, he stands rigid and unknowing. A robot waiting for marching orders.

"Hello, Dr. Jackson." He barely moves his lips. The rest of his face just sits there. And he has a lot of face. A large, loose-jointed man, with a head bigger than it should be, he can nonetheless disappear when not attached to the discussion. I keep expecting him to dominate, given his size, but he uses his body as a place to hide within.

"Hi, Elroy. How you doing today?"

"Do you mean, will I kill myself?"

"I suppose so." He pulls away and before he can become a statue I call out, "Stay with me now, Elroy."

"Everyone I know is trying to kill me. Why should I bother to kill myself?"

"Good question. Does that mean no?"

"Sure it does. I'm okay now. I won't die. Although I might as well be dead. Can I leave the hospital now?"

"Sure. But maybe we have something here to offer you."

"I don't think so." He lifts his head up and looks me in the eye for the first time. There's the start of a twinkle, but it quickly fades. "Do you think there's a way to put more kindness in the world?"

"I'm not sure. I'd like there to be."

"But you don't know how?"

"No. I wish I did." He looks down again and I somehow feel responsible for his change in mood. "Do you know a way?" I ask.

"I used to think I knew a way, but now I don't remember. Do you know what I like to do the most?"

"No, Elroy. But I'd like to."

He flashes the first happy expression I've seen from him, a slight upturning at the corners of his mouth. "I like to hang out with children. You know, at playgrounds. But they mostly stay away from me. I guess their parents tell them to. Why?" Oh, Elroy. On the verge of tears and pathos. And I just let him cry. I couldn't stop it in any case.

After a few minutes he says, "I'm better now. Can I leave the hospital?"

"I'd like to see you again. Have a few talks."

A glazed look crosses his face and three quarters of Elroy is no longer with me. "I'll think about it. Now I want to go back to work."

As a security guard. Nights. Afflicted by the national disease, loneliness. "Alright, Elroy. Think about coming back to see me."

I go to see Eve and try to explain to her about the letter I'm going to send to the court about her assault. They want to know about her competency to stand trial and her criminal responsibility. Terrific.

"Look, shithead," she begins. "No whipass scumbag is gonna tell the judge that I'm crazy."

"Well, Eve, we've only got two choices. We can tell them that you're crazy, or we can tell them that you're a criminal. We ought to figure out which is better. Maybe if you're willing to come here for treatment they'll let you out of jail."

Eve starts pacing and shaking her head. "Shit, Dr. Jackson. Those people are out to screw me. All I want is a place to sleep and a little time. Why the hell can't I have that?"

"I'm with you, Eve. And you're more likely to get it if we say you'll come to the day hospital. Otherwise they'll put you in jail."

"Nah. They won't give me six months' probation for a little assault in a bar. You gotta do something bad to get put in jail."

"Why don't you let me write the letter and we can go over it. Okay?"

"Sure, Doc. Say. Do you think I can sleep here tonight?"

"Why's that Eve? I thought you had a bunch of places to stay."

"Course I do. I just thought this would keep me off the streets for a while. You know, protect the public. I wouldn't want you to get in trouble if I go wild. It'll be on your conscience. I don't have a conscience."

I can't help but to laugh at that. I pull on my beard and try to look analytical. Failing that, I tell her, "I think I can stand it."

"Well, alright, Doc, but I'm in bad shape. How about letting me sleep here?" She sinks down in her chair and starts to look very sad. "I'm real depressed, Dr. Jackson. I need help. If you don't let me stay here, I may kill myself."

"Well, Eve, that sounds bad. But don't you think you'd be more comfortable at home?"

"Home? What home?" She let that slip out. "If I'm crazy like in that letter you'd let me stay here."

"That's not fair, Eve. You said you had a place to go."

"Shit, Dr. J. I'm desperate. I'm really worried about what's going to happen. I do think about killing myself and I can't sleep and I'm afraid I'm going back to drinking. Help me out on this."

Eve makes a very convincing argument and as I agree to let her sleep in the hospital for one night I am struck by the knowledge that I really do not know whether I am being manipulated or if she really means anything she says. I am starting to learn, however, that all mental illness does not have to be psychosis. Eve is not a healthy person.

Then it's time to visit with Ecaterina. Out of the day hospital and back home, she has agreed to come in to decide if she will see me as an outpatient. With Jerry, that'll give me two. And I will not worry about her killing herself. I won't. I promise. Please.

Ecaterina is stunning. Her dress comes just below her knees, but is slit up one side so that her entire thigh is exposed. The side she turns to me. The top of the dress, made from some sort of clinging material, is cut to expose the legally permissible amount of breast. She obviously is wearing nothing beneath the dress, at least nothing that manages to conceal anything. I don't know if she spent any time in front of the mirror this morning, but I doubt she always looks that way when she wakes up. A jade pendant rests between her breasts which draws attention to that spot. It also reminds me that this is therapy, not a date and that this is a patient, a sick woman. But Jesus, what an act!

Sitting in the chair and crossing her legs, she extends her hand toward me. I take it and we shake, and both of us sit there in silence. We play this waiting game for a few, very long moments, as I stare at her and she at me. Finally, she opens with, "How very kind of you to see me today," using a voice normally reserved for houseboys and other help.

"You're welcome."

Again we sit there waiting for something to happen. I've been coached in this by many supervisors. The trick is to let the patient bring up the topic, wait it out, get things in their terms. Except we might be here forever. So I try a trick someone suggested to me.

"It seems very hard to talk today." Sort of a reverse layup.

She fixes a hard stare on me and then closes her eyes. Practically swooning in her chair she moans, "It's awful, darling. Just miserable. You can't imagine."

"Try me."

Flashing a "give me a break" look, she continues. "I don't know if I can take a new psychiatrist. My last one was such a dolt."

"A dolt?" Why is she saying this to me? Why aren't we talking about her suicide and hospitalization and everything else?

"You know, he's stupid. Or is that some kind of game?"

"Ecaterina, how does this relate to our sessions?"

"I decided I didn't want to see him. He didn't do me any good anymore." She takes off her hair band and shakes her head, then runs her fingers through her hair, combing it. She puckers her lips as if to kiss someone, but there is no one else there but me.

I know this is a lie, or as we say in psychiatry a distortion, but who wants to argue? "What does that have to do with seeing me now?"

"I'm just trying to get our ground rules set," she responds, now leaning forward on my desk and slightly leering at me. "What should I say to you now?" she continues.

Starting to sweat, I sit quietly for a moment, trying to figure out which part of Freud is going to help me with this. I know he described the patient, and I know that when he hugged a patient it brought about a cure, or something like that but this hardly seems the right course at this point. Anyway, Freud saw his patients for a lot longer than ten minutes before he had a cure. So what is the technique? Drugs aren't going to get me out of this, and neither will being a blank wall. What to do, what to do?

Naturally, the first thing to do is to get comfortable. I say to her, finally, "Do you think you could sit back in your chair?" as I loosen my collar.

She smiles, feeling she has won a round and sits back. "Dr. Jackson," she says in a very pouty voice, "can you help me?"

"Help you with what?" Shoot, I thought we were going to talk about her suicide attempt and hospitalization and her anger and this stuff is completely out in left field.

"Help me get better."

"From what?"

She stares at me and tries to suck me into her seemingly very gluey world. "I need you, Dr. Jackson." Somewhere between a plead and a demand.

I shake my head inside and try to reconstruct this. Okay, it's sexual. She's very attractive and exudes sexuality. She's acting like we're in a bar. So I have every right to feel nervous. Of what? She's not going to attack me. Or if she does I can defend myself. Physically, at least. Aha. So we feel nervous because we can't mentally defend ourself? Do we perhaps feel a strong sexual attraction, too? And that would make me feel nervous wouldn't it? So I drop back and punt.

"Don't you think we have set ground rules during your stay at Asylum?" My comment is so far away from her affect that even Ecaterina seems surprised. So surprised she tells the truth.

"I would hope," she says, with a ton of self-pride, "that that dismal period could be left in the past. I was just upset about being abandoned by my mother. I want to get on to the future with you."

"How do we do that?"

"We need to restart our therapeutic relationship." She smiles.

Terrific. What is going on here? Time to interpret. "Are you concerned that this therapy not end up like the previous one?"

"Of course. He was an idiot." She begins to purr again. "I'm sure I'll be able to work something out with you." How wonderful, I think. I'm sure you are.

I manage to extricate myself from the room by pleading a prior appointment and make a regular time to see her the next week. As she leaves, Ecaterina turns to me and says, "This was marvelous. I can't wait to see you again." Right.

Molly can barely keep from laughing out loud as I tell her of the session. "What did you expect, Max? You're in a room with a beautiful woman who is making a pass at you and you don't think you'll get a bit nervous? What are you like with Zoe?"

"I just didn't know what to do. I don't like being seduced at the office."

"No? That's unusual. Most people like being seduced anywhere it happens." She puts a hand up to silence me before I can get out a routine protest. "Slow down, Max. All I meant was that you're normal. I didn't mean you had to like it."

"It was just such a bizarre situation. I felt very attracted and didn't know how to handle it. Part of me wanted to tell her to leave the room and another part wanted to keep watching to see what was going to happen. But it all felt very suspicious and somewhat dangerous."

"Let's try to separate the parts. Remember, it was her, not you. Unless I guess wrong about you, you didn't make a pass at her."

"Of course not," I say, with a little indignation. "I'm not that much of a rookie. I know you can get in trouble for that."

"You'd be surprised, Max, how many psychiatrists do forget what is going on. Sex between patients and their doctors is all too common. But that's not what happened here. None of your actions were wrong. So you must be anxious about thoughts."

"I suppose so. It got very hot in the room."

"So you're going to punish yourself for your thoughts?"

"Of course not. But it was impossible to do therapy when all I could think about was avoiding some sexual trap that was being set for me and what the trap was and so on. I got disoriented and couldn't do the session."

"So you backed off?"

"Yup. I backed into her last therapy."

"Not such a bad choice. At least it was safe. But what was on your mind?"

"The seduction. And the strangeness of it."

"Then why not talk about that?"

"About being seduced?"

"Say something like, 'I feel you're trying to seduce me.'"

"And then what will happen? She'll probably just deny it."

"Then ask her to guess why you would feel that way. After all, you don't normally feel seduced by your patients."

"But what if I run against a brick wall?"

"That's alright. You have to keep reminding yourself that no matter how you feel you are still the doctor. She's the patient. The interpretation that counts is the one you offer her. She is there to hear that, no matter what she thinks. If she comes to you as a patient, then you have to be her therapist. If you can remember that, then both of you will benefit."

"Just keep plunging on, saying what I think, eh?"

"If you felt someone was threatening you, you wouldn't let it slide?"

"No way. And this is similar, right?"

"Right," she smiles. "I've got to run now. Don't let it unnerve you. It happens to all of us. We can talk more at our regular meeting."

Zoe, where are you? Lurching around the house, half naked and dead tired after a hard night of partying, I search for my wife. Finally, after scouring the house, I stumble across her in the living room and drag her to bed with me. She also looks a little green around the gills, but otherwise seems pretty happy. "I'm gonna be a doctor, Max!" she sings out. "Yeah for me!"

"Yeah for you," I agree. "Now can we talk about me? We've been celebrating your joyous occasion for days now and I still can't figure my life out. If that's okay with you?" I hope the sarcasm isn't too heavy.

"Whadda ya want to talk about?" Her head seems to flop a bit, but the words come out intact.

"Well," I slur. "I can't figure my work out."

"Don't try to analyze it. Just describe it."

"Life doesn't make any sense. People get hurt."

"So what?" She rolls on her back.

"My patients are so unhappy."

"So is everybody."

"So what?"

"Who said they should be happy?"

"It would be nice."

"For you?"

"Sure. For them, too."

"That's the breaks. Life can be a painful son of a bitch. You got to take your happiness where you can find it."

"Mental patients almost always seem unhappy."

"AAARRGGH!" She sits up. "All sick people have reason to be unhappy. It's horrible to be sick! And your patients are sick. They're not the ones in an existential crisis. You are!"

"Hey, cool it. You don't have to yell at me."

"Sure I do." She falls back on the bed. "It's like you don't want to believe they have a disease. You can't rescue all the sick people in the universe. They have a disease. Let go of the fantasy of changing people into new people."

"So I'm weird. But these patients have all had pretty bad luck. And whether it's their parents or their social status or their chemistry, they do ask meaningful questions."

She sighs. "Look, Max. Stop talking about it. You're a doctor, they are sick, you try to help them. Their lives have been blown away by a horrible disease. And they ask existential questions. So do cancer patients. And you want to help them. That's great."

"But they'll still be sick when they have their questions answered."

"Bingo. Although Shirley is no more likely to find those answers than anyone else, with or without your help. Give 'em drugs, give 'em hope, give 'em peace on earth. You're still not a magician. Unless you haven't told me everything they taught you in school."

"You're telling me it's not my fault that Elroy and Simon are sick."

"Of course not, silly."

"That's how it feels inside sometimes. They sit there in agony and say such painful things and I want so much for them to be out of their misery and I care so much for them. I don't want to just push drugs at them. I'd like Elroy's world to have a little more kindness."

Lying down with me she whispers, "That's one reason you're a good doctor. And you'll be a better one when you stop denying the reality of their misery and sickness. That's the context you have to work in. You can't turn your patients into clones of your reality."

"You know something, Zoe? You could get a good job in this field."

"Go to sleep, Max. I already have a good job in this field."

6

Depression

"Homeward bound, I wish I was, homeward bound . . ." The Paul Simon tune is playing in my head as I slump in my chair, trying to shut out the external stimuli. I'd put on my Walkman, except Sandra would get angry. We've been running through all my patients, trying to sort out what should be happening to whom and I'm barely staying in touch. Too many meetings.

I sit up as she says, "Max, it's time we took care of Tam. The current situation is intolerable." She starts munching on a candy.

"Hard to get me to disagree with that. I've said since day one that this wasn't going to work out."

"What's going on with him now?"

"Let's see." I reach over for some candy and get set for a fight. Sandra crosses her arms and legs and steels herself for the expected angry onslaught. So I start calmly. "He's in the ICU. He's still mute, but that hasn't kept him from peeing on the floor and smearing shit all over the place. He's usually naked and never wants to bathe. The other patients are scared of him, which makes sense. His brother still holds out hope for a miracle cure, which is something of a miracle in itself, since we've tried every known drug on him already, and over the past three months have not been able to get any communication going. Truly, a case that all psychiatry should be proud of."

Sandra holds her serious expression. "Well, I agree with you now. We've got to send him home. This is too much. I think I can convince the staff. You need to convince Sam."

"Do you mean it?" I bounce out of my chair. "You'll be with me on this?"

"Of course I will. That's my job. I'm your chief."

"Thanks, chief."

She lets her arms relax a little and asks, "So how are you doing, Max?"

"What do you mean?"

"How is the year going, what is it like for you now?"

"Do you mean am I having a good time?"

"Well, how are things with support and getting along with people. Do you feel so unsupported as before?"

"Uh no. I guess not. Actually, things seem sort of friendly now."

"Any idea why?"

"Not really, I guess I'm a bit more open and calm. Also, I'm not so angry. And I'm trying to deny my feelings less and accept reality a little more."

"Glad to hear it, Max. You've been doing a very good job."

"Thanks, Sandra." Now what do I say? Where does the line between boss and friend come? Is this an authority figure or a buddy? "Thanks a lot. Coming from you that really means something." And now she looks embarrassed. I continue, "But I'm feeling a bit depressed, I suppose. Have I been acting down in the dumps?"

"Don't sweat it, Max. Everyone needs a break."

Oh, God, Sandra, I need one so bad. I'm getting sadder and sadder and more and more lost and this job really wears me down.

Jerry is waiting to see me. Our meetings have gone well, at least in my book, and it looks like we're about to get to the meat of the material. Jerry is more comfortable with seeing me and happily, so am I with him.

He strolls to the office, his pipe not lit, at my request. As always, he stands in the doorway waiting for me to invite him in to sit, which I do. Tapping his pipe on his hand he coughs, as I wait for him to begin the hour. Jerry still seems quite confused about the fact that this is his time that he can do anything he wants with. He sits and waits for direction from me at the start of each session, as if there were a right way to do this and a wrong way. Not unlike how I felt when I began this process myself a few hundred years ago.

At length he begins. "Ah, this was a pretty good week, Dr. Jackson."

"Oh. That's nice. What was good about it?"

"Nothing special. I did very well on my exams. I think I'm in the top third of my class."

"Congratulations. That's important."

"What's important?"

"Being in the top third of your class."

"Oh sure. The higher you are in your class, the better the chance is of getting the job you want. At least, that's what they tell us at the law school."

"Sounds good," I say, wondering if I could come up with something a little more profound.

"It is good. I think. I'm not sure what kind of law work I am looking for. Somedays I think I want to do legal aid but others it looks like corporate law would be much more exciting."

"What are the pros and cons of each?"

"I'm not so sure. I guess I have to decide what I want to be when I grow up and then I can decide what kind of lawyer I want to be."

He smiles at me and I respond, "That makes a lot of sense," which produces a chuckle from Jerry.

"Do you think a lot about what you want to be?" I ask him.

"Oh yeah. All the time. Sometimes I want to be a world-famous lawyer and other times I just want to hide in some small town and lead a quiet life. I swing back and forth to extremes. Sometimes I dream about not being a lawyer at all.''

"What do you dream about then?" I ask.

He sits there and says nothing, first curling his mouth into a smile and then wiping it off his face as fast as possible.

"What's the joke," I ask, trying to keep my own voice as light as possible.

He continues to sit there silently, but it's hard for him to keep the smile off his face. I sit there with him and at length he answers, "I just had a funny thought."

"When I asked you what you wanted to be when you weren't a lawyer?"

"Yes."

"Is it possible for you to share it with me?"

"I guess so."

"Well, let's give it a try."

"It's just that it's so silly."

"Some of the best ideas anyone ever had were sort of silly."

"What do you mean?" he asks, but I'm wise to this.

"Is it hard to tell me what the idea was?"

"No . . . okay. I was just thinking that if I could do anything, I'd like to be an astronaut." As he says astronaut his face clouds over and he seems to shrink within himself.

"Is that a scary thought?"

"No," he says, then starts to cry.

"It seems to make you sad," I say after a piece.

"Yeah," he sniffles, "but I don't know why."

"It's too sad to even think about," I say, trying to deepen the emotion.

"I don't know. It's just that when I think about all the things that I could have been and all the things that I'm not I don't know what to make of myself. My father always said I'd be a great lawyer. Maybe I will be. I don't know. But I never tried anything else." His voice has softened and rather than being a wail is more wistful. He starts to sob again. "I don't know what to do with my life. I don't know if I'm living it for myself or someone else."

"And that's a very sad thought."

"Yes!" he almost shouts and then looks around, embarrassed. "I'm sorry Dr. Jackson. I didn't mean to yell at you."

"You didn't mean to?"

"No, of course not. I wouldn't shout at you."

"Why not?"

He smiles now and you can almost see the little light bulb go on above his head. "You mean why am I so inhibited?"

God, I love it. A patient who is actually going to do some of the work in here. Wow whee. "It's inhibiting to be here?"

"Well sure. I don't know what you expect and I want to be good . . ." He pulls up short as he hears what he said. Pausing, he thinks then starts over. "I don't know what I want." He shakes his head and looks sad again.

"So sad to think you might be living your life to fill other people's fantasies or desires?"

And the tears start flowing like water over the dam. "Dammit!" he shouts over his tears, "I can't stand this. I can't stand any of this. I hate being me. I want more out of my life. I want more." He breaks down again. "Really I do," he cries.

"You want more," I repeat.

"I'll just never deserve more. I'll never deserve anything. I mess up everything I try to do. I'm just a loser."

"That's pretty strong. Who gave you that message?"

"What do you mean?"

"Did you figure out you were a loser on your own or did someone tell you?"

"I'm not really a loser." He pulls himself together. "But I'm so confused about what I want. I spend all day just thinking about my life and about what I did in the past and what might happen in the future and none of it is good thoughts. I don't even have a girlfriend."

"And that's pretty sad, too?"

"Sure it is. Except I don't know anyone I want to be in love with anyway. I'm a loser at love, too." His face falls once again.

"A loser?"

"Yes. It's like we talked about before. I just can't get things together with women."

"Uh huh." I was wondering when we'd get to this. Or should that be said out loud?

"It's not that I want to be a virgin. I mean I've had offers. Plenty of them."

"Congratulations."

"No. I just want you to understand. It's not that women don't find me attractive. It's just that I don't find them attractive."

"No?"

"Well, I guess I do. Oh God, it's so horrible to be with a woman. I get so flustered and can't think of a word to say."

"Sounds awful."

"Oh, it is. I broke up with my girlfriend." He pauses and I wait. "She left me."

"Why was that?"

"I don't know. She's sort of an ass."

"What did you like about her?"

"Lots of things. She was pretty and smart and lots of fun. She made me feel great. Always said I was good looking and a great guy. Who wouldn't like that? I sure did."

"But she was an ass?"

"Not really. I guess I made her feel bad. I kept pushing her away when she wanted to be close. But I was so scared."

"What finally happened?"

"I told her I didn't want to see her anymore."

"I thought you said she left you?"

"That's when she did. She didn't have to go, you know. After all, she could have made me keep her."

"Is that what you wanted?" I ask.

"I don't know what I want. But I was sure she was getting angry at me for turning her down and I knew that if we stayed together much longer she would become furious at me. That's what always happens."

"Did she say she was angry at you?"

"No. Of course not."

"Then how could you tell?"

"I don't know. I could just tell. Things seemed so tense when we were together."

"Do you want to see her again?" I ask.

He sits and thinks and tears start to come but he keeps them in. "Yeah," he says softly, "I guess so. But how can I?"

"Why not give her a call?" Am I making a direct suggestion? "What if she won't talk to me?" Before I can answer he says, "I know. The worst that can happen is she'll say no. That's what my father always says."

"Sometimes fathers make sense."

"Okay. I'll do it." He is almost whispering and looks so sad that you would have thought he was on his way to a funeral, not a potential date. And anyway, why am I acting like a date service?

The clock says time is up, but with Jerry so sad, I hate to leave. So we sit there for a minute while he pulls himself together. "Am I getting better?" he asks as we stand.

"Better than what?" I respond.

He brightens a little. "Do you think I'm crazy?"

"I'm starting to think you always want my opinion more than yours. Why don't we talk about it next week?"

"Okay," he says, and shakily walks to the door.

And then it's time for my meeting with Simon. Now that he's out of the day hospital and on his own, both of our expectations for him have gone up quite a bit. He desperately wants to get his band together. So I presume we will talk about this. And am seemingly correct when he enters the office, on time for once, saying, "I feel my creativity is gone."

Simon looks depressed. He dresses in gray from head to toe and his huge mass intensifies the picture. He looks like the union representative for obese cat burglars. Except he doesn't have the all-knowing glint in his eyes. Nonetheless, there is a far-off quality that seems a worthy substitute. As he speaks to me he strokes his hair, staring into the distance behind the wall. And I say to myself is depression better than mania?

To Simon I say, "How can you tell?"

Still fondling his locks, he responds, "I don't know. When I'm manic I feel so creative. I feel like there is nothing that I can't do. Now I'm blah. I don't even want to wake up in the morning."

"Sounds pretty depressing."

"It is. It's very lonely too. All day long I hope that my friends will come and see me, but they never do. But I keep waiting for them. Do you know what I do? I make meals for them and I believe that they will come someday." His voice starts to rise as if to fend off an expected challenge. He begins to cry.

"It sounds so lonely."

"It is lonely. I want to have a life filled with people."

"What happens if you make a friend?"

"That's very confusing. I make the wrong friends." Again he raises his voice and seems on the verge of either tears or an explosion. But I want to know more.

"What happens?"

He looks at me accusingly. "You know what happens. You'll never be my friend even if I want you to like me so much."

"And that makes it hard to come to see me?"

"No. I like to come here. But I can't trust you. I like you. I wonder if you love me. Or is this just a job?" He again cries. Now Molly has briefed me on this. I'm not supposed to duck or interpret the way he feels for me. That would just be evading my responsibility. I need to find out what is going on in his mind and see what that teaches me about him. This stuff about wanting a father or someone to trust sounds important. So . . .

"Tell me more about how you feel about me." Ooh. Too raw.

"Well, I think you're attractive. And you're one of the only people who listens to me. You're not like some woman who ignores me when I walk down the street."

"Who's that?"

"It could be anyone. At least you listen to me. I've got no one else I trust."

"That must put a lot of pressure on these sessions."

"It does." He sniffles. "I don't know how to show you that I like you."

"You do care for me?"

"Yes. Of course."

"And you don't know how to tell me?"

"No."

"Why not just say it?"

"It seems inappropriate."

"Why is that?"

"Nothing could ever happen between us. You'll always just be my therapist. My wishes will never come true."

"So why can't you tell me you like me?"

"I just told you." He starts to pout.

"I understand you're disappointed that we will never have a relationship except in therapy, but I don't see what makes it so difficult to tell me you like me." Circles and circles, where does it end?

He nods his head and a thin smile comes across his face. "You mean I can like you and not be in love with you?" I do?

"Is that how it feels?"

"Yes."

"And what is that like?"

"It's sad." He starts to cry. "I'm angry that I can't have more of you. But it's nice to come here and see you." And then the mad face returns. "But it's so sad. There are no other people I can love!"

"That's very hard." No kidding. This whole session seems pretty hard.

"When I look at you I see my father who abandoned me, who left me alone, who moved on while I stayed in one place. People have always been leaving me. I remember when I was little that my father would go away to work in the morning and I could never be sure if he would come back."

"Can you tell me more about your father?"

"He's a good man, except that he left my mother. He loved me and he wanted me to do well, but he couldn't ever tell me. And then he left. He left just as I was getting to know him. He left before I could ever tell him that I loved him. Or that he loved me. I know that he does love me. He always sends me presents. It's just that . . ."

"He left you before you were ready?"

"Yes!" he explodes. "He left me and now the only way to keep him is to think about him and have fantasies about him and I don't want to have to do that but it's the only way!" His words are starting to run together as he gets the manic flavor to his voice and I want to push on but see he needs a break.

"And you're angry and sad about it." With emphasis in the sad. Big sigh. Why am I feeling so sad?

"Yes. Don't you see? If I give up my thoughts, I lose him."

"Yes, Simon, I do see. It sounds like a very hard choice."

He dries his eyes and looks me straight in the eye for the first time. "I don't get it. What's my choice?"

"You can choose whether to stay in the past and right those wrongs in your mind, or to move on to the present."

"But I want to get back with my father. I want to have him as the great man I want him to be."

"That's fine."

"He left me!"

"It sounds awful." Too awful, Simon. Can't we talk about something else?

"It was. He was awful. Of course it drove me crazy. My whole life is so depressed."

"It's so hard to think about change."

"How do I change me?"

"By realizing that you have a choice. The future need not be preordained. You can move into the present and try to have a new relationship." Who am I kidding? What the hell kind of answer was that?

"You mean give up my feelings? They are all that I have. Why should I trust someone to be nice to me? I can trust me. But not you." I pass him the tissues while I look at the clock and thank heaven we're near the end of our time. I want to end this session on a clear note, so I say, "It's okay to mourn the past and the pain that's there. But you have to let go of it or else you'll never move on."

"I don't want to give up what I have."

"As long as you choose. Let's talk more about it next time."

"Yes, alright. I want to."

"Well, Molly, how did I do?"

"You seemed to have a good session with Jerry. What did you think?"

"Oh, I liked it. I think we're getting somewhere."

"Do you find that you have an easier time of it with healthier patients?"

"I guess so. Why?"

"What makes it easier?"

"Well, it's a real pleasure to have a session with a theme and a line of reasoning that I can follow and things like that."

"And what was that theme with Jerry?"

"He seemed to have real insight into the fact that his own issues with negative feelings about himself influence the way he thinks others view him. I thought that was important."

"So do I. But things were not so clear with Simon. What were you trying to get at?"

"I wanted to show him and have him understand how his feelings about me are rooted in his past."

"And do you think you accomplished that?"

"What do you mean?"

"How did he seem at the end of the session?"

"There wasn't much change, but there seemed to be a lot for him to think about. Should there be more? I never do know how to evaluate what is going on in these sessions. I always feel like I'm flying by the seat of my pants. I keep hoping that by some magical miracle I'll be hit on the head by the right phrase and then the patient will be all better. But that never happens."

"That's your need to feel omniscient and omnipotent. Intellectually you know you can't save the patient, but in your heart you'll take it as a personal insult if he doesn't get better. As you did when Ecaterina overdosed."

"So how do you know if you're doing the right thing?"

Molly shifts in her chair to give her quite pregnant belly a new position to lie in. She seems supremely calm and collected, acting as if she indeed is omniscient, that she has figured out all these issues for herself and is merely imparting them to me. I know that isn't true, but wow, it sure feels that way. I wonder if this is what my patients feel when they are with me? Or do I praise myself too highly?

Molly ducks my question and poses a different one. "What were you getting at with all your emphasis on choice?"

"I wanted to point out that there is a freedom to choose. That mental health, while it may be a disease, still left you in a position where you could ask questions about your life and make real decisions about how to live it. I thought it would be good to offer the possibility of a patient having some control over his life in spite of disease."

"How does the issue of control and choice apply to Simon?"

"Well, he acts like it's all the fates, that the world has conspired against him, which is true to some extent, and that there is nothing that he can do to help himself. He acts so out of control. I want to get at that."

"Why do you think it bothers you so much?"

"What do you mean?"

"His being out of control, or at least feeling out of control. That's a pretty normal reaction when someone is ill. Especially if the person is depressed. Hopelessness and helplessness are part of the entire depressive picture."

"So that means I shouldn't go at it from that angle."

"Let's try to figure out what you were after."

"It's like I said. I figure that if Simon can feel like it is possible for him to make a choice about his life that will result in an improvement, then he will have benefited mightily."

"That's certainly true. But is he truly able to do that? I worry, Max, that you are asking him to do something that you are trying to accomplish yourself. I wonder if the issues around choice have a lot to do with your own work with patients."

"I'm not sure I get you." Or want to.

"You seem to be having a lot of self-doubts about psychiatry, a lot of questions about the pain you feel and the pain your patients are in. Perhaps you're wondering if you made the right choice."

"It's been a very hard month, that's true. Hell, it's been a very hard year. And my denial has been falling apart, and I can't even seem to get angry anymore and I feel a little like I'm just a robot, doing a job. And the hours are lousy and the patients are so sick and the workplace is totally high pressure and Zoe is going to med school. Whew. Maybe I don't have any choices. I sure thought that I would when I went into this field. It looked like the place in medicine where you had the most freedom to be yourself."

"And why doesn't it?"

"I really don't know." And all of a sudden I'm sitting there in her office bawling my eyes out and I don't know why and I'm feeling awfully embarrassed, but there seems to be nothing I can do about it and anyway Molly isn't telling me to stop it and it is a relief. She hands me a tissue and I dry my eyes and say, "Jesus, I don't know what that is all about."

"As a guess, Max, you're feeling depressed." She smiles. "Tears often mean that."

"Do you think I caught it from one of my patients?"

"No. It's a pretty normal thing to happen to a first year psychiatry resident. You stopped projecting out all your anger at the system or your bosses or your patients and now you're blaming yourself for the ills of your patients. 'If it's not the world, it must be me.' It's as if you are looking for someone to be in control. And as Simon well knows, being depressed is one way of hanging on to the illusion that you are running the show. Even if you're running it into the ground."

"But I don't feel depressed."

"No? How do you feel?"

"Pretty normal." And then I start to feel the tears well up again and I'm afraid. Where is that coming from? "Molly, this job is so depressing." I put the emphasis on "job" but she hears "depressing."

"Max. It's fine to feel depressed. Everyone does. And you no more have to talk yourself out of it than you have to talk Simon out of it. Sit with the feelings. And give yourself some time off. Write a paper or something. Take a break. You don't have to carry the whole world on your shoulders."

Thanks, Molly.

The lobby is fifty feet high and if flooded would serve as a decent replica of the Coliseum on Navy night. Smooth marble coats the building like some sort of flypaper and busybodies rush everywhere with books galore. The quiet is what you'd expect from a library, especially a medical library. Two huge spiral staircases reach from the ceiling to the basement with no visible means of entering on the main floor. Crossing past the glass cases filled with incredibly valuable books and medical *tchotchkies* I seek out the librarian to get some directions.

"Excuse me," I say to the first person wearing glasses. "How do I get to the reference room?"

She peers over the half rims and says, "Do you have an ID?"

Oh good. A stress experience. "Yes I do."

A moment of waiting then, "May I see it?"

I pull the thing out of my wallet and try to remember if anyone at Asylum has ever asked for it. No way. On the other hand, Asylum doesn't look like this place either. If the patients there were as well taken care of as the books in the library, it is possible they wouldn't need the hospital anymore. Or at least they could have a better time.

She examines the picture and my face, tries to decide if under the beard I really am who I pretend to be (a question I have also asked) and points to an elevator in the corner. "Go down one floor. Someone will help you there." Then she turns away and resumes ignoring my confusion.

With much to do, I sit at the reference, the Index Medicus, a guide to all medical knowledge and journals and such of the previous few years. Now all I have to decide is what I want to research. Research is, after all, the way to get ahead and make it in academics. That is why I came to the Great University in the first place. I think. Anyway, everyone else I know is writing a paper, so why shouldn't I? Why did I come here? What am I doing?

So what to read up on? There are many great topics. Like, "Eighty-seven different new drugs to cure depression." Or, "Eighty-seven new side effects from drugs that treat depression." How about, "Stress and the psychiatrist?" Lots of good material around on that. Or there is the more esoteric stuff. Munchausen's syndrome. Multiple personality disorders. Mass murderers with brain tumors. The history of psychiatry at Asylum.

Abandoning the Index, I wander over to the shelves to see if there is a good journal to give me some direction. Settling into one of the very plush chairs that must have come from alumni money, since the State has nothing like it, I begin to peruse. This is more like it. To huddle away in the quiet corner of a world of books, far from the mad crowd, a moment of peace. Psychiatry looks so mellow on paper. Scholarly articles on the treatment of schizophrenia. How to set limits on a borderline patient. The poor efficacy of therapy with a sociopathic patient. Wonder what Eve would say about that? Probably agree. And a very interesting article on psychiatry in the late 1800s. When we called ourselves alienists. There's been sad people forever.

From a corner of my brain I hear this horrible beeping noise. Yawning, I reach to turn off the alarm clock. Why am I wearing my clothes? Why am I sitting in a chair? Another few seconds to orient allows me to figure out what all these journals are doing on my lap as I snooze away in a corner of the library. Nicest part of the day. I turn my beeper off and go to the phone. Sandra questions, "Where have you been? Eve has been going wild." No rest for the weary.

I run to the day hospital and see all six feet of Eve standing by my office, fresh from her court appearance.

"Look, Dr. Jackson. You eat shit. You're a real scumbag. You know? My social worker don't do nothing to help me. Just give me more damn forms that don't do nothing. I'm sleeping on the streets! You ever sleep in the snow? Get all soaked to death? Look at me!"

"Uh, Eve . . ."

"Forget it, Doctor. I think I'll go back to stealing. Yeah, that's what you want. I can have as much money as I want to. Fuck. I'd rather go to jail than come here to see you. That what you want? I should have taken a year in jail instead of having to come see you!"

"They'll really put the screws to you if they catch you breaking the law now. No probation next time."

"Yeah? Well, it's your fucking fault! You told the judge I was crazy. If I'm so crazy how come I ain't sleeping in the hospital? Dr. Jackson, I need to stay here. All I do on the streets all day is drink. If I drink I'll hit somebody. Is that what you want? Why didn't you tell the judge that?"

"Eve. I didn't tell the judge anything. All I sent in were those forms you signed for."

"Hey, Doc, I can't read. Okay? Shit! I want a new doctor. I'm gonna talk to Dr. Watson and get me a new doctor do something for me. Get me someone who doesn't want me to go to jail. Hey, man! I'm sleeping in the streets!" She storms out of my office as I sigh. She had that tiger-in-the-cage look, pacing back and forth, that I am all too happy not to deal with. The room seems twice as large after she's left.

Frankly, I wish Eve would talk to Dr. Watson. Maybe he'd have more luck than I do. "Look, Sam," I say. "She's sleeping in the streets. She's not eating. She's losing weight. She can't read or write. All she ever learned how to do is scare people."

"I know, Max. She threatens you every week. Didn't she tell you last week that you were a, 'dead man?' "

"Okay, Sam. But this woman has nothing. She'll be dead or in jail soon. And she hasn't actually hurt anyone here. Maybe we can help her."

"Sorry, Max. No way. Eve is not staying here overnight. It's hard enough on the staff having her come to day hospital. She disrupts every situation she's in. She's sucking you into her system but you've got to be firm."

Sucking me into her system? Sam has got to be kidding. Who knows how Eve lives? Certainly not me. I don't know from rats and hunger and hate, from not being able to read and being sexually abused. I don't claim to understand the system of a twenty-eight-year-old woman whose life plan is to steal two thousand dollars and escape to the hills to live on roots.

"Sam! Her problems are not just in her head. There are real environmental issues involved here. How do I train a scary illiterate tattooed woman with no income or job prospects to succeed in the world?"

Sam sits there and says nothing so we remain in silence. Finally he replies, "Changing the world isn't your job. Helping Eve cope with it is. And giving her a place to hide won't help."

"Baloney! Society isn't willing to try and it's my job to tell her. Well I'm with Eve. Up yours!"

Eve is waiting for me in the hall outside my office. "Can I borrow a dollar?"

"Sure, Eve." I give it to her without thinking, too preoccupied by my encounter with Sam. What the hell is true?

"You people have ruined my life and there's no way to pull it together again. Okay if I sneak into the cafeteria and grab some food?"

"Sure, Eve." I look at her distractedly and add, "Try to stay out of trouble this week. Okay?"

"I will, Doc. See ya tomorrow." And she's off and running.

I go back to Sam's office to apologize, ready with a canned speech about stress and confusion and so on, but he waves it all away. "Real problems are something that have to be dealt with. But therapy, even with a patient like Eve, has to follow certain rules and parameters. And a patient like Eve will make you forget how sick she is as she makes you remember how sick the system is. But she still is sick. If you put her in Beverly Hills right now, do you think she'd do well?"

"Well of course not. But . . ."

Sam cuts me off. "I don't have anymore time now, Max. But remember, you're a therapist. That's why your patients come to see you. No matter what they say."

Ecaterina sashays into my office and says, "I can certainly understand why people are helpless if the only way they deal with their problems is through psychiatrists."

Not knowing where this is coming from, I ask, "What do you mean?"

"I mean it all seems so stupid. Problems, always problems. I can't stand my problems. I'm sure you can't stand me either."

"How do you know that?"

"You know very well the answer to that."

"Can you share it with me?"

"Why do you act so cold?"

"Cold?"

"God, you make me so angry." She turns her head away from me and stares at the pictures on the wall. These sessions get harder by the minute. We can get hopeless together.

"Ecaterina," I say, "what are you feeling now?"

"I am feeling nothing. I am trapped in an existential nightmare. I cannot live and I cannot die. I can only go on living in pain. And you make that pain more overwhelming."

"How do I do that?"

"I don't like this therapy. I think I will leave it."

"Can you share more about that?" As long as we're getting nowhere.

"I just can't stand it. Anyway, you'll leave me just like my other therapist did. You all do."

"I'll leave you?"

"Of course. You're just a resident. I know how this works. What's the point of getting involved if it's all going to end soon?"

"You know, Ecaterina, I'm going to be here for at least another two years. That will be a lot of time to get work done."

"It's not enough."

"You know," I infer, "it seems like you're saying that these sessions are important to you and you're afraid of losing them." Oh boy, an interpretation.

"Bug off, Dr. Jackson. I don't need you and you don't need me. We're nothing to each other."

"Oh?" And a significant pause.

"Look, Dr. Jackson. I know how this works. I'm going to fall in love with you and then you're going to leave me and then I'm going to kill myself. I don't want that to happen."

"I don't either, Ecaterina."

"How do I know that?"

"You don't. It will take a long time for you to learn to trust me."

"I need someone to love me. I'm very lonely."

"And so you'll fall in love with me?" Why are all my patients falling in love with me? Didn't they have any problems before they met me?

"It's not just you. It's everyone."

"You fall in love with everyone?"

"Sort of. But none of them love me back."

"What happens?"

"We go out a few times and then they want to make love except they want to do something disgusting and then . . . Oh, I don't know."

"Something disgusting?"

"They want to sleep with me. I hate that."

"What about it?"

"All of it. Don't you understand?"

"Not really."

"Why should I be tempted if I can't have it? Why must I always want that which is beyond my reach? My last boyfriend, do you know what happened? I'll tell you. We went out a few times. For dinner. And every time we went out I could just feel him leering at me. I could feel his hot breath when he spoke and feel his eyes undressing me. He wanted me. He really did. And when he would take me home it was all I could do to keep him from coming in after me. The entire experience was horrible."

"It sounds terrible for you."

"It was. He was disgusting."

"What does it mean to be tempted by something you can't have?"

"I told you. He was disgusting."

"Why couldn't you have him?"

"I didn't want him."

"I'm confused."

"I loved him from a distance, but when we went out he wasn't what I imagined."

"Because he wanted to make love with you."

"No!" she shouts. More softly, with anger, "Because he was disgusting."

"What did you love about him from a distance?"

"He was a beautiful man. He looked so gentle." There is a singsong character to her voice as she speaks. "He had beautiful eyes. I truly loved his eyes. And his voice was low without any growl in it. I thought he was at peace with himself."

"You thought of him often?"

"Oh yes. I dreamed about him all the time. I dreamed he would put his arms around me and carry me away to a magic cloud and love me forever."

"But when he tried to touch you, you were angry."

"It's not the same thing," she protests.

"How was it different?"

"He was disgusting."

"It sounds like the reality of your fantasy coming true was frightening."

"I wasn't frightened. I was just horrified. I was . . ." She starts to falter in her speech and finally says, "I knew he'd just reject me if we slept together. I knew he was an asshole just like the others. At least in my fantasies I get to keep the man."

"You knew he would reject you?"

"Yes. Like you will."

"What is there about you that makes you so easy to reject?"

"I don't know." She starts to sob. "I just feel so horrible. I do. I feel horrible now. I felt awful then. I know that nothing is ever going to work out. It never does. I'm cursed." We sit in silence as she cries.

"You indict yourself so harshly," I say, as gently as I can. For the first time I have an understanding of this woman's sadness. "You push people away when you feel so bad."

"That's not it, oh maybe it is, I don't know, I can't talk right now." She continues to cry as we sit together.

After minutes that seem like days, as I grow sadder and sadder, she comes to my rescue and says, "You know, Dr. Jackson, I really want to be in therapy. I'm not going to quit right now."

"That's good, Ecaterina. I think we can accomplish something here."

"Will I see you next week?"

"Of course. I'll be there."

Sadly, though, the depression hangs in the office after she leaves, and I can no longer blame it on my patients.

Molly tells me to cheer up. Spring is just around the corner and I'm having a tough year but everything will be alright.

Eve crying is a very strange sight. It is as if all the outer layers of denial have been stripped away in one instant and all that is left is a shivering, sobbing, totally out-of-control woman. There is virtually nothing left of the previous Eve I know so well. Rather, this is a one-day-old child, lost in the world, looking for a home. She sits down and continues to cry. After a few, very long minutes I say to her, "Eve. What happened?"

She continues to sit and another minute later tells me, through her tears, "My family threw me out."

"That's bad."

"I love my mother," she explains. "I love her more than anything in the world. You have to understand my mother. She's a good woman. She's my mother."

"And she threw you out."

"That shit! She doesn't love me the way I love her. I love her more than she loves me. I do everything for her. I live for her. And this is all I get? I love my mother!" Her voice is angrier but she still cries and gets sadder and sadder.

She looks up at me and speaks, in a very soft voice, "Dr. Jackson? How am I ever gonna get what I want?"

"What's that, Eve?"

"I want to be loved and to have people and to be in a better place in my life. I feel like I got nothing and I'm empty. I want to feel whole." This speech has drained her of every ounce of strength she had left and she collapses in the chair and sobs quietly. We remain in tableau as I think about where to go with this incredible insight on her part, when Eve turns to me and says, "I'm not gonna get violent, Dr. Jackson. I'm not gonna hit anybody. I'm not gonna kill myself. But I need someplace to stay." And she says, with the tears flowing still, "My family threw me out. I love my family."

"You can stay in the hospital, Eve. I'll set it up." Great. This will go over real well. But what is there to do? Impossible patients get themselves and you into impossible situations, where there is nowhere to go and no one to help out when you get to wherever it is that you are. As I sit and watch Eve cry, the room fills up with incredible feelings of sorrow and loneliness. And she goes back to the dayroom while I call the dorm and I am almost paralyzed with sadness.

A trip to the snack bar for a Snickers to cheer me up and it is time for my last meeting of the day with Sam. To discuss things in general, but mostly Tam. "Come on in, Max," he says as we enter his office. There is a spider-to-the-fly aspect to the way he says, "How have things been for you lately?"

"Okay, I guess. Actually, I've been a little depressed."

"Do you want to tell me about it?"

"Not much to tell. Work is getting me down a bit."

"I've noticed that. I've been meaning to talk to you about your work, only there hasn't been much time recently."

What the hell does that mean? "What's up, Sam?"

"I've been wondering if you're finding any difficulties with your work here."

"Why? Are you?"

"How do you see things?" Discussions between two psychiatrists often have few direct statements in them.

"Look, Sam. What is going on!?" It's good to see that I still have some of the old anger left in me.

"Why so angry?"

"What is this? Chinese water torture? I came here for a discussion and I'm getting the third degree. And I don't even know what you're talking about."

"Max. You're obviously angry and depressed and as your advisor I'd like to know what is going on with you."

"Nothing is going on. It's a hard year and I'm feeling angry and depressed. What the hell is so bad about that?"

"Does it interfere with the way you care for your patients? Because I think it might."

"I don't think it is. How would you know, anyway? Spying on me?"

Sam laughs a little, but not enough to convince me that people haven't been talking about me behind my back. But why so frightened? Why not talk to Sam about what you feel? After all, even though you've disagreed about patients in the past, he's always been a good listener. But a lingering doubt remains. Can I truly trust this man? He's my boss.

"I don't need to spy, Max. You haven't been doing your charts, you've been missing lots of meetings and right now you look like you're at the end of your rope. So to speak."

"Look, things have been tough. But I don't really want to talk about it."

"Why not?"

"Because I am depressed right now and I don't want to blow up at you and oh shit . . ."

"Look, Max. It's my job to deal with this. You can't hold it in all the time. You're not in therapy, which is your choice, but it is my business if your mental state is affecting your performance here."

"It's just that I don't know what to do sometimes. I either feel like there is nothing I can do to help anyone or else I feel that society and the hospital and the whole world are so messed up that there is often no purpose in helping anyone. That's too strong. But you know what I mean."

"I think I do. It sounds like you're dealing with your own feelings of not being omnipotent."

"What do you mean?"

"Look at it as if you were a patient. Or as if you were looking at a patient. If someone decides that the universe is against him, we call that person paranoid. It's an expression of an inability to deal with conflicting feelings within you, so you project out those feelings you can't tolerate and set yourself up against them."

"So now I'm a paranoid?"

"No. But almost all residents will go through a position like that of the paranoid. That's because you do in fact have a lot of real issues arrayed against you. And your omnipotence crumbles in the face of this. So it makes sense to imagine an all-powerful world that is causing your misery."

"But I'm not paranoid. I'm depressed."

"Which is normal, too. If projecting out your anger and other feelings doesn't work, then you can bring it inside and decide that the reason you're not getting done all that you want is because there is something wrong with you. And then you feel depressed."

"So I'm doomed to spend my days flying back and forth between paranoia and depression?"

"In a way, yes. But that's a major thing you're here to deal with. When you stop feeling that you have to save the world and really believe that the patients have the illness and you won't be able to rescue them, then, both your depression and anger should get a lot better. Although there will always be hard days."

"Omnipotence, denial, repression, rescue fantasies, anger, unexpressed rage; I had no idea I had so many problems before I came here."

Sam laughs at this and continues. "Go into therapy if you have to. Remember, your work has to go on, no matter how bad you feel."

"Thanks, Sam." I think. "So can we talk about Tam now?"

"Sure."

We rearrange ourselves in our chairs in order to start this discussion from a fresh point, as we've moved from the advisor role to the boss one. At least I know better how this one works.

"I don't think we're doing him any good. Frankly, I think he's in as bad shape as ever. It's been four months and I really think he deserves to be back with his family in Thailand."

"I agree with you, Max."

"You do?"

"Sure. You did what you could. But where he goes is up to his brother, too. You need to work it out with him."

"Great, Sam. I'm glad we all agree." What good could have possibly come from all this?

And that's all there is to it. Four months of daily struggles with

patient and staff and that's it. I don't know whether to be glad or
angry. Or depressed.

Zoe and I are in bed. I lie on my stomach and she begins to
massage my back, touching it lightly with the tips of her fingers. I
want so much to relax, to let the tension out, to leave work at the
hospital and focus on the pleasures of life. But it is of little avail. I
remain tight as a drum and can barely feel those lovely hands
pumping life into a tired body. "Max," she asks, "tell me what's
wrong. Your lying there is pathetic."

"Pathetic," I moan. "That's right. I'm pathetic."

"Ah. My poor baby. Tell Zoe what it's all about or I'll stop
rubbing you."

"No! Don't stop. You're my only hope. I'm depressed. My life
is awful. Psychiatry stinks. I don't know what I'm going to do with
my life."

"My, my," she says. "Did we have a tough day at work?"

"Oh Jesus, Zoe. It's not just a tough day. It's a tough life. What
am I going to do? No one gets better. I do nothing for anyone.
There's no hope for any of my patients or anyone."

"Poor, Max. What is he to do?" She is talking in pit-a-pat
phrases just to get my goat. And of course, it works.

"Zoe! I'm serious. This isn't working out. I think I'll quit."

"Okay."

"What do you mean, okay?"

"I mean I'll love you anyway and it's okay with me. I don't need
you to be a psychiatrist to be in love with you and have a happy
life."

I sit up. "That's nice. I'm glad. Cause I'm serious. This has
been an incredibly awful week. I think I'm catching a depression
from my patients."

"Frankly, Ace, I suspect you were able to come up with one on
your own."

"Everything is so lousy!"

Zoe sits up with me. "Stop for a second, Max. Let's try to look
at this in small pieces. Are you sad to be a psychiatrist?"

"I don't know. It's better than medicine."

"That's good. You used to direct all your anger at the hospital, as if it was the cause of your misery. Is that not true anymore?"

"I can't seem to get very angry. All I feel is hopeless. No one will ever get better and nothing that I do will help them. I don't think the hospital does too much, except get the mental patients off the street, but I guess that's something."

"So you don't think it's the hospital that's ruining your life?"

"No."

"Good. Now, is it the patients? Are they ruining your life?"

"Of course not."

"What does that mean?"

"It means that they are sick and all they want is to get better. I haven't lost it so bad that I blame my patients for wanting to get better."

"Well, we can put that off for right now. If it's not the patients and it's not the hospital and psychiatry is better than medicine, then all that's left is you."

"Right. Thanks a million."

"So what do you have to be depressed about?"

"I don't know. Actually, things are pretty good. I have a good job, I'm in love and in bed with the most beautiful woman in the world, and I live in a nice enough place. We've got great friends and we get to travel and see the theater and all sorts of other stuff. No one is threatening me. I just got a massage." Zoe smiles. "There really isn't anything that's bad. Except I feel awful. Hopeless. Helpless. Worthless."

"Tell me, Max, do you think this has something to do with my getting into medical school?"

"Why would you think that?"

She lies back down and stares at the ceiling. After a moment's thought she replies. "As I recall, your depression and my med school acceptance happened about the same time. Do you remember?"

"As I recall, it was you who seemed upset at that time."

"You're right, Ace, I was. But I was anxious and excited, not depressed. Maybe you're worried about what will happen to us if I become a doctor, too."

"Are you doing insight-oriented therapy now?" I try to sneer, but it comes out very shallow.

"Listen to me, Max. I'm going to be working very hard and you're going to have to do a lot more work in keeping us together. In fact, you're going to have to figure out a lot about your entire life and the way you want to live it. I wonder if you want to do that."

"Of course I'm worried about med school. It's incredibly hard and I'll miss you all the time. But I want you to be a doctor. What amazes me is that you are so elated by it all and so idealistic about what it will mean for your life."

"Could you be a little clearer on that," she says with extreme deliberation.

"Ten years ago, when I started this whole mess, I had no idea what I was getting into. You know how everyone is always asking if you would do something over again? Well, I ask myself that all the time. I'm an okay guy. I could have done a lot of things. But I chose this. And I wonder why. I was so incredibly idealistic when I went to med school. I was going to save the world. And I felt ground down by the studies and by reality, whatever that is, and by the sheer horror of human illness. And I'm lying here in bed, moaning for myself, while you get ready to embark on this course with rosy visions of the future."

"Are you jealous?"

"No. I don't think so. I just can't figure out what is going on."

"What's going on is you're depressed. It's not impossible. But stop it. Or you'll make me depressed, too. I don't want to hear all this lousy stuff about medicine and psychiatry! Sometimes I think you do it just to make me worried about my future. Would you do that?"

"Of course not. Maybe we should just go to sleep. Okay?"

"You know, Max, maybe it's not work at all. Maybe it's the position of the planets or the moment of your birth or the alignment of your spine. Maybe your entire life isn't based on being a psychiatrist."

"I know it's not. I need some sleep."

"If you put less energy into being crazy about your work, you'd have some left over for other fun activities."

"Not tonight, love. I'm pooped."

She growls and rolls over. "Goodnight, Ace," she says to the wall.

Rounds are not the horror show I had expected. In fact, with Sam's backing, no one has any real objection to Tam Luck leaving the hospital with his brother to hopefully find a more culturally appropriate kind of mental health than we can provide here.

Lucy, his social worker, and I meet. She calls up Tam's brother, Ho, and with the help of an interpreter arranges the discharge. It seems that Ho was as frustrated as I was and is happy to have Tam back. He knows of a Vietnamese psychiatrist here in Boston. Why didn't we think of that?

Only one thing remains. Trying to explain this to the patient. I put in a call to his brother, Ho, to expedite matters. He arrives with an interpreter, a friend.

Tam is speaking again, but I don't think it's French and Michael, Ho's friend, doubts if it's Vietnamese, either. But he starts to explain to Tam what is going on. Tam is again in a quiet room, secluded from the rest of the ward. He has nothing on except a pillowcase, which is wrapped around his head. And he grins and grins. As Michael explains, patiently I suppose, although I can't understand a word of it, Tam continues to sit, motionless, grinning. After a few minutes, Michael shrugs his shoulders and we leave. "Well," I ask, "do you think he understood?"

He shrugs again and shakes his head. "I do not know."

Ho and Michael leave the unit and I walk to my office. Under the circumstances, it's tough to be elated about this particular discharge. Normally, there is a feeling of satisfaction that comes when a patient is well enough to go home. Now, there is nothing but a sour taste in my mouth. I don't know if it's a feeling of frustration, but there it is. Four months here and all we did was lock him up and drug him up. And I know that this is not a usual case and everything else that people say to me, but it sure is a pain in the neck. Ah well. Maybe it's me.

As quick as I can I duck out of the ICU and head down to my office to hide. Oh, sweet peace. My mind starts to wander to depression and sadness so I pull out my list of daily activities. There are items like: call patients' parents, call social worker, get blood levels of lithium, see in session, have team meeting, plan discharge meeting, arrange school placement, and so on. At least half of my time is taken up in meetings, and half of what is left is spent on the telephone. So I start to do the daily chore of list management but it seems a poor way to end a depression. Picking up the phone I shake my head and turn to the pleasures that await me.

7

Fear

In the dream, Zoe and I are in a castle with old, brick walls. Everything is quiet as we search for family and friends and can find no one. Then we are on a beach, gorgeous and long, again with no one there. Looking up I see that the beach is now crowded but there is no one I can recognize. A group starts to chase me and Zoe struggles to keep up. We turn behind a rock and stop because we are all alone again. We realize that we are at a banquet at Asylum. Everywhere around me is food but we cannot advance to the tables. I am very hungry and try to go around the barrier but it leads me back to the beach and we lie down, unfulfilled. I wake up in a sweat.

Looking over at Zoe she still snores lightly. I reach out to touch her face, not wanting to disturb her, but she awakens anyway. Smiling, she entwines herself around me and, putting her head on my shoulder, falls back asleep.

With just the barest touch of warmth in the air, I shed my winter coat and start to dream of spring. Perhaps, I think, my mood will improve with the weather. Perhaps the warmth heralds a new spring. They tell me at the hospital that admissions go up in the spring. That depression is most common in the spring. So maybe a good mood now means I'm not the patient after all. Maybe this is the message that a nice spring will pull me through. I hope. It's much too early for the crocuses. But I can still look for a bud here and there.

"Molly," I ask, "what are the benefits of all this? I'm losing track of why I went into this business in the first place."

"I can't answer that for you, Max. That's one you have to figure out for yourself."

"And if I don't find the answer in my own backyard maybe I never lost it in the first place?"

She laughs. It's a nice, throaty laugh that seems to come from the heart and I am instantly envious. Where is the pleasure coming from? We do the same job. Sort of. What is the secret that she knows that I don't? How do you figure out happiness?

"Very funny," she says. "Actually, in psychiatry you don't even have to look as far as your backyard. We settle for somewhere between the head and the heart."

"Well, why are you so happy when I get depressed all the time? Is there something wrong with me? Do my patients cause it?"

"Max, let me tell you, I've been in the pits of depression. Who hasn't? Anyone, including you and all your patients, who have allowed themselves to experience feelings, have experienced depression. I was in analysis for five years. There were many days when I thought that I was as low as a depression could get me. But then I got lower. And if I was with a depressed patient, I could carry around their depression for days."

"Terrific. So that's the club I've joined. But I don't see you being so sad. Certainly not like I feel."

"Well then at least we know therapy helped me." She laughs again. "Seriously, I get depressed. But I know how to bounce back up again. When your emotions take you, or Simon, or Ecaterina, or anyone down, you plummet till you hit bottom. But for most everyone, and I'm sure for you, there is a bottom. And the trick you need to learn is how to hit the bottom and then bounce back up. I can do it in minutes now."

"That's fantastic! I've been wallowing in sadness for a month."
I start to get a little excited and ask, "How do you do it?"

"Therapy helps. But you'll learn. And when you do you can
share it with your patients. The trick isn't in teaching people
never to get depressed again. Bad things happen and that's the
way it is. But you can help them to realize that they can be happy
again and not have to take the rest of their life to find it out."

"That makes sense. I never thought about it that way. I'm
always trying to convince my patients that they don't have to be
depressed. Maybe I'd be better off trying to help them get
through their depression a little quicker."

Molly gives a knowing smile that makes me quiver and agrees.
"Additionally, it allows you to recognize, acknowledge, and help
the patient bear the pain."

"And I don't struggle with them?"

"Exactly."

I'm a little buoyed by the time I head back through the hospital
door. I can bounce back. I'm depressed because of real life events
and I'll be better. I am. I am. Sandra is waiting for me on my
arrival. "Max. Come into my office."

Plopping down in the chair I work a smile on my face. "How are
you feeling today?" she asks.

"It's lovely outside," I reply. And it is. As the day has gone on
the sun has emerged. We stand at the window and peer at the
courtyard, which for the first time in months is filled with patients, huddled together in groups, talking, or walking around in
circles. How many months ago, nine, ten since this all began?
Sandra breaks through my reverie with a touch on my shoulder
and an invitation to sit down. "Are you feeling more relaxed?"

"Making the attempt, Sandra. I'm learning that I don't have to
be depressed all the time."

"Good lesson. When you figure out the answer, tell me, alright?" She stretches out and puts a satisfied look on her face. I
get the feeling that she's heard this before.

"What makes you think my advice would be useful?"

"Well, Max, I sometimes forget how painful my first year was. I rarely think about it, let alone talk about it. But I still have incredibly low moments and feel quite intense emotions, that I never really remembered before I did my residency."

"You know, Sandra," I say, "sometimes I feel that I need these emotions if I'm ever going to understand how my patients feel."

"Could be. I think you're doing a fine job here."

"How's that? Things have felt less than excellent."

"Perhaps your standards are too high. But at least you're not subjecting others to the ridiculous pressure that you put on yourself. It would be nice if you could let up a bit on you. The patient is the sick one, remember? Everyone goes through miserable periods here. When you sit with a patient you sit with unbelievable emotion. Of course you go a little nuts. It's like any stress experience. Speaking of which," she changes track, "how are your patients doing?"

"Everyone is pretty much unchanged. I got my two nursing home patients back to the nursing home. All they needed was a few weeks to cool out and get some space from their stressful environment. I think the meds helped too. Simon is perking along. He's still depressed and I don't know if I'll ever get anywhere with him, but at least he comes to therapy and we've got an alliance of sorts."

Sandra cuts in. "Don't underestimate the work you're doing with him. He's a tough patient and has thrown some real powerful stuff at you. The depression alone is impressive, and the psychotic transference is also very strong."

"How do you define his psychotic transference?"

"He seems to treat you as if you had all sorts of magical powers that aren't true. Basically, you seem to be a part of his craziness. That can be very intense to sit with."

"Agreed. And the sexual stuff he throws out is pretty wild."

"Speaking of sexual stuff," she replies, "how is Ecaterina?"

"Frankly, I think the therapy may be going well. She's not exactly what I expected, but in the last couple of sessions I think I've gotten a grip on what's happening."

"Well, that would be good. She certainly is interesting."

"Yeah, if you like cobras. Magda stopped calling me. It probably means that she'll be back here in a few weeks."

"Perhaps," Sandra says. "She may be stronger than you think, just using her calls to you as a way of making sure she has a line in to the hospital."

"Could be. Shirley is still totally bonkers. A person without a clue to what's going on. Every day it's a new fantasy. It's amazing. Eve is still Eve. Hasn't killed anyone yet. But boy, she can really put the fear of God in me."

"Frankly, Max, I'm under a lot of pressure to have you discharge Eve. She misses most of her groups and the ones she goes to she is totally disrespectful of everyone else there. What do you think is the reason for her to stay on in the day hospital?"

Rats. I was hoping no one would ask me that. "I'm not totally sure. She seems to be able to open up and trust me more since we started treatment. And she hasn't made any criminal acts, or at least known ones, in months. I think she sees the day hospital as a place she can go without fear. Which is a new thing in her life."

"I appreciate that, Max, but what good are we doing her now? She really is very disruptive for the other patients and it's not fair to have two sets of rules, one for her and one for everyone else."

"Why not? We're supposed to be a hospital, here to help people." My voice is rising in volume and I start to feel the anger rise with it. Goddamn all these rules! "She needs a different kind of treatment than someone who is depressed. Damn, she needs all the help we can give her!"

"Slow down, Max." Sandra, thanks be, manages to stay calm while I boil. "I want to help her as much as you do. I just don't think we do her any favors by letting her break the rules. I think that's the wrong message to give. Why don't you discuss it in team meeting?"

"Fine. I will. That's what we were planning on today, anyway. But I doubt I'll get many allies."

"Don't be so sure, Max. I've said it before, but if your emotions are going crazy, talk to people. That's what this profession is all about."

"Right, Sandra," I say as sarcastically as I can muster. "See you later."

I'm left standing in the doorway, kicking myself for turning down help, when Lucy, Eve's social worker, walks on by. "Going to team meeting, Max? It's time." Maybe it's the weather, but everybody's smiling.

"You're looking nice, Lucy."

"Thank you, Max. But you've been down a bit lately, haven't you?"

"I suppose so. Has it been that obvious?"

"Not really. But we kind of miss your humor around this place. It would cheer up everyone to have you part of the team again."

"I hadn't realized I had dropped out."

"Maybe it's not you. Maybe things have just been disorganized lately."

We've arrived at the conference room and go in to meet the rest of the group. Team meeting each day anchors the process of making up care plans for patients. We sit and decide what to do with whom and who is going to do it and then we all hope it happens the way we planned it which it usually doesn't. Lately, I've been treating these meetings as a great imposition in my life. Primarily, I suppose, to distance myself from all the pain. At least that's what Sam says. I'm not so sure, but here I am.

There's a big crowd today, perhaps because Eve is such a wild and woolly patient. In addition to Lucy and me, Kathy, the head nurse, Jill from activities, Irv, the mental health assistant, Sandra, of course, and a host of other staff members. Sam has been briefing me on how to handle this meeting. "Max, the thing is that you are an authority and you have to make decisions. People count on you to be a leader. That's different from being authoritarian. Accept who you are. People will listen."

Sandra has been reinforcing the message in a different way. "Remember," she says, "these people are your friends and best allies you have. They can make your life a lot easier if you let them."

Everyone says good morning and a few jokes are made and

Lucy calls the meeting to order. "We're going to talk about Eve today. Max, do you want to start?"

"Sure, Lucy. But why don't you list the main issues, first." A strong, cautious beginning.

She pulls out a big yellow card divided into many areas with lines and circles and so on, on which each of us in the room at some time has placed our ideas about the patient. This is our team planning card. "From the top," she begins, "we have one, antisocial behavior, two, difficulty with relationships, three, poor home situation, four, disruptive in day hospital, five, poor schooling. These are the main ones. Should I go on?"

I smile, since everyone in the room knows that to go through all of that would have us meeting sometime till June. "That seems like a lot. Why don't we start by trying to figure out what has been useful to her here?"

"Good idea, Max," Kathy begins. "I think we should focus in on Eve and the day hospital." I can't tell if there is hostility in her voice, but I say nothing. Kathy continues. "Frankly, she's been a pain in the ass. There seems to be no way to get her to follow any of the day hospital rules and she certainly sets a bad example for the other patients. I'm not sure if she should be here any longer."

"What happens when you try to discipline her?" I ask.

"She either threatens you or walks out. Most of the staff are pretty frightened of her. I'm not sure you recognize how scary she can be."

I laugh in spite of myself. "I think I understand that, Kathy. I'm the person who sits with her in my office and gets threatened. I'm the one getting the late night phone calls threatening to blow my head off."

The room focuses in on me and is silent for a minute. Lucy breaks the silence by saying quietly, "You know, Max, I didn't know you felt that way about her."

"What do you mean? How could I feel any other way?"

"I don't know," she responds, "but this isn't a feeling you have shared in here before."

"Well, it's true. That woman scares me to death." I start laughing and then everyone is laughing and suddenly I'm feeling a little better.

Jill asks me, "If you're so scared of Eve, why do you keep treating her?"

"What do you mean? I treat her because she's sick."

"Half the world is sick. She's no sicker than many of the rest of them. Why put all this energy into Eve?"

"Hey! I think we help her. Isn't that enough?" And I start to feel worse.

Kathy joins in. "It isn't if she's a detriment to the rest of the patients here."

"I'm not sure that she is. Perhaps it's everyone's fear of setting limits on her that's the biggest problem. Maybe if she could be treated just like any other patient none of this would happen."

Sandra says, "Max, it sounds as if you're not feeling supported by the rest of the staff."

"Well, I guess I don't. I think I'm really trying to do something for this patient and all I hear is how bad she is."

"It's not the same as us saying how bad you are, Max," Lucy replies. "Everyone here thinks you're trying to do an incredible job with Eve. Many people would have given up on her long ago. But that still doesn't make it any easier on the rest of us who have to deal with the mess she leaves behind."

"I know that," I respond, not really having thought about it until this moment. "But what are we going to do to help her?"

Kathy says, "You seem to be suggesting that we need to set firmer limits. What do you propose?"

"Treat her like any other patient. If she misses a day, suspend her. If she disrupts a group, suspend her from the group. Make her re-earn her privileges if she can't stay within the rules of the day hospital. Just don't let her intimidate you. I know she's scary. But that's her disease. We need to treat her just like we'd treat anyone else who is frightening."

"But she's different," Jill begins. "She's not psychotic. Sometimes she's just disruptive for the hell of it. She threatens other patients and I think she may be stealing. We can't treat her like anybody else. It takes three men just to keep her from beating up another patient."

"I know she's a pain in the neck, but . . ."

Kathy cuts in. "Max, listen to us. We feel as badly about Eve as you do. But she's been here for over a month and things are still terrible in trying to handle her. I can't run the floor with her here anymore."

"You know," I say, "I get a different view of her in therapy. I really feel like I'm seeing some change there. And now I hear people saying we should ask her to leave the hospital."

Lucy asks, "How would that make you feel?"

"Rotten. I don't want to abandon her because of the limits of the hospital."

"Max, it's not a failure by you. Sometimes the hospital isn't the right place for every patient. If she is improving in therapy with you, great. You can continue that. But it's simply not working in this framework. We have limits on what we can do."

"So do I!" I start to shout and then cut myself short. Listen, I think, listen. Pay attention.

Jill follows up her earlier question. "Why do you want to have her here so much?"

"I don't know. Where else can she go?"

Lucy, switching to social worker role, says, "There really isn't anywhere. Her family has cut her off, she has no money, her friends, few as they are, are a bit crazy themselves. When she leaves here she goes on the streets."

"Oh, that's terrific."

"Max," Sandra says, "that's no reason to keep her here. This is a hospital, not a shelter."

"So we throw her on the streets?"

"No, we discharge her from the hospital."

"It comes to the same thing."

"It's different. We're a hospital. We can only do certain things. And one of them is not picking up all the homeless people in Boston and giving them a place to sleep. We all would like to be able to do that, but we can't."

"Why not? I feel like I'm doing my best."

Irv cuts in between Sandra and me. "Max, you're not the only person here with compassion. We all get sad when we can't fulfill all the needs of our patients. But we have to consider doing the most we can do. Psychiatry is not perfect. There are lots of people we care about but can't help. Eve may be one of them."

"Max," Kathy says, "you have to consider the other patients. There are fifty-five people on this ward and every Eve makes it twice as hard to care for them. And we can do something that will help them. We do have therapies that will work. We need your backing to do our job. And one way is to understand how Eve affects everyone else here."

"I get the feeling that everyone in this room feels put upon by this patient. I'm no exception. I just don't feel ready to throw her out yet."

"We're not asking you to throw her out," says Jill. "Just to consider what is really best for her and the entire ward."

"So what should we do?"

Sandra says, "Let's talk to her about discharge." And everyone else agrees. Lucy then continues, seemingly for the group. "Max, we admire your sticking up for Eve. It's not easy to be her therapist and advocate and we respect you for it. The more you let us work with you on it, the smoother it will go for all of us."

"Alright, Lucy," I say, and the room utters a collective sigh. "I don't like this, but I'll try it out. But I'm not just kicking her out on the streets."

Sandra says, "We'll work that out when we need to. Are you concerned that your meeting with Eve will be a problem?"

"Not if you like explosions."

Endless thoughts tumble through my mind, like will Eve beat me up, what am I going to do, and where have all these people been the past few months? Or where have I been? Feeling alone when I didn't have to? Am I keeping Eve here out of fear? Or do I truly think we can help her? Sandra is leaving the room and I catch up to her. "Gotta moment?"

"Sure," she says, and we head back to her office.

"What did you think of the meeting?"

"How do you mean? I thought that a pretty good conclusion was reached."

"I still feel we can help Eve here."

She leans over and puts her hand on my arm. "You can work on that, Max. But you have to do it in the context of this ward and all these people. Is that so hard?"

I smile, then reply, "Not too hard. But difficult."

"Keep an open mind, Max. There's a solution if you keep things open."

Shirley is sitting in a chair beside my office door. "Excuse me, Dr. Jackson," she says. "May we have our session now?"

"Of course, Shirley. This is the time we always meet."

We enter the office and she spends a few moments trying to decide which chair to sit in. After completing her deliberations, she takes the chair that she sits in every week.

"Good morning, Dr. Jackson, how are you today?"

"I'm fine, Shirley. Why do you ask?"

"I ask because that is what there is asking for."

"Uh huh."

"I have a number of questions that I want to ask you this week."

"What are they?"

"Those tiny dots of light in the sky, are they planets or moons?"

Now, the big question: should I interpret this or not? Nah. Let's talk. "Actually, Shirley, they're stars."

"What do you mean, stars?"

"You know, like the sun."

"I think they're planets."

"Oh. Why's that?"

"Because that's what they look like."

"How can you tell with them being so far away?"

"I can't tell, it's what I think."

"Oh." We're silent for a moment and then she says, "Why do you think they are stars like the sun?"

"That's what it says in the science books."

"How do you know they are true?"

"How do you know anything is true?" This gets her thinking and we're quiet for a full minute before she responds.

"I don't know if anything is true. I know that I have many messages to carry to the world. But they are painful messages. That seems to be true."

"It's good to question?"

"I think it is good. If they were stars then they would have to be too far away. If they were planets or moons they could be closer. I don't know if it is too far away."

"You could look it up."

"How do I know the books aren't lying to me?"

"You don't."

"So what good does it do to look it up?"

"You tell me."

"It doesn't do me any good. I have to question to be me. I have to think and I know what I think."

"Thinking is what makes you you?"

"It makes me an independent person."

"Independent from what?"

At this point she starts flapping her arms as if she's a bird trying to take flight. I assume that means we're on the right track. "Shirley, when you do that it seems to me that you are thinking or feeling something that's unpleasant but important."

"I'm thinking about the Russians."

"How's that?"

"Why do you hate my electrodes?"

"How's that, Shirley?"

"You want me to give up the voices of truth."

"And?"

"That's it."

"Can you tell me more?"

She begins to snarl and can't get the words out. She sort of coughs and wheezes and then just sits there. Feeling like I've already got a lot of information from her, I decide to back off. "How are things at home?"

"I don't have a home."

"I mean with your sister."

She stops squirming and stares at me. "How is your family?" she asks.

"They're fine. Why do you ask?"

"You know all about me. Let's talk about you."

"This seems pretty unfair, doesn't it?"

"I'm getting a feeling like I'd like to tear you to pieces."

"Do you feel angry at me?"

"No!" This is a half laugh/half scream and then Shirley is standing and asking, "Is it alright if I leave now? I want to stop."

"Do you know why you want to go?" I ask, hoping she'll connect her feelings to her actions.

"No, Dr. Jackson. I just want to go." And she leaves pouting. Yeesh. I have to find a better way to end these sessions.

I sit there and start to scribble the process notes for the hour, my record of the pearls we have exchanged.

Jerry, as always, is punctual. He smiles as he enters my office and begins to talk before he has hit the seat. "Dr. Jackson, I had a great week. I really want to thank you. Wow, this therapy is okay."

Isn't this nice? "That's great, Jerry. What was so terrific?"

"Lots of things. I didn't worry at all, and school went fine and things just seemed to be so easy. And I called Belinda and we went out again."

"Belinda? Is that your girlfriend?"

"Yeah sure. Didn't I tell you that? Belinda. She's great."

"Tell me about her."

"She's tough to describe, but I really like her. And she likes me. When I'm with her, I am just so relaxed, so comfortable. It's like a new morning." He grins at his own analogy and looks at me. "I must sound like a dope. It's just that after we talked last week I called her up and she said we could go out and things have been great."

"How did you feel when you asked her out?"

"I was nervous. Really nervous. I was so afraid she'd be angry at me. I got pissed at myself before I was able to call her. But I got it together and it went pretty good."

"What was the call like?"

"Well, it was fine. I couldn't believe how easy it was."

"She didn't hate you?" Why not get to the point? Anyway, the happiness is terrific to see. Why not try a little humor?

He laughs. "No, I guess that was all in my head. Besides, if I can forgive me, I suppose anyone else can, too."

"Glad to hear it. So you're not such a terrible person after all?"

"Boy, not around Belinda. You know, Dr. Jackson, I think I'm in love. How can you tell if you're in love?"

Wow. If I could answer that I've got a great career. "What does it feel like to you?" I ask.

"It's a hard thing to describe. But, for the past week, I've felt as if any problem or any difficulty that I had could just be magically cured by just being around her. And I think about her always. I play with the letters in her name and imagine presents I can buy her and spend hours of my time not studying at all, simply thinking of her. And I'm not angry at myself for that. It's time well spent." He exhales and sinks back in his chair.

"That sounds like love," I say. "Definitely."

"I thought so, too. I'm going over to see her after our session. I told her all about you."

"Oh?"

"Yeah. How you helped me and all. She thought I'd never call back, not after what an idiot I'd been when I broke up with her because of, uh, sex."

"Is that still a problem?"

"Not yet. I'm worried about it though." He squirms a bit.

"What have you done the past week?"

"I told her a little of what we talked about last week and how much I liked her and everything and she seemed to accept it. She didn't push herself on me at all. It helped me relax so much. I can see her in such a different way now. I always liked Belinda, but this is too much."

"You were able to relax when you told her how you felt?"

He puzzles for a second. "Yeah. When she knew the score, things were fine."

"So what makes you worried about the future?"

"Well, I figure we're going to make love soon. All things considered, I really want to. But, I'm worried. I mean, this isn't easy for me."

"No. You said last week that it was hard for you to get close to anyone."

"Yeah. I get nervous and flustered. I really feel on the verge of panic. But it's not just with women. It happens anytime people put any pressure on me. Anytime any authority figure tells me to do something, it's like I have to do it or I just won't be able to sleep. That's part of the whole problem I'm having with deciding what I want to go into. I don't know whether I want to be a corporate lawyer or not, but there's no way to avoid it. At least that's how it looks to me."

"You're being forced into it?"

"I know it sounds stupid, but you don't know what it's like. The pressure at school is so intense. All the professors and deans and advisors, everyone is steering me to the big firms. No one wants me to branch out on my own."

"Isn't it possible that you have to break away without their help?"

"What do you mean?" He sounds genuinely confused.

"Do you feel so controlled by them?"

"Not controlled. That's not the right word. They just have a lot of power over me and it's awful hard to make the right decision with that kind of pressure."

"Uh huh." We sit in an awkward pause.

"You don't believe me," he says. "You think I should be able to work this out for myself, live my own life, make my own decisions. Well it's not that easy."

"No it's not."

"Yeah. It is. I want to though."

"Like you did with Belinda?"

"Huh?"

"Like you got what you want with her?"

"How is it like that?" Confusion again.

Oh good, another interpretation. "You may be afraid to be honest with people. Afraid if you tell them the truth they will reject you. So you either try to avoid them physically like Belinda, or act like a different person than you feel, as at school. You'll be happier at school if you can express your real self." How was that?

"I get you." Alright. "But I don't want to go too crazy at school. I mean I don't want to get thrown out."

"Is that who you are?"

"I'm not sure. I mean I'm not sure I know who I really am."

"You seem to want to find out, though."

"Sure I do. I get your point. You don't have to rub it in. But I'll try it."

"Try what?"

"Being myself."

"Good luck. And congratulations about Belinda." And as he exits I am filled with wonder and confusion. Does this stuff work? And how?

The calls today seem to roll off my back pretty easily and no major crises are in sight as four o'clock approaches, and I can see the end of the week finally arriving. But it's been pretty calm and there are mostly exciting things to look forward to. Like this year ending. Residents' meeting is all that's left today and it usually is relaxing. But my arrival there is delayed by a visit to Sam's office.

Sam starts. "Max, we need to talk about Eve."

"It's okay, Sam. We discussed her in team meeting this week and I think everything is fine. We're going to have a planning meeting and work out what should be done within the next few days." I sit there proud of myself till Sam cuts in.

"Max, what are you talking about? Have you heard from Eve today?"

"No. What's up?" I don't like the look on his face.

"She's in the ICU, Max. The police arrested her. She threatened to kill someone. The police brought her here."

"Oh hell! Who did she threaten?"

"It seems the police are claiming that she called the senator's office and said she would 'get him' if the police didn't leave her alone. I guess she was picked up by the cops a few nights ago and she felt hassled. Didn't you read about it in the *Globe* this morning." He pulls out a copy of the paper and turns to the Metro section. PSYCHO TO SENATOR: WATCH OUT reads the headline. As I scan the article it becomes apparent that Eve, or whoever made the call, is in a lot of trouble.

"Sam, it doesn't give any names here. How do you know it was Eve that did it?"

"I just got the call a half hour ago from the district attorney. Apparently she left a return number that the senator could call her at when he had time."

"She left her number?" I asked incredulously.

"Yes. It's part of her pathology. She doesn't think things through very well."

"How could anyone take this seriously, Sam? She was just blowing off steam, I'm sure. Although one never knows."

"Well, we're going to find out."

"Why us?"

"Because she was our patient and that means, at least in the eyes of the court, that she's our responsibility."

"This is the negative side of assuming that we know what's best for people?"

"Very funny," Sam says dryly. "In the meantime, we've got a hot situation on our hands. I had Eve put in the ICU with the court's approval for an evaluation prior to arraignment and the senator's office is breathing down our throats. What do you think we should do?"

"Well for one, I'm glad I'm not in your shoes."

"Anything else?"

"Sam, I don't see how it could be our fault. After all, we did more for her than anyone could have expected, not less. Let's face it, in most cases we would have just thrown her out on the streets. Instead, we tried to give her treatment. I hardly see how that makes us liable."

"Well, I agree with you, Max. But the courts have a funny way about these things. Threats by psychiatric patients are not taken lightly. Our first job, it seems to me, is to do a thorough evaluation of Eve. Let's try to make our points clear there."

"But she didn't hurt anyone," I remember to note.

"Luckily, no. Thank the stars." Sam sighs and wipes his forehead. He really has moved too high in the hierarchy to have to put up with this stuff. "She seems to have just been enraged and made a stupid phone call."

"Do I have to do the evaluation?"

"She's your patient."

"Yeah, but she may get a little teed off at me after all this fun. If she thinks I'm working for the system or to lock her up, things could get hairy. Hell, they already are."

"Be careful. And see her only with a security guard present."

"Will you see her with me, Sam?"

He looks at his watch and then nods. "I've got a few minutes now. Let's go."

"Hello," I say, "Eve?"

"Yeah, Dr. Jackson. That you? And Dr. Watson? Hey, the boss and his boy."

"Hi, Eve. We need to talk."

She stares at me as if I was the devil himself. "Dr. Jackson, I'm gonna kill you! You told the police where to find me! I'm gonna kill you! You're a dead man! I'm gonna get me a piece and blow your head off! You're dead! You understand?"

Gee, this is fun. "Eve, I don't know what you're talking about. This is the first . . ."

She cuts in. "Forget the lies, asshole. You're dead!" She swings her arms wildly at me as I back away, petrified.

"Eve," I shout, "stop this now!" She pulls back for a moment then verbally charges back in.

"You set me up Dr. Jackson. None of this would have happened if you hadn't forced me to be in this hospital in the first place. Now they think I'm crazy and I'm going to kill you." Holding her arms to her sides she advances toward me again as two mental health workers step between us. Thanks, guys.

I turn to Sam for support as Eve stands and looks menacing. He takes me by the arm and we back off of the unit together.

Great time I'm having. "Sam," I plead, "get someone else to do this evaluation. Why don't you do it? I'm scared to death."

"Don't worry, Max. Security here will protect you."

"Sam, this is a little too intense for me. I've put up with a lot from Eve, but now I'm really scared."

"Look, Max. Take the weekend off. You'll feel better on Monday."

He turns his back, signifying the interview is over and I find myself all alone in the hall. I don't want to die for my job. I don't want to die. It's not worth it. It's really not. Oh God, what am I gonna do? Should I tell Zoe? This will scare her as bad as me. Should I tell anyone? What do you do when a crazy woman is on your tail? Desperately, I go to our residents' meeting and blurt out the whole tale to them.

"Oh my God, I'm scared to death. What if she kills me? Do you think I should change my phone number? What am I going to do now? This isn't the way to do a psychiatry residency, living in fear. She threatens the senator so they lock her up where she can threaten me."

Bobby offers me a cup of coffee and a donut. "Here, have something to eat, you'll feel better."

"What is this, a trip to my mother's? A bunch of psychiatrists and all you can do is feed me!" I'm starting to get a little wild.

"Slow down, Max," Sandra says. "No one is going to kill you. What exactly happened?"

So I repeat the story of my visit with Eve and how terrified it made me feel and then start eating ravenously. Denise says, "Hey, we'll be around. Nothing horrible is going to happen to you. Eve never really hurt anyone, did she?"

"Just a cop," I mumble. "That's how she got to Asylum in the first place. She beat up a cop." I can see it in the papers now: STUPID PSYCHIATRY RESIDENT SHOT BY FORMER PATIENT. "Staff says, 'We told him not to treat her.' "

Eric gives me a pat on the back and tells me, "Hey, nothing is going to happen. She's in the ICU. And you can see her with someone else in the room. There's really nothing for you to worry about. All you have to be is careful."

"Good point," I respond. "I'll just be careful. Does anyone here want to walk me to my car tonight?"

"One thing you can be glad about," Bobby says. "At least Eve doesn't have any family to set on you. Otherwise she wouldn't be so angry at you. She'd be angry at them."

"That's right," says Denise. "This is really her way of letting you know how much she likes you."

"She certainly has an unpleasant way of showing it."

Sandra says, "Well, at any rate, you have found out what an important person you are in her life."

"That's terrific. Just great. But she's crazy. I didn't have anything to do with the police. She's just nuts."

"Or else she's a sociopath who is going to take no responsibility for her own actions. And you're the handiest person to blame." Bobby gives me another donut as he says, "In addition, she knows you too well. Sociopaths are good at that. And she figures that as long as she's suffering in the ICU, she can make you suffer out here. I bet she is sure that you'll be scared to death by her threats. That's what she's good at. You know that. So she's just manipulating you. It's your mind, not your body that is in danger here."

"Okay, I'll buy that. But what am I going to do this weekend?"

"Max, take a vacation," Sandra says. "Go away for a couple of days and relax. Everything will be here when you come back."

"I will," I say, still quaking from the encounter and the way that I got twisted. Does it ever stop, these feelings of confusion and manipulation? When will I feel at ease with whatever my patients say? How to separate what is said to play with my brain from what is real? Or perhaps more importantly, how to not get twisted by any of this stuff, while remaining able to hear it sympathetically and kindly?

The moon hangs over Mt. Monadnock, just about to slip behind the peak. It's snowing in New Hampshire and the temperature continues to fall. There is already a foot of snow on the ground and the moon, mountain, and falling flakes conspire to produce a paradise of white, an envelope of quiet and solitude broken only by my periodic giggles when Zoe touches my feet. Pine trees stand in the evening shadows, their branches reaching out for any glimmer of light. As Zoe gets up to turn on the gaslight and I throw another log on the fire I inwardly sigh. Why not this always, why not keep the solitude and peace? What do you say about someone who has a job that beats his head on the wall?

"Penny for your thoughts, Ace."

"Oh, Zoe. I just feel fine. You're the best thing that ever happened to any person anywhere."

"Thanks, love. But I bet that faraway look had to do with something else."

"I was thinking about the job, about Asylum. Mostly I was thinking about me. Why I do it. What good is it. What do I get out of the job and the people and everything."

"Did you come up with an answer?"

"Not even close. It's funny. I don't feel so depressed anymore. In fact, I am getting some satisfaction from all of this. Getting Ecaterina out of the hospital. That's worthwhile. Talking with Shirley. I liked that and I think I can help her. Even my sessions with Simon seem to be going somewhere. But I still feel so unsettled. Less depressed, but somehow no more secure. If that makes sense."

"Do you think you're still frightened about Eve?"

"Not much. The things that people said to me about her ring true. I don't think she's going to hurt me and I can control the situation I see her in pretty well. Although I worry about you. What if she stakes out our house?"

"That's sweet, Max. But I feel alright."

"Doesn't stop me from worrying, you know. It's hard to tell fear from paranoia. I'm not sure where all this leads."

"Where would you like it to lead?"

"I'd like to be a good doctor. I'd like to be able to help my patients. And I'd like to be happy in my work. Like in the *River Kwai*."

"We can probably do better than that. Do you mind if I give you a few observations?"

"No, I can handle it here." It is a three-story log cabin with no electricity or inside plumbing on the top of a mountain. Our car is parked a mile away and there is simply no way for the outside world to get here. No Eve. No one. And as cold as it is outside, the wood stove is fired up and the warmth makes the house seem as much like a womb as I'm likely to find. So I may as well feel safe here.

"Max, you do seem to be in better shape. Your depressions are shorter and more directed. You seem to complain less about the job. I don't know why, but you're talking about your fellow residents in much more positive ways. So maybe this has been a good process for you. But you still seem to be hurt by it. You still come home from work each day with a look of pain on your face and some anger in your heart. I wonder if there isn't something you haven't let go of, some fantasy or hope or anger or I don't know what. I'm not a shrink. But it's only when we get away that you seem to find an inner calm. I wish you could feel this way at work as well as on vacation."

"So do I love, so do I."

And so on Monday, I am prepared to try and figure out what that elusive something is that's missing from the job, or me, or both.

Simon strolls into the office, ten minutes late, saxophone in hand and sinks into the chair. As always he looks sad. As always he is moving slowly, face drooping, a cup of tea in the other hand. Like him, I now believe in the value of a little mania. Anything to get him out of this never ending depression.

"It was a horrible weekend," he begins.

"You look sad."

"I am. I had thought of killing myself and everything seemed very intense and I didn't know what to do. I tried to call you but the hospital wouldn't give me your number." He starts to sob softly.

"You missed me."

"I wish . . . I just wish there was some magic. Something that would make the sadness disappear, like a dream I can wake up from in the morning."

"But I thought you don't like pills."

"I don't like pills. I want magic." He smiles a little as he says this, so I decide to try the pills once again.

"Why not try medication? It might be better than this."

"No never. It'll never help me. I'm too sick." As I've seen too often before, he starts to raise his voice and uncontrollable emotions rise to the surface. I brace myself for an onslaught, but he calms down. "Maybe I'll try it. Some other time. I don't know. I'm just so depressed and sad and I can't get any of my music done. I'm trying to play, but I can't."

"What makes it so hard?"

"I want to make beautiful music." He sighs. "I want it all the time. I carry my music everywhere with me, but then I don't know if that's me carrying the music or the music carrying me." He half grins and looks pleadingly at me, as if looking for some sort of confirmation. When I say nothing he continues. "I try to capture people in sound. But I worry that might destroy everything."

"What would be destroyed?"

"I need to be intimate with someone," he blurts out. He stretches out in his chair and starts to run his fingers through his long hair. "But relationships never last. I guess I destroy them all." He cries.

"And I'm one of them?" More transference?

"No, no," he says. "You don't understand. It's just that sometimes, usually, I can't judge what's going on too well. I get afraid that people might want me and hurt me and then I don't know sometimes if even that would be better than being alone. Do you see?"

"You describe a great aching pain."

"I'm in agony!" he wails and breaks down for minutes, sobbing with his face turned to the wall. "But I have my dreams. Even without hope I have my dreams."

"Is that a good thing to have?"

"How do I know? I don't know. I have to keep my dreams or else I might lose everything."

"And this world is too painful?"

"Even my dreams are painful. I dream of a world of beautiful music lovers and then I'm afraid that you will hate my music."

"But those are just dreams. I can't read your mind."

"How can I be sure of that? How?" He begins to cry again. "Max. I mean, Dr. Jackson, are you going to leave me like my father?"

"You're afraid you might lose me?"

"Everyone else leaves me. Even my parents."

And as I say, "Simon, I'll tell you when I'm leaving, I won't just disappear," I think to myself, yes you're right. I'm going to leave you. I'm just a resident and I'm here temporarily and sooner not later I'll be gone too. And a small glimmer of what my job is and how it's different from my life begins to seep in.

I daydream about separating my job from my life or at least learning which is what and where it doesn't separate and miss most of what Simon is saying. He doesn't seem to notice and when our time is up he thanks me and looks in my eyes as if to ask, "You'll be here next time, won't you?"

I sit there drumming my fingers on the desktop, feeling vaguely guilty about missing so much of the session, but not wanting to get too involved. Is he drawing me in? Or do I respond to neediness so intensely? Or both? Molly! Help me now. Are things too complex to try to understand everything at once? Or is this just his version of free will? Can he choose to be happy? Can I choose to be happy? Can I start to believe it, that somehow I can affirm a desire to be free, and so can my patients? I just don't understand their barriers yet. Or my own.

Ecaterina is late for her appointment. Our last session, which I saw as sort of a breakthrough, given that we seemed to get to real feelings behind some of the acting out, has prompted her to miss the next two sessions. And now I am concerned that she will never return and I will lose one of the few patients who at least speak in a language that I understand. Not to mention that I feel like I must have done something wrong in order to precipitate her departure. Molly tells me to calm down, that this sort of thing happens all the time in private practice and that all it means is something to do with Ecaterina. I shouldn't expect every patient to be able to sit with affect, no matter how empathic I am. So she tells me that I don't have to be the perfect therapist and Ecaterina doesn't have to be the perfect patient. Psychiatry can handle it.

The phone rings and it's Ecaterina. "Hello, Dr. Jackson. I can't make it in today."

"Why's that?" I ask, nonchalantly.

"I don't feel well. I'm under a lot of stress."

"That sounds like a strange reason not to see your therapist."

She laughs and agrees. "But I just don't think I can handle it."

"Is that why you didn't come in the past two weeks?" I ask, springing the nonexistent trap.

"I don't think so," she says. "I was just very busy. So many things came up."

"Uh huh," is all I can manage.

"But maybe I just didn't want to come in. Maybe I should stop therapy."

"Do you know why you feel that way?" I certainly have a theory. We're getting something done.

"No. I guess I feel like we're not getting anywhere."

"Hmmm. Do you want to come in so we can discuss this?"

"I don't know."

Time to get forceful. "I think it would be a good idea if you did."

She hems and haws and agrees. "Next week at our time?"

"I'll see you then, Ecaterina."

The phone rings once more as I finish my process notes on the call and it's Sandra to tell me that Eve has returned from court after her preliminary hearing and is ready to be readmitted to the ICU. I dash up to do the paperwork and ask Eve a few questions. Somehow my resolve not to see her has vanished with my fear. Realistically, I hope.

"How are you?"

"Shit, Dr. Jackson, I'm fine. No problem. How you doing?"

"Eve, why did you threaten me last week?"

"What do you mean, Doc? I like you."

"Eve, you said you were going to kill me."

"Hell, Doc. Can't you take a joke?"

"It's not funny Eve. One more time and you can find yourself a new doctor."

"Shit, Dr. Jackson, be cool. Everything is okay."

Maybe it is Eve. Maybe it will be. "For right now, Eve, you'll be staying in the ICU, until we figure out what to do."

"I need privileges. I need to get out of here."

I don't have the energy to argue and go back to my office.

End of the day and I'm tired. Hell, it's been a long one and all I have to do is check on my new patient, an ax murderer in the ICU, here for a court evaluation for competency, and then I can go home. She's a very strange patient.

"Whirr, whizz, blip, blip, blip. Whjiozzzz!" She has a very high forehead which shines in the light. Her entire face stretches out and seems to become a simple plane with no features. Then her eyes shut briefly, mouth clamps tight before everything flies open and starts all over again. She looks a lot older than her twenty-five years. A self-contained unit of madness, she sits in a chair, making bizarre noises and rocking back and forth. Lights on, nobody home.

The paper from the court had said commit for up to twenty days to evaluate competency to stand trial. The newspaper headline was more to the point. WIFE SLASH MAKES HUSBAND TRASH! it screamed. Edna was seemingly stronger than she looked, having done in her husband with one solid ax blow to the head. However, it was the slicing of hubby into neat three-inch cubes and then putting him in a big trashbag that had really impressed the papers, as well as the courts. Not to mention the fact she sounded like a robot from the 1939 World's Fair. "Hello, Edna, how are you?" And the only reply is, "Bzz, whirr, glip, zing zang a wheeee!" Then the eyes and mouth slam shut before springing open to start all over again, like a hoot owl at midnight.

"Shoot, Sam," I had said. "What the hell do I need twenty days for? This woman is clearly nuts."

"So why did she do in her husband? Try to figure that out." So I sit with her in the ICU, although she might as well be on another planet. Since Tam has left, this has been a quiet place for me. One patient tries to bum a cup of coffee, another cigarettes. I read in the papers that the nicotine and caffeine somehow interact or counteract one another. Which makes sense watching the copious quantities everyone here consumes. It is other hungers that will never be quenched. And in the background there is this woman going, "Whizz, whirr, blip, wheeee!" And Sam barely smiled when I told him that the only way to find out why she killed her husband was to find the three-inch piece with his mouth and ask it.

Turning to her once more, I resolve to get some sort of communication going. "Edna, what's happening?" She totally ignores this. "Talk to me Edna." Again no response. I tap her knee. Not a thing. I pick up my chair and move around in front of her, so there we are face-to-face. I put the chair down and tap her knee again. Still, I get nothing from her. "Edna, this is your doctor. Speak to me."

Sighing, I close my eyes and rub them, trying to force this too long day to a close. I'm tired and sleepy and need a break. I open my eyes to give it one more try and see a blur moving very fast toward my face. Before I have a chance to fully get my lids up, the fist smashes me on the left side of the head and my glasses go flying across the room. I reach up to where the fist was to grab it but it is no longer there. Dazed, I don't see the other fist heading toward the right side of my head till it is on me. I get slammed back into my chair as Edna stands and I try to move back out of her way, nearly blind from the blows and loss of glasses.

I hear a huge noise behind me as patients start to scurry away and I am tempted to call to them for aid. In the milliseconds while waiting for the next blow I scream, "Attendant, Attendant," as loudly as I can, in a desperate attempt to get help. Edna kicks me in the shin as I stand up and then leaps at me, nails bared, hoping to gouge my eyes out. I stumble backward, fall over a chair, and land in a heap on the ground. Finally, after a wait that seems hours two burly men show up, grab her, wrestle her to the floor, then down the hall and lock her in seclusion. A nurse asks me, "How long should we restrain her?" Dazed, I answer, "Forever, I don't know, ask someone else," and collapse into a chair. All I can think of is where are my glasses? I get down on my knees and start crawling around the floor searching. Frustrated, I see Ty coming into the unit, likely in response to the alert that had been called during the rout of Dr. Jackson and wave to him. Gently, he tells me to sit and he'll find the glasses.

He brings over three broken pieces of plastic and glass and says, "This is all I could find. She really walloped you, didn't she?"

"Thanks, Ty." I say no more, just sit there, not able to figure out how I feel or what just happened. Ty asks me, "You all right, Doc? I mean, you don't look so hot."

"Am I bleeding?" I ask anxiously.

"No, I didn't mean that. You just look sort of out of it. Let me tell you about the first time I ever got punched out." And he proceeds to tell me about some street fight when he was a kid and got ambushed behind school and on and on and pretty soon he's got me laughing at I don't know what.

"You know, Ty. This is the first time I've been in a fight since I was thirteen. Hell, I built my whole life around being civilized."

"Civilized? Shit. There ain't no such thing. You got to be careful or they'll get you. They will."

We walk out of the unit together and down to my car and Ty tells me, "Take it easy, man. It's tough to get hit. Take it easy." And as he predicted, the glow of good cheer vanishes immediately upon getting into the car and is replaced by a feeling of being lost in a maze of confusion.

I got hit. Oh Christ. That bitch. She hit me. I wanted to hit her. But I couldn't. Or I didn't. I don't know. What happened? That bitch. All I was trying to do was help her. Jesus, I'm on her side. And she hit me. What an asshole. Damned if I'll ever talk to her again. But what if I have to? What if Sandra and Sam make me? I won't. Up theirs. How could they possibly do this to me? Those bastards. I didn't come here to get hit. Where were the attendants in the ICU? If they were doing their job this never would have happened. Why do I have to do everything by myself? Hell. My eye hurts. I wonder if the retina is detached? I wonder if it's going to swell up? How could the courts send someone like this to a mental hospital? What did they have in mind? This woman is dangerous. She killed her husband. They should lock her up and throw the key away. Oh my God. Oh my God. I could have been killed. Where was security? Isn't this their job? Isn't this why they are called security? My head hurts. My face hurts. I should have hit her back. But you're not supposed to hit patients. Or girls. Who invented that stupid rule? Damn. I got hit.

I pull up to the house and go inside. I'm still feeling dazed, hating the world, angry at everyone, when Zoe meets me in the hall, not yet knowing what has happened. "Max," she says, "I'm so depressed. I just got my first medical school tuition bill. I don't see how we're going to pay it."

I stare at her and walk by to the living room to sit on the sofa. I fix the expression on my face that says, "Go away, I'm cold and uncaring," but Zoe takes the risk and approaches.

"Is something wrong, Ace?"

I turn toward her and keeping my voice at a tone just above a whisper start to whip her with it. "Is something wrong? Is something wrong? You stupid moron. You idiot. Do you think I want to hear about your med school tuition? Do you think I could care less? Is that supposed to be the most important thing in my life? I'm getting beaten up so you can go to school and all you can tell me about is your depression? Well, stuff it."

Zoe stares at me, her face becoming almost as blank as mine. She reaches out to touch me, but I brush her hand away and stand up. She stands with me and asks, also in a whisper, "What do you mean, beaten up?"

"I got punched. What the hell do you think I mean?" I raise my voice slowly till it becomes a shout. "What the hell else could it mean? I got punched out by a goddam patient and it hurts and all you can talk to me about is money!" As my voice climbs toward a scream, she backs away, half in terror, half in pain, as she studies my face for signs of the blows.

"Oh, Max. That's horrible. Are you okay?"

Amazed that she stays with me I continue to scream. "Who knows? Who cares?"

Zoe struggles silently as I watch her, her fear and sadness

finally bubbling into anger. "Max! Shut up! I'm on your side. I'm your friend! I didn't hit you!"

I can hear her with half a mind and know she is right, but I just don't know if I care. At least I'm getting to hit in this fight. "You don't care! No one cares! Just leave me alone. Okay? Get the hell away from me!" And I storm past her into the bedroom, slamming the door shut when I get there.

Lying on the bed, consumed in tears, I hold a pillow over my face and try to clear my head. Zoe enters the room, looks at me, and says, "You're a crumb," then walks out the door.

8

Sublimation

I really like my waterbed. It rocks me gently to sleep and wraps me in warmth all night long. So I could tell by the feel of the bed that I wasn't at the hospital. But why was I alone? Where was Zoe? After all, I was the one who had to sleep by myself in the hospital and anyway I wasn't there, I was definitely home. I felt around the bed with my hand and she persisted in not being there, so I cocked my ears to see if she might have slipped out into the kitchen to make me some breakfast. Alas, no sound could be heard. In my half-awake state I rolled under the covers and tried to forget it all, which was a complete failure, as I remembered the previous evening and freaked out. "AARRGGHH," I cried to myself, "where is she?"

I staggered out of bed, took a long look in the bathroom, convincing me that Zoe had every right not to be there and then began a search of the apartment for some sign of her leaving. Unfortunately there was none. Why couldn't I have been a little more tactful? It wasn't her fault. But why did she have to storm out on me? Or did she? I can't ever remember details after a fight. Wandering into the kitchen to get something to eat, I scratch my head and wonder what to do now. First eat. That may make a decision easier. Food is a good answer, the return to the womb, the return to Mother. Food will make me strong, give me the strength to face the day, to return to work, and cope with everything. Why would I want to go back to work anyway? That's where the asshole is, that stupid shit who hit me. I don't want to ever see her face again. I want to kill her. That stupid dope! Slow down. She's crazy. It wasn't her fault. You have to understand her problems. And so on. But none of that sticks. And why should it? It's not my fault she's crazy. I didn't make her that way. Why should I have to suffer?

Meanwhile, where is Zoe? This isn't like her, to go away like this. I know I wasn't the most sensitive guy in the world, but she could understand, couldn't she? Opening the refrigerator door, I see a note. "Max, you're a rat, but I love you anyway. I'll be home after work tonight and we can talk. Try not to be such an idiot. Love, Zoe." Well, it's a bit better than I could have gotten. But this is an awfully lonely house.

And how the hell am I going to deal with work? Just prowl around the floor where people beat you up if you aren't careful? Aren't careful? Victim blaming? I bet I get to hear a lot of that.

I obsess my way down the stairs and into the car and out to work. By the time I get there I am totally confused, but no calmer. So much for obsessions as a defense.

Kathy meets me in the hall and says, "Hi."

I turn to her and say, "Hi," and keep on walking. So far so good, but I can already feel the swell of anger building up in me. And after giving it to Zoe yesterday, I don't know where it's headed today. And I thought I was over this particular stage.

Ducking into my office, I seek the peace and solitude of a closed room and begin to plot how to get through the day without any confrontations. My reverie, though, is soon interrupted by a call from Sam. "Morning, Max. Can you come down to my office so we can talk?"

"What about?"

"About Eve. Are you alright?"

"Of course I'm alright," I practically shout. "Why?"

"Just come down to my office. Now, okay?" This not being a real question, I don't bother to give it a real answer.

As I enter Sam's office I resolve to keep out of trouble. He swivels in his chair and turns to me as he talks on the phone and holds his hand up to silence me till he is finished. After a moment he hangs up and says, "What are we going to do with Eve?"

"Who cares, Sam. I don't know. Let's lock her up and throw away the key. Then none of us would have any of these problems."

"Max, you don't seem to realize this is a very serious matter. We could all get into hot water if the media tries to make a big deal out of this."

"Big deal. As long as I don't have to talk with her, I don't care what we do."

"Of course you'll talk to her."

"No chance. She threatened me too many times. I'm not risking my life for her evaluation. Forget it."

"Max, we can protect you."

"Like you did last night?"

"What do you mean?"

"Like the way you protected me last night? When I got the stuffings beaten out of me?" I am shouting now.

"When did that happen?" Sam replies, as nonchalantly as possible.

"Last night. Do you think I'm lying to you?" Down boy, down.

Sam swivels back to his desk to read the evening report of hospital activities, while I sit in my chair and steam. I didn't know before I arrived that I would refuse to see Eve, but there has to be a limit somewhere.

He swivels back to me and asks, "What happened?"

"I got punched out by that new wonder drug of a patient you assigned me. Mrs. Ax Murderer! What the hell do you think I was referring to? A walk in the Combat Zone?"

Sam looks thoughtful and responds, "Max, I'm very sorry to hear this."

But my rage is not to be contained. "Sorry? What do you mean you're sorry? What the hell good is that supposed to do me?"

Sam continues in his soft voice. "I understand you're upset, Max. You have every right to be. But that doesn't mean you can shirk your other responsibilities here. And that includes seeing Eve."

"Forget it, Sam. You've put my life in danger for the last time. I don't need anymore liberal bullshit about responsibility and power and the use of authority. I've had it up to here," gesturing with a slashing motion across my throat, "with all the goddam rules and regulations. You ever been hit? Have you?" I scream.

"Of course I have been," he replies calmly. "It's awful. We can talk about that if you want to. I think we should. But it's not related to Eve."

"What do you mean, not related? I just got beat up by one of the so-called patients we admit to this hospital and now you want me to see someone who has threatened my life and you don't think they are related? Is that the kind of support that you and Sandra have been promising me exists in this hospital? Well, screw you! I mean, I mean, is this the best you can do?"

Sam looks at me pretty indulgently given my level of outburst, but refuses to discuss it now. Ass. "Max, we need to talk about your getting hit. It's an important issue. But we need to decide how to handle Eve right now. There is very little time. The people of the state have a right to us doing our part in cases like this."

"And I don't have any rights? Is that the point? I'm a punching bag for Edna and for you and for the state and now I'm supposed to be one for Eve too? Well you can forget it. Just write it off." And before my brain knows what my body is doing, my feet are carrying me out the door and back to my office.

Right. What an idiot. Let him do the goddam evaluation himself if it's so important. My heart beats a little faster as my brain begins to swirl. All these years of doing just what authority figures told me to do. All those years of school, of which this is something like the twentieth year, constantly pounding into my brain, "Do what you are told or you will suffer." Now I have to do things for myself. For my own life. I have to take care of myself. No one else is going to do it. I'm an okay person. I have a right to my own life. They've messed with my head long enough! And now I want to choose what I want to do and if I don't want to be killed, I won't. Now I can do what makes sense to me. I've had enough! They don't even care if I get killed! If it makes sense to me, I'll do it. That's my only rule.

My reverie is broken by Shirley knocking on the door. "Dr. Jackson," she says, "I need to talk to you."

"Okay, Shirley, let's talk." Just put the other stuff away. Get it out of your mind. At least you can help Shirley.

"Dr. Jackson, I left the hospital today."

"That's good, Shirley," I say absently. "Did you have a good time?"

"It was alright. But a little strange."

"A little strange," I respond by rote, missing the panic in her voice.

To myself I say, concentrate, dammit. Do her and yourself a favor. If you want to be independent, if you want to do your best, then you have to stay with each individual patient. Stay in touch.

"A little strange," I repeat, trying to get into the scene.

She smiles and giggles at me. Her mouth opens to huge dimensions and she growls out, "It was real strange. I took a walk."

"Where did you go?"

"Well, first I went to the dry cleaners but they didn't have my clothes."

"Was that surprising?"

"No," she says, then starts to frown. "Why should it be?"

"I don't know, Shirley." Just the facts, ma'am. "Why don't you tell me more."

"Then I went to Boston Trust." Her eyes narrow as she leans forward on her chair. For the first time in a long time she actually looks serious. But it's a peculiar sight, with her shoulders hunched, head drawn in, and a look of wariness in her eyes.

"What happened there, Shirley?" I'm starting to share the feeling of strangeness.

"Do you really want to know?" She tries to sneak back into a groan but I want to know what is going on. I say to her, "You were going to tell me about Boston Trust. It sounded important." And what do you know, she refocuses. A new talent shown.

"Oh yes, it is."

We sit there in silence till I decide to press on. "Tell me about it, Shirley."

"Well, Dr. Jackson, I was standing there in the parking lot of the bank and I realized that all those nice cars were the cars of the people who owned most of Boston and the world. It seemed to me that these were the people whose view of reality was what got me into so much trouble." She pauses for breath and then continues. "So I decided that I had to break all the windows in their cars. And then everything would be even." She smiles in a half-serious way as she tells this story, not sure whether to retreat into her electrodes or stay tuned in and find out what makes sense to me.

My first thought naturally, is, "Oh my God, another criminal to deal with." This is followed by an internal smile, which I hope doesn't show, as I think, "Right on. Give those authorities what's their due." Then I remember that I'm an authority now and I have to see Shirley as an individual who needs my help. So forget the rules she breaks and try to focus on feelings.

"You must have been pretty pissed off," I say.

"Why do you say that, Dr. Jackson?"

"Because breaking windows in cars is an angry thing to do."

"Like when I want to attack you?"

"Exactly." I tremble slightly and ask, "Are you planning to do that now?"

"No, Dr. Jackson," she sighs. "What's angry?"

"When you break the windows on other people's cars, that's angry. When you want to hurt people, that's angry."

"But those people always try and tell me what to do."

"It's hard to follow the rules of a society and you get angry."

"I get real angry and it's not fair."

"No, it isn't fair, but you still have to play by the rules. Otherwise you end up back here." I hope Sam never hears me say any of this.

"I have these crazy feelings, Dr. Jackson. I feel different things than I think." She smiles large and giddy, flashes an out-of-control look, then snickers, "I'm crazy."

"Because your feelings and thoughts aren't the same?" A working definition for schizophrenia.

But we've gone far enough today. She starts to cackle and croak as her words become incoherent. After a few minutes she calms down and says, "What holds up the moon?"

"Shirley, let me ask one question before we stop. What did you do in the parking lot?"

"What did I do?"

"Did you break the windows?"

She giggles and says, "Of course not. I came back here to talk to you."

Whew. "Good choice, Shirley. We can talk whenever you want. Don't break any windows." Advice I should ponder myself.

"I know that Dr. Jackson." She smiles at me and leaves the office.

It's noon but I just can't take it anymore and want to blow it off. I put a sign on my door that refers everyone to Bobby and head out. I don't know what to feel anymore. Bobby asks me, as I walk out the door, "What happened to you last night? I heard you got hit."

"I did, Bobby. Some son of a bitch patient punched me out and Sam says it isn't important enough to talk about now."

"That stinks, Max," he says. Bobby is a good therapist.

"Yeah. It does. I don't know why the hell I work here. I think I can do better at something else. Like being a lion tamer or sky diver or something with a little less pressure and danger."

"Why don't you take the rest of the day off? I can cover for you here."

"Would you?" My God, an ally. "Great, I need a break. I left a sign on my door saying you would. I have to decide if I'll ever return."

"Sure, Max. Take as long as you want. I'll handle things."

So I'm in my car driving home at noon (thankful that I still have windows) and notice that this is a really fine day outside, nothing like the crazy day going on inside my life. Birds are actually chirping. Blooms are everywhere. It's warm enough to take my coat off and sit a spell on any bench around. But it's all so incongruous. The world I experience is unlike the world inside my head. This one feels and moves and vibrates and is a unified whole. My thoughts seem so jumbled and split and crazy. Suddenly I wonder, is thinking the opposite of happiness?

I wish I was with Zoe now. She'd say something to me like, "Max, getting hit was a warning. It's a message to you to pay attention. It doesn't mean your life has to fall apart."

"I know that, Zoe," I would say. "But nothing seems solid. I can't get a firm handle on how it all works."

"Nothing is solid, Max. The world has a conscious reality as well as a physical one. That's the whole point of your profession. The reality that you inhabit is not the same as anyone else's. The solidity it gets comes from you."

"You're right, of course. It's just that I don't know where to start sometimes."

"You can only start one place, Max. With yourself. Just be yourself. You're okay. Everything else will follow."

"It's a mad world. Sometimes I feel on top and sometimes I'm crawling along the bottom. How am I different from my patients?"

"Max," she would say, "you're not different in the ways you think you are. We're all people with full emotions and feelings. The way you're different has to do with the individual you are. You don't have to try to be unique, you are."

"But why is the hospital so strange?"

"Just relax," she says as her voice fades away. "There are no answers, only questions."

I see a parking spot as I drive past the Charles River and pull over to stop. Climbing from the car I feel a warming breeze coming up from the south and wonder if spring has come. Then I turn off the wonder and feel the breeze. Feels nice. In Jamaica, when I would ask someone to predict the weather for me they responded, "What am I, Jesus?" with a big smile. So what? Do I look like Jesus? Why must I want to know what is happening and when and what sense it all makes? This year hasn't changed

what's out here at all. Is that what makes it so important? Being
outside? I could be more like the water, more like a river, flowing
and moving, existing and growing. Maybe then things would go a
little smoother. As I try to tell my patients all the time. And they
don't listen and neither do I. You have to feel it.

I start to walk down the river. For an early spring day, at
noontime, there's a big crowd. People standing around, many
looking slightly befuddled as I do, wandering the banks of the
river. Skyscrapers loom on one side, buildings reflecting off other
buildings. A concentrated mass of city and people and problems.
And a stone's throw away, on the Charles, I'm standing in a park,
then sitting on the grass, listening to the quiet. Same world. Is
that crazy? Is that a bizarre concept? All split up. Glass buildings
and parks and rivers and mental hospitals and people getting
beaten up. And where is Shirley and her magic electrodes to tell
which version of reality is real?

But I know the answer to that one. I have to tell Shirley, not the
other way around. The state gives me the right to. Pays me to do
it in fact. The courts, my patients, my supervisors, my schools, my
parents, my wife—all give me the right. Even insist I act on it. So
the only person who won't let me choose my own reality is me.
Months of mental and physical abuse. Mental and physical abuse.
Over and over.

So I walk back to the car to cool out. Stopping at a liquor store
on the way home I pick up a six-pack, hunker down with some
very loud music, and get set for the afternoon. It's just fine to be
me and things are going to be just fine.

Poor Zoe has had a hard day at work, fretting with her own
problems with bosses and too much work and dealing with her
future which is pretty scary for her, since it now contains going to
med school. On top of that she has had to spend a goodly part of
her energies trying to resolve her anger at Max. Which hasn't
been easy. Her internal process went something like this:

Anger: How could he do this to me? What a jerk!
Denial: Maybe it was my fault. Maybe I started it.
Depression: He hates me. What will happen?

Bargaining: There must be some way to resolve this scene.

Acceptance: My poor love. He's coming apart at the seams.

This is all mediated by a deep worry. If we can't deal with only one of us being in medicine, how can we deal with two? Come to think of it, this is the first confrontation we've had about medical careers. Certainly didn't go very well.

But Zoe is basically sane and decides to let it all hang until she can deal with Max in person. Indeed, as she has been teaching him, it is much better to let go of things you can't fix than to hold on to them and worry. Nonetheless, Zoe still wasn't sure how to deal with Max upon her return home from work.

Humming softly, she enters the apartment and breathes a sigh of relief, happy to be on familiar turf. And there curled up on the sofa is Max, fast asleep, beer cans strewn about his feet. She goes over to the couch and touches his head gently, caressing him and pulling him closer to her. He awakens and sees it is her and dissolves.

"Oh, Zoe," I exclaim, trying to pull my thoughts together. "I'm so glad it's you, Zoe. It's you."

"Of course it's me, Max. I left you a note. You knew I'd be here." Glancing at the beer cans she remarks, "It looks like you got home early to wait for me."

"Oh, Zoe." I get upset as I remember my anger, my voice tense, shaking at times, unable to take a deep breath.

"Hey, Max. It's okay. I love you."

I shake my head to clear it, fail a few times, then make an attempt at a speech. "I had a horrible dream. Horrible. We were driving down a street together and you said you had to duck into a house for a minute. When you didn't come I went into the house and you were lying on the floor. You wouldn't move although you could talk and I didn't know what was happening. A huge man threw me out of the house and I couldn't get back in, no matter how hard I tried."

"It's okay, Max. I'm home now, I'm here."

"I'm glad," I say, falling sideways into her arms. "Oh God, Zoe, I'm so sorry." The words start to tumble out now. "I feel so bad about last night. And about the year, I guess. You've had to put up with so much from me and you've had your own scene to deal with and it hasn't been fair, I know that, but I've had to go through so much myself this year and sometimes I just didn't know what to do."

"It's okay, Max."

"I love you so much. You're wonderful, do you know that?"

"I know it, Max," she says with a grin. "I'm going to make us dinner now, Max. Just pass out on the sofa while I'm in the kitchen." And off she goes, wagging her finger and her bottom, which I'm too messed up to pay attention to. My loss. Physical reality has its own rewards.

Luckily, there is little hangover when you have confined your drinking to the previous afternoon. By the next morning, things are relatively peaceful. So on arriving at work, I could not only resolve to keep things on an even keel, I could also try to smile and act as if everything was fine. As if I knew whether I wanted to be there at all. As if I had no doubts about psychiatry at all. But it was time to separate psychiatry doubts from personal issues. And me with them. So as I had the previous day, I slunk into my office without disturbing a soul and sat and waited. After a pause to reflect I called Bobby.

"Hi guy, how are things?"

"Max? You sound better. Was your day off worthwhile yesterday?"

"It was fine. Better. Things are alright now."

"I'm really sorry about your getting hit," he says. "I was frightened all day myself."

"Yeah. I wish they'd get rid of that patient."

Bobby laughs then sighs. "I wish they'd get rid of all of them."

"Bobby," I ask, "do you want to just chuck all this psychiatry stuff ever?"

"You bet I do, Max. But I always decide it's worth the pain."

"Why's that?"

"Well, I enjoy being with the patients. And it's a good way to be a doctor. And it's a pretty fun job. And sometimes people get better and then I feel happy. I'm glad I do this."

"That's nice to hear. I wish I could be so enthusiastic."

"Don't worry about it, Max. It'll happen."

"Yeah, I suppose, Bobby. I've got a patient coming. I'll see you later."

The patient coming is Ecaterina. At least I hope she'll be here. Another missed week and I might start getting nervous. But if she comes, at least I know I won't be bored. None of this constant looking at the clock wondering if the session will ever end. Ecaterina holds my attention.

Today she does show, wearing the fifties look; toreador pants, hair in bangs, straw hat and skintight sweater. All designed for who knows what, but quite possibly for me. Which seems more apparent as she sits and says, "Do you like my outfit?"

These are the moments I feel it all turns around. Do I stay neutral, brush it off, interpret it, turn it back, find an affect, ignore it, something else? And although I've read many books by this point, I still have nothing close to an answer to this dilemma. As many psychiatrists as there are, there are different styles. If you don't do what feels most comfortable to you, then it won't work. If I sit there anxiously trying to figure out what to say, then neither of us will be comfortable. I have to make it flow from my heart, which is much easier said than done.

"Yes it is nice," I say. "Did you wear it for me?"

This seems to startle her somewhat, but she recovers quickly. "Why Dr. Jackson, what a nice thing to say."

"What's that?"

"That you like my outfit."

"Well, I'm glad to make you feel better. Should we end the session now?"

She looks at me as if she's uncertain if I'm serious or not, decides not, and giggles. I also can't figure out why I'm saying what I am, but it seems to fit. So on I go.

"What brings you here today? Surely not to talk about clothes."

"What do you mean?"

"It's just been a long time since our last session."

"I need to talk about my depression." As she says this she pulls a handkerchief out of her pocket, to use, I suppose, in case of tears. However, Ecaterina isn't showing a touch of depression in her face. Her look is basically blank.

"You're feeling depressed?"

"Of course I am! Didn't I just say that? Wouldn't you be if you were me?"

"What is there to be depressed about?"

"Are you serious?" she practically shouts. "Look at me. I'm old and ugly and awful looking. You must hate the way I am."

"How did you get that message?"

"What's that?"

"That I hate the way you are."

"I don't need to get the message. It has to be true. Don't even try to deny it. I know."

"You've received that message before?"

"Of course. From everyone."

"Everyone? Anyone in particular?"

"I've heard it all my life."

"So it goes back to when you were a child. You've felt you look ugly and awful since then."

"Yes! I said that!"

"That sounds very depressing," I say. "If you heard it that far back even your parents must have told you that you were ugly. That's truly awful."

She nods her head in agreement. "It was awful. It really was. My mother said horrible things to me. She was a pain in the ass my whole childhood."

"And you get pissed off just to think about her?"

"You bet I do. She was the worst. God," she belts out the word, "I hate that bitch!"

"And you just want to shout it to the world."

"I do. She told me I was ugly." And here Ecaterina's mood starts to shift. Her face draws in and the color drains from it. It is as if she has seen a ghost, but isn't sure if that's what it really was. "I am ugly." She starts to cry. "Look at me. I'm awful to look at."

"Is that your voice speaking or hers?"

She sniffles again. "I don't know. I can't tell us apart. All my ideas must have started with her. Isn't that what all you therapists believe? All I ever get to talk about in therapy is my mother and I don't want to talk about her anymore. She was a bitch and now she's gone and I don't want to deal with her at all."

"Good riddance to her?"

"You bet. Let's forget her."

"She might as well be dead," I say.

"She will be soon," responds Ecaterina.

"Oh? Why is that?"

"She had breast cancer diagnosed about six months ago."

"That must have been a painful time for you."

She straightens her face and gives a half smile. "No. It was alright. The bitch deserves it."

"It's funny to me that you hadn't mentioned this earlier."

"What do you mean?"

"Well, I talked with you in the hospital about your family and we've met a few times and, usually, the terminal illness of a parent is something that patients mention to their psychiatrists. Perhaps it had something to do with your first admission here."

"I suppose you think it means something important."

"It might. What do you think?"

"I think you're an idiot. You know how awful this is for me and you continue to rub it in. Why don't you lay off a little? Jesus. You remind me of my mother. Always picking at my faults."

"If I remind you of her, this therapy is going to be difficult for you."

"Everybody reminds me of her sooner or later. You just got there sooner." And she begins to cry, first softly, then louder, then sobbing in fits, moaning slightly. At first I can't tell if it's an act or if it's real, but the more I watch, the more real it becomes. After minutes, she pulls herself together and before I can say anything, tells me, "That was very unladylike, wasn't it? You must think I have no control at all."

"You put a lot of thoughts in my head, Ecaterina. I'm all for your crying here if you need to. If I have a judgment to make, trust me, I'll tell you. Okay?"

She gives me a weak grin and for the first time I feel like I've connected with her in a positive way. Then she wipes off the grin and fixes her face. "Things are very strange in my life right now."

"What's going on?"

"I got a job. An acting job. In a play downtown. It's a small part, but a good one. It will let me act. And that's so important to me. I'm truly a marvelous actress. But I'm nervous."

"Nervous about what?"

"I'm not sure. That's what makes it so tough. I'm a little afraid of the director. He's so macho and smooth and I think he may like me."

"What's that like for you?"

"I think it's alright. But who knows? Every other relationship gets screwed up and when they do I end up suicidal."

"Have you been suicidal this week?"

She looks aghast. "Oh no. Of course not. I didn't mean that. I'd tell you if I was. I'm just worried."

"It's a frightening situation?" It is so great to talk about something else besides her feelings for me. So great to talk about her real life.

"Yeah. I've had so many others like it."

"And what are you scared of? What's so horrible?"

"It all is. I just can't decide about him. If he asks me out, what should I do?"

I know I should be trying to find out what's behind the fear. All my supervisors tell me that. Locate the emotion and find out what's behind it. Yet today I feel so much like I know about fear. "It's a very terrifying situation," I say.

"Oh boy, it sure is. I feel like I'm going to dissolve." And she dissolves, using her handkerchief to dry her eyes when her tears have stopped. "Whew," she sighs. "I carry around so much tension. I fight the world all the time."

"That's a tough way to go through life. You must be pretty exhausted."

"I am. All I need now is a rest."

"Will you give yourself one?" I ask.

"That's a good idea. How do I do it?"

Now I'd like to answer this question with a question, and the end of the hour dictates I find a good closing place. So I respond, "Isn't that what you came here to find out?"

"I suppose so. You know, I'm not sure anymore why I come here. But I like it. I'll keep on coming. Sorry I missed the past few weeks. I was scared of being here. Everytime I thought of it, I got sort of jellylike inside. Maybe I'm a little afraid of how I feel here."

"How's that?"

"Warm, I guess. I get worried what you'll think of me, or what I think of me. It's hard not to be able to pull the wool over people's eyes."

"It sounds like you're getting something out of this."

She stands and moves to the door. "I sure hope so. I can't go on this way forever. It really hurts." Oof.

I'm left in my office, playing with my pencils and writing process notes. What will Molly say about this session? It seemed terrific to me. Maybe I'm becoming a better therapist. At least it took my mind off the problem at hand. Which is that it's time for team meeting, and I don't really want to face the group. A blowup on Eve is to be expected.

The same crowd is there as last time, but no one is smiling. My refusals and anger with Sam have obviously become common knowledge. So nobody knows what will happen next. Neither do I.

Normally, it's pretty easy to fade into a wall. After all, I spent a sizable piece of my youth at dances wanting to be unnoticed. But this was not to be on this particular day. If you had put a chair in the center of the room and had a spotlight over it I couldn't have been more conspicuous. Or at least that's how I felt sitting alone there while everyone else in the room stared at me. We had a special visitor at the meeting, Sam, which also was a bad sign. Lucy led off. "Things have moved quite fast with Eve since our last discussion. I think we need to draw up an alternate plan."

All eyes focus on me as I clear my throat and say nothing.

Our head nurse, Kathy, then comments, "There is no way in

the world I am letting that patient back on this unit. She's a menace." Others nod their heads in unison.

Lucy says, "This seems to be a general opinion, that Eve is inappropriate for the day hospital. Do you agree, Dr. Watson?"

Sam also nods his head then says, "I wonder what Dr. Jackson feels about the treatment plan?"

I fidget then search for the middle ground, thinking, you bum. Then I say, "If no one wants her here, then it doesn't make any sense to have her here. Who wants to tell her?"

Lucy replies, "That's usually the job of the primary clinician."

"Usually," I respond, "but Dr. Watson and I have already discussed why I think this case may be unusual. Isn't that right, Sam?"

"Why don't you explain your position to the group," he says, "so that we can all understand it."

"Well, Eve's been threatening me and I don't feel safe with her. So I don't plan to talk with her."

"The hospital can provide security while you see her," Kathy says.

"I don't think so," I reply. "It certainly wasn't able to provide security a couple of nights ago."

"Max," Sandra interjects. "I hardly think that is relevant."

I turn on her angrily. Raising my voice I demand, "What do you mean not relevant?"

"We're talking about Eve right now, not other patients who have a history of violence. We can protect you."

"I don't believe it!" I can feel my blood starting to boil and I don't want to be so angry, but they keep pressing on.

"With the proper precautions, we can provide safety," says Sam.

"Are you implying that it was my fault I got hit the last time?" I ask.

"No one said that, Max," says Sandra. "We just said that you don't have to be worried."

"Look at my eye," I shout. "It's all swollen. And I don't have to worry?" I check around the room scanning the faces, wondering where I can get some of that teamwork that is so highly promised among my peers. And people do indeed look sympathetic. But the room remains quiet.

We all sit there in silence and Sam says, "Maybe the three of us can talk about this later."

But I want my support. "Don't try and isolate me. What happened to me could happen to anyone. Any of us in this room could get slugged tomorrow. Or hurt even worse. We all read the papers. Why are you trying to force me to see someone who has threatened me? What's the point?"

Jill, who has been quiet, responds. "Max, I can see how upset you are and how important this is to you. If you truly are worried about your life when you see Eve, perhaps you shouldn't have to. But I agree with Sandra and Sam, the hospital can provide security."

Lucy echoes much of this and adds her own sentiments. "It's awful to get hit. I got attacked by a patient once and didn't want to ever return to the hospital. I thought I might quit my job. But in time I felt a lot better. I don't think it was my fault that I was attacked, but I take a lot more precautions now than I ever did before. And so will you, so you'll be safer."

Kathy says, "I remember that last meeting we had about Eve you told us about the threats and no one was willing to take some of the weight off your shoulders. I apologize for that. It's no fun to have someone threatening you. And maybe we can work out something about your seeing her."

Feeling a little cooler, I try and explain. "It's not that I don't want to do my job. I just think that someone has to be able to say when enough is enough. If I've been wrong about Eve in the past, I'm sorry. But I don't intend to get killed for my job. And I think my risk from Eve is greater than anyone else's at this point."

Sam has heard enough. He wants to stay in control of the meeting. He stands and he says, "I appreciate everyone giving their viewpoint to me. When we meet later on, this will help me make a more informed decision. Thank you." And he goes to the door and leaves.

The tension is gone and we move on to other topics, as I space out. All of a sudden it's easier to melt into the floor. Sandra grabs my arm as the meeting ends, however, and pulls me back into her office.

"Max," she says, "let's talk. What is going on with you?"

"What do you mean?"

"What was that display in team meeting?"

"Oh that? Just feeling supported by the group."

"Why didn't I know what was going on?" she demands.

"I don't know. Why should you?"

She looks truly shocked and angry. And then on the verge of tears. "Max, I'm your chief. Couldn't you come to me with this problem?"

"I guess not."

"Why? What happened?"

"I guess I didn't think I'd be given the help I needed."

"Haven't I been in your corner in the past?"

"Yes, you've been pretty good about that. It's just that this has been a hard month for me and you sit in meetings like that and I don't see you being on my side at all. I know you're my chief. Sometimes you don't feel like it, is all."

"I'm really hurt to hear you say that, Max. I don't think it's justified. I have to think about the operation of this entire ward. So I can't run meetings with just your feelings in mind. But that doesn't mean I can't hear what you're saying."

"I'm not so sure about that," I say. "Maybe your job makes it impossible for you to give comfort to people after they've been hit without offending someone else."

"You feel I'm afraid to offend Sam so I don't support you?"

"Bingo, Sandra."

"That's totally unfair." Her voice is touched with outrage and hurt. "I spend most of my day protecting you and all the other residents from the administration. And when I can't I help you as much as a person can. And if you had come to me after getting hit and discussed your fears about seeing Eve again I think a lot of the pain of the past few days could have been avoided." She seems so sincere so I get sad and start to mumble.

"I didn't know what to say. It was awful getting hit." And all the feelings of being impotent and helpless and furious come rushing back to me and I start to get choked up. "Jesus, Sandra, it's been a very hard year. Sometimes it feels so lonely."

Sandra nods sympathetically. "It's been hard for me, too, Max. I'm really sorry you feel so all alone." I slow down to a sniffle and then start to sigh. "Don't worry, Max. It's also been a wild year."

"I would much rather like you than be angry at you," I say. "And you know, I usually do feel pretty bolstered. Sometimes things are so crazy I get paranoid or depressed or who knows what."

"It's okay, Max. One problem that we all have here is feeling isolated. All our problems seem so huge and no one has the same perspective so the tendency is to take on too much and feel all alone with it. But if you want to throw things around, I'm the person to do it with."

"I'll try it, Sandra."

"Thanks, Max. I appreciate that. Now what are we going to do about Eve?"

"Couldn't someone else do the evaluation? It's not that I won't ever see her again. It's just that things are too intense for me right now."

"Will Bobby do it, or one of the other residents?" she asks.

"I don't know. If I can get someone to do it, will you arrange things with Sam?"

"Sure, Max. And by the way, don't be so hard on Sam. He's under a lot of pressure, too. Everyone at the hospital is. All the jobs here are as stressful as yours. That's what you're training to do. That's what you're learning how to handle."

"Thanks, Sandra."

"Think nothing of it. By the way, you did well in the team meeting. You led with your face, but the rest of the team seemed to understand. It was good you were honest. That's a big part of getting along here."

"Okay. I got it. No more lectures, today."

"No more lectures, Max. Let's talk again later today. I'll tell you what Sam has decided."

I meet Bobby walking down to the coffee shop and ask him to do Eve's evaluation. "No problem," he says. "You can owe me one. It's nice to see you cheerier than yesterday."

"Have you got a minute?"

"Sure, Max." He flashes a crooked grin and asks, "Your office or mine? Which one of us needs the therapy?"

"Hopefully neither of us. Things are just so confusing and I need a little space."

"Why don't we go to my office?" he asks. "You could use a change of scenery."

We sit in his sanctuary, which looks much like mine, although the personal touches are different. Bigger plants. Japanese wall hangings. An oriental rug. The little backboard on his wastebasket is a nice touch.

"I gotta tell you, Bobby, getting hit was a bizarre experience."

"What was the worst thing about it?"

"It was just so infuriating. I became enraged. I wanted to kill her. I really did. It wasn't like a fight when I was a kid. It wasn't even like getting beat up. It was just a horror show. Everything about doctors and patients and everything else just seemed turned upside down. This was my patient and I wanted to kill her. Really kill her. It makes it sort of hard to be a therapist."

"Well," Bobby says, "you're not the only one who ever wanted to kill a patient. I myself have felt pretty angry at times. And as I recall there were a few times when you wanted to do Ecaterina in. Until she tried it for you."

"Thanks, Bobby. I really needed that."

"Hey, we're all going to lose a patient before long. We know that."

"I just don't want to lose one by my own hand. But it was so infuriating."

"How have you dealt with it?" he asks.

"You know, it's funny. On the whole, getting punched out has helped put the year in a bit more focus for me. After the initial shock I've felt okay. And some of the bullshit here seems less important. It's like I know the worst and I survived it so now I can get down to business."

"That sounds like a good way to go. I could use more focus myself."

"I'm sure there are easier ways than getting beat up. Although it does have a lot of shock value. Besides, I learned a valuable lesson, that this stuff is real, and that the pain that is going on here is the real thing."

"I know that's true," he says. "I struggled with that for months. It was so hard to see my patients' illnesses or comprehend the symptoms and there are no lab tests like in the rest of medicine. It took me months to get a grip on the seriousness of this stuff."

"It was always easy to see how crazy the patients were."

"I don't mean that. The ICU has got to be one of the most intense experiences around. But I couldn't emotionally feel what my patients were saying. It was all so irrational and crazy. I rejected a lot of it out of hand."

"Is that why you found the drugs so handy?" I ask. "Are they a way of distancing yourself from the pain?"

"I don't think that's fair, Max." He frowns. "I use them because they work. And you use them, too."

"I'm not saying medications don't work. But we use them to treat symptoms that seem crazy. We don't use them to treat the disease. Shirley has been on medications for years and is still sick."

"So what's your point?" he asks.

"I'm not sure. Only that there is more to all of this than meets the eye. You never know if you're doing something for the patient or because of how you feel. If you give them to hospitalized patients they stop having hallucinations and being off the wall and get out and even home. So I guess that's working. But I still don't like them. And I'm not convinced that we're treating what we want to. Our patients are still in such horrible agony. For so many, life is a miserable thing to be suffered through. How do we help them have meaning in what they do?"

"I don't think we can, Max. I don't think that can be our job at all. We're doctors who have a limited number of tools at our disposal. All we can do is use them the best we're able and hope things turn out better."

"Maybe," I say, "but I don't want to buy that yet. I'll go along with prescribing medications. Anything that gets patients out of the hospital and back to their lives is something I'm in favor of. But there seems to be another issue. Mental illness can't be understood solely on the basis of its symptoms. You can only understand it in terms of the life and function and family and situation of the person with the symptoms. We should try to put ourselves in our patients' positions a little bit before we go off at them. Honestly, some of the psychiatrists I hear act as if they've never felt a depression or had an obsession or a crazy thought. All they talk of is the reasoned approach and measurements of things I can't pronounce. But this has been a very personal experience for me. It's only by feeling what my patients feel that I've grown a bit more comfortable with prescribing to them at all. Hell, the more I can feel, the easier it all gets. If you just take away the hallucinations and the delusions, awful as they are, it can't be seen as a real cure. When I was struggling with Simon, this was a major part of my confusion."

"But you ended up getting him to take the drugs."

"And it didn't cure him. It's only now, after talking for months, that we're starting to even understand what the problem is. And he is racked by pain and misery. And that is his sickness just as much as his delusions. Psychotherapy works, too."

"So do you have an answer, Max?"

"No. I suppose not. Even though I'm convinced that antipsychotic medications are necessary and helpful, I don't have to like them. We all need to keep searching for more."

"If Edna had been on meds, maybe you wouldn't have been hit."

Good point. "I guess you're right. And I don't want to get hit ever again. Once was for clarity. Twice would be excessive."

"Sounds good to me, Max. I'll try to do without the experience, if you don't mind." He looks at the clock and says, "I've got a patient coming, I'll see you later."

"Of course, Bobby," I say. "We can talk more about this next week."

9

Anticipation

Jerry looks great when he enters my office. Even better, he seems relaxed. At least more relaxed than when we started all this therapy stuff, a million years before. The gorgeous day, a late spring wonder, is reflected off him in so many ways. Perhaps he is noticing how wonderful the world can be.

"Hi, Dr. Jackson. I had another good week. I really did. I've been looking at summer jobs and there are a lot of them that I want."

"Great." I smile and nod and wonder where we are going.

"So," he says, "how are you today?"

"Fine thanks. How do I look?"

"Fine. Yeah." He seems embarrassed by this exchange and the glow fades from his face. I pursue this. "What just happened?" I ask.

"I'm not sure. I guess that was a stupid question to ask. I never know what to say."

"Never?"

He giggles and frowns. "I know sometimes. I don't know what to say today."

"What makes today so hard?"

"Well . . ." He pauses and we wait while he figures it out. "I have something I need to talk about."

"What is it?"

"It's hard to bring up."

"Uh huh." Déjà vu.

"Uh huh?" he asks, quite angry. "Is that all you can say, 'uh huh'?"

"What makes you angry about that?"

"It's like you don't care what I have to say."

"And that makes you angry?"

"Sure. Of course it does. I sit here week after week and spill my guts to you and all you can do is sit there and say uh huh all the time. How do I know if you're listening?"

"You had something important to tell me and then you got angry. I wonder if the two are related."

"What do you mean?" Still angry.

"You became angry instead of telling me what was on your mind. I wonder why?"

"Boy, you really like to pick at me. I don't know why I come here to see you. And I pay for it, too. Maybe I am a little nuts to go through this."

"You're wondering why you come here?"

"Yeah." He sighs. "That's what I wanted to talk to you about." He pauses again and we wait. Finally, "I think I want to quit therapy."

"Uh huh," I say, keeping my face as blank as I can while I wonder what I did wrong. "Can you share with me why you want to stop?"

"I think I've got enough out of this. I have," he insists.

"I'm pleased to hear that. What has therapy been useful for?"

"A lot. An awful lot. I'm really indebted to you, Dr. Jackson. I've got a girlfriend and I'm not so crazy about law school and I can almost deal with my father."

"That all sounds very important. I'm glad you got so much out of this. But why do you want to quit?"

"I've had enough. Don't you think I deserve a break?"

"Sure. Is that the only reason to quit?"

"Well, summer's coming and I've got a lot of things to do. I'm getting along terrific with Belinda now and she wants to spend more time with me. All in all, I'm busier now than I ever have been. It's not that I don't think that this is valuable to me. Therapy has been unbelievably helpful. No problem there. It's just that there are so many other things to do."

"This one hour really eats into your plans, eh?"

He shakes his head. "It's not just the hour that I'm here each week. Therapy takes up a lot more of my time. I think about being here often during the week. It takes up lots of my mental energy."

"What do you think about?"

"What do you mean?"

"When you think about therapy, what do you think about?"

"Being here, what I'm going to talk about. Sometimes I have a feeling, like, oh yeah, I don't have to be worried about any of this, it'll be okay, and then I figure that I'll be able to talk about it here and so then therapy is on my mind."

"You think about what you will deal with here?"

"Mostly. Sometimes I worry about what you think of me. I figure I've said enough jerky things in this office to last a lifetime of knowing me."

"So why would you want to give up therapy?"

"I just said. It takes up too much of my time and I've already got enough out of it." He begins to get angry again.

Time to interpret, I suppose. "While it sounds like coming here has already been useful to you, you also seem to have some unresolved feelings."

"Like what?" he interjects, with vehemence.

"Are you angry at me?"

"You're disagreeing with me."

"And that makes you angry?"

"Of course."

"Why's that?"

"What do you mean? I come to you for a little help and now I say that I don't want it anymore and you tell me I do. Wouldn't that make anyone angry?"

"It seems to make you angry. I don't know about anyone. I'm hearing that you want to be heard right now. And we should talk about that. Whether you stay here or not is your decision. I do want you to have my opinion."

"Don't worry. I have it. I should have known you'd want me to stay. You probably think I'm totally crazy and need to stay in treatment for years. You probably think I need to take medicine and who knows what else." His anger has been replaced by sadness.

"Those are frightening thoughts."

"You bet they are. I don't know what to do anymore." He starts to tighten up.

I want to say, "Maybe this isn't the best time to drop out of treatment," but it sounds too harsh. What I come up with is, "There is still so much pain to deal with."

"I know," he sniffles. "I'm tired of having all these depressing thoughts on my mind." He dries his eyes and continues. "Mostly, I like coming here. I am doing a lot better. For sure. And I never would have got together with Belinda otherwise. That's been just wonderful."

"Good. Things are going well?"

"Unbelievable. As a matter of fact, we spent the night together on Saturday." He pauses.

"How did it go?" I ask.

"Dr. Jackson," his face lights up, "you wouldn't believe how well it went. Fabulous. Sex was no problem at all. I mean, I was a little worried at first, but then she helped me relax and then . . . no problem."

"Congratulations. No wonder you feel like you deserve a break from all this talk."

"What do you mean?" he asks.

"It was hard for you to tell me about your experience."

He sits quietly and seems to recede from me. After a minute he returns. "I thought you might think it was a silly thing to talk about. I mean, why should you care about my sex life?"

"Why would anyone care?"

"Well, my family certainly never would!" He expels the words.

"I mean, my father would have told me it was a stupid thing to talk about or else laughed at me and asked what took so long. He is such a royal bastard."

"And it's scary to think I might act like that, too."

"Yeah, of course." He leans back in his chair and sighs. "How do I know what the hell is going to happen here? I don't know if I can trust you."

"Trusting can be a pretty big risk. Although it sounds like it worked with Belinda."

"That was different. We're . . ." he searches for the right word, "intimate."

"It seems a real relief to find that with her."

"You bet. I can trust her, mostly. At least she didn't laugh at me. Of course, there was nothing to laugh at."

"Unlike here?"

"What do you mean?"

"You said your father wouldn't have treated you with respect and you're afraid that I may be similar to him. That I may laugh at you or put you down. Perhaps that's part of why you want to quit."

"Hell," he says, "I don't really want to quit. It's just so difficult to come in sometimes. I get so anxious."

"I'm glad you're going to come back and try to figure out why." I see that our time is up. "Next week?"

"I'll see you then, Dr. Jackson. Thank you." He leaves the office, dripping with sweat.

"Molly, how did I do?"

"More importantly, Max, what were you doing?"

"I was getting him to stay in therapy."

"Why?"

"Because he can still benefit from it."

"So could much of America, but you don't drag them into your office and demand they stay."

"That's not fair, Molly. This isn't the same thing. He came to my office first. And anyway, I think that leaving was just a cover for something else. When we got down to brass tacks, there was a bigger piece of him that wanted to continue than to stop."

She grins. "I was just pushing you the way you pushed him. I agree that it was right to encourage him to open up. This issue of when to terminate therapy is a crucial one and should always be examined very carefully. Often a patient will want to quit before you feel he or she is ready and that sets up a difficult situation. You need to figure out what was prompting him to leave in the first place and then approach the issue with caution. What was behind his desire to stop?"

"It seemed to be a transference type situation. He was afraid that I'd react to his good but intimate news with derision and that kept him from wanting to share it. He treated me as if I was his father."

"So this was transference?"

"I thought so. What do you think?"

"It's possible. You needed to address it directly. My guess is that he's having many angry and other disagreeable feelings when he sits with you and wanted to distance himself. He was running from the feelings and you need to get him to sit there and talk about them and feel them."

"And the anger was a way of separating. Of going away mad?"

"Probably. It's also a way of being intimate. He accused you of not caring enough about him. When you stayed with him after he got angry and continued to ask him to stay, he felt you cared."

"So I should continue to get him to talk about his painful feelings while in therapy?"

"Sure. All patients terminate eventually. But if you help them work through their transference feelings, then you will have gotten to the heart of the process."

"Thank you, Molly. These sessions seem to go well, but I still don't know what's happening half the time."

She laughs and picks up her knitting. "Don't worry, Max. You'll get it."

"I'll be on vacation next week, so I'll miss our meeting."

"Enjoy yourself. Forget it all."

Poised in midair, I can feel the wind rush by me as the adrenaline starts to pump. I have run to the end of the dam without thinking, since a moment's thought may destroy the attempt, the fragile courage, so desperately shored. The jump happens without hesitation and by the time I hit the water twenty feet below my head is swimming faster than my body. The shock of the water is cold and forces the last ounce of epinephrine out of my adrenal glands and makes me start kicking and moving my arms as I head to shore. But not before I look around at the onlookers, proud of myself and smiling. Zoe is cheering and friends are applauding and I feel a little sheepish to be so pleased with myself. The swim to shore is leisurely. The water seems warmer than it is, rushing down the mountain, freshly frozen only hours before. But the warmth within cannot be touched by the temperature without. And I pull myself back on the rocks to sun and gather my courage for another leap.

Zoe throws me a towel and I lie back to get some heat and feel my heart still pounding. Who are all these people? Drunk with the exhilaration of the jump, I am almost in love with the whole group. No one is talking about psychiatry. In fact no one, although they all must have jobs, is talking about work of any kind. Is the look on the faces that of escape or relaxation? Or from a rush on something they can do themselves? Like flying off rocks into outer space. Zoe is smiling at me as I open my eyes to her. No one else is paying any attention at all, as all are watching the next leaper, as each in turn becomes the show and the center for the group. And my adrenaline calms down a little and my heart goes a bit slower and I am on my feet climbing up the rocks again for another dive.

Lunch is a camp lunch, since we are all at a camp of sorts. Not the camp I remember as a child, what we used to refer to as military camp. All I can remember of it is standing in line, getting inspected, and hearing reveille at some ungodly hour. I'm sure there was horseback riding in there somewhere, but in my memory it is the rules of camp I can recall. I always wanted to do something, more activities and less rules. Now it is different. Rather than seeking stimulation, I avoid it. I can spend a week in

Vermont, at a beautiful lake, just fishing and sleeping and playing games and eating. And there are no rules at adult camp, no counselors to tell you when to go to sleep. And on that one day, when I seek excitement, I am flying through the air toward an icy stream below while a bunch of strangers cheer me on. I like adult camp. I really do. I don't even mind cleaning the cabin.

When we played charades, the girls were much better than the boys. (It's too hard to think of ourselves as men and women.) The ladies simply knew what they were doing. And how in heaven's name was I supposed to know how to act out *Seven Brides for Seven Brothers?* Somehow Zoe had spread the word that, as an understanding psychiatrist, I would be a wonder at the game. She simply doesn't understand the job yet.

Dr. Grill looks around the room and starts to talk. The words tumble out of his mouth quickly, like they were hot coals, too painful to hold on to any longer. But he speaks them as pearls, demanding we hang on to every burning piece of information that he delivers.

"The only thing that you have when you enter a psychiatry residency is your defenses. In fact the only thing you have in your entire life is defenses, but that's another story for another time. As you're all about to move on to the next year of your training and will become the teachers for the group of residents to follow, I thought you should hear about what the residency process can do to someone." We all groan and someone shouts out, "We know, we know," but the lecturer flashes a look and goes on.

"Psychiatry is a field that's well known for stirring things up. And stirring them up at the hardest time in the strangest ways. There are things you can't be taught in books. Important things that you need to know. Primary among these is how you, as an individual, will be manipulated. By both your workmates and your patients. But especially your patients." He flashes a wry grin and adds, "When I manipulate you, it's for your own good."

Continuing, he says, "One of the first responses that we generally see in working with such difficult patients is paranoia. The general form that this takes is a resident assuming that a certain patient has been given to him or her in order to embarrass the resident in front of his friends and colleagues. The patient is only the agent of the humiliation. The reality is that the world, or at least the hospital, has conspired to ruin his or her life by setting up such an impossible situation. This is usually the reaction seen at the start of the year when no one seems to be getting better.

"Sometimes, when the stress seems to be getting especially heavy, we see regression. At this point the resident is liable to do almost anything. But basically, we can expect to see a person who is holding her breath till she turns blue, expecting the system or the patient or the whatever to change for him. One thing I can assure you, this will not happen." He pauses for only a second, then plunges on. No one has beeped themselves out of the lecture yet, so he knows that he's holding our interest.

"Obsessions are another great trick in coping with the first year experience. Certainly, all of us are very good at obsessing or else we would never have gotten into medical school, let alone through it. So you will often see a resident in the throes of a massive obsessive crisis. This is the person who needs to get everything done, is at the hospital till ten o'clock every night, and feels constantly guilty about not getting the work done." A few people in the audience, including myself have started to turn a bit pink as we identify ourselves in the lecture. Sensing this, Dr. Grill cautions, "These are normal defenses I'm talking about. They help you get through a tough year. And they're better than some others you might have tried." Having piqued our curiosity again, on he goes.

"One of the most dangerous defenses we see used is that of identification. In this, the resident sees herself as the advocate of the patient and starts to act as if she must defend the patient from the staff. Not only does this do the patient no good whatsoever, since if all he needed was an advocate he would be unlikely to have come to a mental hospital in the first place, but it also is bound to get the resident in very hot water. First, you will make mistakes. Then you will find yourself isolated. Then you will start to feel like it's the hospital, not the patient who is crazy. Disregarding politics, this is not a healthy or a happy way to spend a year of your life. Residents are in a poor position to be friends to a patient. They need a doctor much more than an advocate.

"Some people deal with the stress and anxiety of working in this situation, with the incredibly long hours and incredibly sick patients, through the technique of spilling. This has the effect of using every meeting and every encounter in the hospital as a therapy session. In moderation, this can be useful. That's why we have residents' meetings and weekly sessions with chief residents. But when you try to turn the entire hospital into a group encounter, you will find that very little work gets done, and that you don't get the therapy you need, anyway. For some people, just getting through the year is enough insight. For others, finding a therapist is important. But trying to get it hit and miss in the halls or in supervision is a mistake.

"One final method of defense deserves mention. This is avoidance. I didn't see it in any of you this year, but occasionally it has been a problem. When this happens there is very little that we can do other than to try to get the resident to get back into the swing of things. Ultimately, some residents simply stop showing up. In less severe cases people don't do their work, fail to get their charts done"—he glances around the room and everyone hangs their heads a bit—"or don't see their patients."

All around the room you can feel the hum of recognition, as we all grab on to that part which applies to us and are both glad that we are normal, but still embarrassed to have been found out, to have had our secrets blown so wide open. Yet the relief far outweighs the guilt of discovery and there is a general sense of happiness that begins to fill me and, I suspect, others. It is a feeling of survival and it is a very good one.

As has become his pattern, Simon shuffles into my office looking like it's the end of the world. Which it usually seems to be for him, I suppose. But I have to admit that I'm finding it a bit tedious to watch him struggle with the same depressive issues over and over. And also to watch him refuse to even consider that medication, which got him out of the hospital in the first place, will be helpful for him now. Molly has suggested that I be tough with him, that I put my newfound conviction to being a therapist and less a friend into action.

"Dr. Jackson, I had a terrible week." He pauses. When I don't respond he says, "I felt lonely all week. I wanted to call you, but knew you wouldn't like it. But these weeks are very hard to get through."

"Uh huh," I respond.

"I really need more therapy," he says.

"What would that do for you?"

"I don't know. Help me, I guess."

"How would it do that?"

"You should know." He sounds exasperated, then falls back into a depressed slow pattern of speech. "I don't know. Maybe it wouldn't do anything. At least I'd get to see you more often."

"And that's what therapy is? A chance to see me?"

Eyes averted, he says, "Yes."

"How does that affect the therapy?"

"Well, you're a lot more than just a therapist, you know. When I don't think about you I feel so depressed and can't sleep and wish I was dead." He starts to sob and says, "I feel so bad most of the time." His words come slowly between tears. "I just don't deserve someone like you or someone like anybody. I'm just going to be sad my whole life."

Now this is my chance. With Molly's words, not to mention Sam, Sandra, and a lot of other people behind me, I don't interpret or go back once again to Simon's awful childhood. Instead, I lead with my best punch. "Simon, when you are this depressed it's very hard for you to live your life and very hard for you to make good use of therapy. I think it's quite important that you try medication."

"I won't," he pouts, still tearful. "They won't help anyway and I'll get a lot of side effects."

"It's possible you'll get side effects. We need to watch for those. But there should also be many benefits from the medication."

"Why are you doing this, Dr. Jackson? It's my decision." Is this the depression speaking or just his character? Who knows?

"Simon, I think I could be of more help to you if you were on medication. And I feel strongly that you should give them a try."

"But they won't help me."

"That may be true, but there is no way to be sure. When you feel depressed, it can be difficult to weigh risks and benefits. Even though it seems to you that there is no hope and that you will get no benefits from meds, this may not necessarily be true."

He starts to sniffle again. "I won't take them. I don't want to talk about it."

"It's what we're going to talk about till we are both satisfied. As your doctor I would be doing you a disservice by not insisting. We've been trying to work with your depression for a year now without using meds and it simply has not gone in the direction it should. So now it's time to try a different method."

"I won't see you anymore if we keep talking about this."

Now is where the alliance comes into play. Molly has explained it to me thusly: "He and you have a real relationship, an alliance that will allow difficult issues and disagreements to be aired and still maintain the therapeutic atmosphere. This is what you've really been doing for the past year in the therapy. You've been developing a relationship that will allow for the greatest latitude in treatment."

"You can find a new therapist if that's what you want," I say. "But as long as you're my patient this is what we will be working on." I soften my voice somewhat and tell him, "Simon, I'm speaking now as your doctor. You come to me as an expert, as someone you can trust to help you deal with your problems and your pain. If you can't trust me or what I recommend, then you're right, you should find someone new. But I think we can work together and I think that medications will be helpful."

He opens his mouth to object again, then stops short. We sit in silence for minutes which seem much longer, glancing at each other, the clock, the walls, then each other again. Finally, I break the quiet and ask him, "What are you feeling now?"

"What will the medication do for me, Dr. Jackson?" Alright.

"I think it will help your depression."

"Nothing helps my depression."

"Uh huh. That's why we should try this. I don't want to give up."

"How long would I have to take them?" he asks, finally lifting his eyes from the floor and turning his face toward me.

"I don't know for sure. We'd want to try them for a few months before making any decision."

"Okay," he says.

Barely believing my ears, I ask him to repeat it.

"Okay. I'll try it. It won't work, but if it's so important to you then I'll do it." His voice chills. "But I don't want any side effects."

I give him the rap on possible side effects and things we can do about them and write out a prescription. He takes it easily and rises to leave the office. "Thank you, Dr. Jackson," he says.

"For what?"

"I don't know," he responds and leaves.

The conflict I expect to find isn't there. I feel just fine about having Simon on medication and I start to wonder what all the fuss was all about. But I am mainly glad that the fuss, his and mine, seems to be ending.

What are my defenses, I wonder, heading home to see Zoe. She just got her schedule for med school and we're taking the afternoon off to celebrate and be together. The fears of being apart as our careers collide can be oppressive at times and an afternoon together is worth much more than the hours involved. Dr. Grill's lecture stays with me as I drive.

I wonder if all the other residents have had as intense a year as me. Residents' meetings have changed. The trust between us has grown, and the pain we can reveal is impressive, but the healing seems to happen alone, outside of the group. Almost all my peers seem healthier than at the start. Who knows the pain they go through? All our talking and I still can barely figure out me.

The nightmares have slowed to a stop. In the dream last night I am sitting alone by a campfire in the pitch-black of night. Then the room is filled with people. I join in a conversation and we are all talking very loud and we all begin laughing and laughing very loud and I almost want to shout that it is too loud but I don't and then everyone is quiet again. I look at all the records on my shelves and we all share our favorite song with one another. I want to remember something but I can't. And then I know it and I wake up and I can't remember it.

Zoe kisses me at the door.

Her smile is precious, hanging on her face as if it is the only possible expression she could have. My smile, which was a little tight, like I was posing for a picture I didn't want to be in, loosens up. I open my mouth to say something but she puts her finger on her lips as if to say, "Shh," and gives me a hug. "Thanks, Max. I needed that." We enter the dining room where the table is set for two. Candles are burning. Aromas fill the room. She tucks a napkin under my chin as we sit. Someday I can do this for her.

My last night on call. The absolute last time I will be sitting up all night in Intensive Care madness waiting out the insanity of who knows what for hours on end while people jabber all around me in a language that I can barely understand. The last night that I will all alone manage assaultive, crazy, sad, and suicidal people who are so out of it that they have to be locked up to protect themselves. The last night that I will meet the police at three in the morning to greet some murderer who is so strange that even the police don't want to deal with him. So why do I feel so nostalgic?

A mad day today. All the patients know that the academic year is coming to a close, and even though I will stay their doctor as I move to the outpatient department, they are still anxious. Like me, they have a general feeling that everything will be different on July 1. Definitely not as different as it was on the last July 1, but very different nonetheless. So the normal tension of just being here has been tightened one more notch.

The morning opened with Shirley. Profoundly paranoid and needy, she hovered at my office door. Each time on opening it we would have a conversation like this:

"Dr. Jackson," she whispers. "Am I alive or dead?"

"How do you feel?"

"I feel dead."

"How did you die?"

"I don't know. There are a lot of enemies out there."

"How can we be talking if you're dead?"

"I don't know. You're the doctor."

"Shirley, I'm busy now. Hold a mirror up to your lips, if you can see it cloud up then you're still alive."

She meets me again in forty-five minutes.

Holding a mirror in her hands, she exhales as I leave my office door. "I'm not sure if it's clouding or not, Dr. Jackson."

"Let me see," I respond. Taking the mirror from her hands, I examine it closely and tell her, "Definitely clouding. Nothing for you to worry about. You're just fine."

"How do I know you're not lying?"

"Why would I?"

"Maybe you want me dead too."

"Then you'd be in a fine pickle, that's for sure."

"Pickle?" she asks.

"Bad shape." I sigh. Looking at my watch and knowing that I am behind schedule, as always, I say, "That's all for today. Don't stand by my office anymore. I'm busy."

She starts to cry. "But I need you." It is a plaintive wail.

I look at my watch again and nod. "I have a few minutes."

"So am I dead or alive?"

We enter the office as I reply, "What do you think?"

"What do I think?" She shakes her head, saying, "You are one sort of crazy psychiatrist, I can tell you that. You are just a crazy one."

"Why's that, Shirley?"

"Why's that? Why's that?" She starts pounding the chair uncontrollably. "Boy oh boy. You are crazy."

"I don't get it, Shirley. Help me understand."

She looks at me and shakes her head. "You're not a spy, are you?"

"That's right."

"Well then you know."

"Share it with me."

"How could I know? You tell me. You can read my mind."

"I can read your mind?" I ask in wonder.

"You're my doctor, aren't you?"

"You bet."

"Well then, that's all there is to it. Jeesh. I can't understand why I even bother to talk to you about any of this stuff."

Partly I want to smile and partly I want to scream and I can't even figure out if I'm doing Shirley any good at all, although my supervisors think things are going along just great. As if she senses my questions, Shirley says, "So how do I deal with my life?"

"What part?" I inquire.

"You know, getting it together, figuring things out."

Amazed by the lucidity of this, I answer, "That's what therapy is all about. First we figure out the questions, then go for the answers."

"Well, that's the question," she says, somewhat exasperated with me.

"What are you figuring out?"

"I want to find life. That's all. Can't I have that?" She raises her voice and starts to get angry, but instead says, "Or maybe I'm dead." Her body shaking, she crosses her legs and starts to sway back and forth.

"Those are very hard things to get, aren't they?" I ask her.

"Of course they are!" she shouts.

"And it's horrible to not get them even when you see me?"

"Of course!" she replies.

"When you work so hard to make me understand?"

"Yes!" She begins to growl and I ask her, "Are you alive now?"

"Of course!"

"Does that make you angry?" I say.

"I'm not angry!" she shouts, snarling at me. "I'm dealing with major truth. These crazy electrodes do it to me."

"What are they telling you?"

She looks at me and shakes her head. "Oh no, Dr. Jackson, oh no. You're one crazy psychiatrist, I'll tell you that, Dr. Jackson. Whew."

"This is important stuff, Shirley. I'm glad you're talking about it."

"Important?" she says. "Of course it's important. It's my life."

"Then let's keep talking about it. Okay?"

"Am I dead yet?"

"Indeed you aren't."

"Well, alright," she says, standing to leave the office. "You know, Dr. Jackson, this session went fast."

"Why do you think that was, Shirley?"

"How would I know? You're the shrink." She leaves the office.

Today was my last juggling group. The composition of the group has changed so much over the year that it seems like each week I am teaching the basic pattern all over again. Leif, a tall Scandinavian type, has been a constant presence for the past three months, given the fact that his delusional system will not go away. Which is bad for him, but nice for me, since I've got him passing clubs with me now, which is a very pleasurable way to spend work time. I explain to him and the others who show up, mostly to watch the two of us juggle, that this is our last meeting. His response is, "Oh," and nothing more. Such is the flat affect.

Shirley is again waiting for me when I return to my office. She has revived the dead or alive question. This time I send her to a nurse to get her questions answered.

Bobby has returned to my office with me after my group. Like me, he is looking forward to the next year, but has some trepidation.

"We made it, Max. Hurrah!"

"You sound like you have some mixed emotions about that."

He laughs and says, "None whatsoever. This has been a tough one. You wouldn't believe what one of my patients told me today." And we get into a can-you-top-this session about our patients, consisting of the various things they've done. These generally go: "My patient said that trees were the source of universal control." "Oh yeah, mine said that Martians were in his breakfast cereal." "That's nothing. I have a patient who thinks that his father turned into his mother and that his mother became a praying mantis." "Listen to this, my patient went fishing in the Christian Science reflecting pool and when he got caught dove in." This can go on and on as we release our anxiety about it all, till eventually we feel a little sheepish and guilty and move on to talking about ourselves.

"Bobby, a great thing happened this week. I got Simon to start on medication."

"Oh? I didn't know you used them?"

"Sure I do."

"I thought," he says, "that they were just a crutch and nothing else."

"Don't give me any trouble. Hey, I've seen these things work. That patient of yours. I think they saved his life. He was going to be a big lump forever."

"You don't have to convince me, Max. I've spent all year trying to convince you."

"No need anymore. They work. I don't like them but what difference does that make? It's so horrible to be sick. And these people sure do have depression. Anyway, I got Simon to start and I think they might help him." I'm positively beaming.

"It is great when you can do something concrete for the patient. This field can be so nebulous. Didn't you like Dr. Grill's lecture? He really nailed me."

"Yeah, I did. I wish we had heard that at the start of the year instead of the end."

"I think we did hear it," Bobby says. "I just don't think it meant anything to us. It was like the man said, some things have to be experienced, not taught."

The knock on the door is Shirley, looking panic-stricken, eyes wide open, mouth hanging ajar, skin pulled taut, shaking like a leaf. "What is it?" I ask, somewhat impatiently.

All she can get out is, "Dr. Jackson, Dr. Jackson . . ."

Bobby leans over and whispers to me, "Great job you're doing with this patient."

"Shirley," I say, "you're safe here. There is nothing to be afraid of. Nothing at all. You're safe. Now go sit down."

She continues to stand there, but nods her head. "Do you understand me?"

She nods again. "Then go," I suggest. She walks back to the dayroom and sits.

"Medicines don't always work," I say to Bobby.

"I never promised they did," he says as he strides from the room.

I get up and go next door to Sandra's office. She invites me in and I sit and munch on Tootsie Rolls, the candy of the week.

"Well, Max." The words are left hanging.

"I'm going to miss you, Sandra."

"I'll miss you too, Max." We both pause in silence.

"Uh . . ." we both begin, then laugh, then stop.

"You go first," she says.

"Okay. I learned a lot from you this year."

"I could see that, Max. You really developed as the year went on. It's hard to believe that the resident who didn't know how to do a mental status exam has turned into a good psychiatrist. But you have."

"You're making me blush. But thanks."

"It's true. And you added something to the ward. I may not have always agreed with what you said, but at least you said it. And you seemed to learn a lot about how to say what you wanted to."

"I did. But that was in no small measure due to you. I can't tell you how much your help meant to me."

"I tried," she says, shyly.

"Well, you succeeded. Your leadership was part of what got me through."

We sit in silence again and then start to smile. Sandra says, "We sound like a mutual admiration society."

"I guess we are. This year brought us fairly close. Hard times and all that."

"You know, Max, that was part of what I like so much about the year. Getting to know all the residents and be close."

"I'm really going to miss you," I say, starting to sniffle. And tears are welling up in Sandra's eyes too. The silence is heavier as we sit there and feel how sad it is to be losing each other, although I know she's just my boss, but that isn't true, either.

"I didn't expect to cry," I tell her.

"Why not?" she says through her tears. "It's sad. We went through a lot together."

"Yeah. I just didn't think I'd feel this way. I expected to be happier that the year was ending." We both dry our eyes and reach for the candy. After a moment, Sandra says, "You can be happy to be moving on and sad at the same time. It doesn't have to be either or."

"Yeah, I guess so. I just spent so much time being miserable or crazy this year that I never expected to feel sad that it was ending."

"But you made a lot of friends and learned a lot about yourself. What could be a more valuable year?"

I laugh and say, "That sounds like a psychiatrist talking."

"That doesn't make it wrong."

"No. And I agree with you. Hell, that's probably why I went into psychiatry in the first place."

"What's that?"

"To learn about myself. It seemed like every week I had a new reason to go into this field. Sometimes it was to help the sick, or to cure them, or for social reasons, or economics, or whatever. But each time I seem to come back to how much being in training has helped me to come to grips not only with being a doctor and a healer, but also with who I am."

"In this field," she tells me, "there isn't much difference between the two. I could see you were in a lot of pain all year. But you pulled through."

"I wouldn't want to do it again."

"You don't have to."

"I'm really going to miss you, Sandra. Our relationship meant a lot to me."

"Me too, Max. Me, too." She gives me a hug and opens the door.

"Thanks," I say.

"You're welcome."

I want to go home, end the year in Zoe's arms, but there is the small matter of the last night on call before it all ends. As if to keep me from having to think about it all, I get an admission as soon as the night begins.

Bonny limps into my office. She is dragging two crutches behind her and her leg is in a cast. Ty stands behind her, guarding me as it were, twirling his finger in circular motions around his ear, giving me the international sign for "crazy."

"Hello, Ms. . . ."

"Just call me Bonny, Doc. Hey, you're good looking. Wanna go on a date with me tonight? No? How about that great-looking dude in the hall?" She turns around, dropping her crutches on the floor. "Hey, you. Yeah, you. Wadda you doing tonight?" She turns back to me and starts whopping her cast with a crutch. "Goddam thing," she says, forgetting I'm in the room. I may as well not be for all the progress I'm making.

"Uh, the commitment form says your name is Bonita."

"That's right, Doc. Call me that. Say, could I get some food? I'm real hungry. I haven't had anything to eat for days. Look at me, Doc, I'm all skin and bones." She gets up and I instinctively pull back, but all she does is lift her shirt up to show me her stomach. "Skin and bones, eh Doc? Hey, wanna see my tits? I got good ones." She lifts her shirt off her head and starts to shake her body, showing off her ample chest.

"Bonny, try and slow down a bit for me." She's up and dancing now, revolving around in circles on the cast, her other leg splaying out, her breasts bouncing up and down. Her cast looks as if it'll fall apart at any moment. And I say to myself, why are we talking now? It's action time.

"Ty," I say aloud, "could you help Bonny here get up to the ICU? I'll call a nurse to come down and get her clothes."

Ty, grinning something fierce says, "I told you, Doc. This was an easy one."

When I meet Bonny in the ICU a few minutes later, she is, mercifully, dressed. However, she is still going at 78 rpm and shows no sign of slowing down, no matter how often I request it.

Talking a mile a minute, hopping all over the place on her one good leg, she is smiling and crying and totally unable to listen to me or talk to me. A quick trip to the record room has let me know that this was not her first admission, that she carries a diagnosis of manic-depressive illness, and that she takes Lithium. I somehow doubt, however, she has been compliant with her meds. She was found directing traffic on an airport runway.

"Bonny," I say, "do you know where you are?" We run through the usual admission questions and such and confirm that she is indeed both manic and psychotic. But she won't let me finish a sentence and none of what she says makes sense to me. With visions of Simon dancing in my head, I say to her, "Bonny. This is your room. You will stay here until you figure out what you want. If you don't need any help from us, that's fine. If you do, we'll be here."

"I won't take your stupid meds!" she shouts. "Look at me, I'm beautiful."

"You don't have to. But our conversations will be brief until we can figure out how to communicate."

"You bastard! I'll scream all night. I'll sit here and rot before I communicate with you."

"That's your decision. I'll see you later." The nurse, new to the unit, looks at me suspiciously.

"Aren't you punishing her for being sick? It's not her fault she's out of control."

"It's not a punishment," I say. "This is what works best for someone in her condition. Space limitation and medication are two of our best tools to get her out of the hospital and back to her life as soon as possible. I know it's restrictive to treat her this way, but it would be far more restrictive to keep her in the hospital for extra months because we weren't willing to treat her."

This was a much longer response than was expected, but serves to end the conversation. As the nurse walks away, I am left scratching my head, figuring out how those words tumbled out so easily.

10

Fantasy

In the dream I am on the top floor of a skyscraper, staring out the window. I try the doors, but they are all locked. I look down at the street and see Zoe there, with a crowd of people, riding on horseback. They come to the building I am in and enter it, then appear at my door. As Zoe enters, she gives me a kiss and everyone pulls out food and colorful streamers from their pockets. We sit down to have a party, laughing and talking and singing.

I awake with the top of the convertible down as we race up the mountainside, the car barely holding the road as each turn seems sharper than the one before it. Zoe's hair is streaming behind her, the wind a roar in our ears. She can't hear me as I turn to her to speak. The red of the car contrasts with the green of summer in the mountains, the green contrasting with the blue of the sky. We flash through in utter silence, as each mile we travel leaves the past year farther behind.

Have you ever had that feeling, always when moving (there's a different one when you stand still), that things are just perfect, that this moment fits you? That you have so much of what you want that you can barely contain all the good you feel inside?

Zoe turns to me and smiles. We lock eyes for a moment, then she turns back to the scenery, absorbing it as I absorb her in it. She has told me this morning about past lives and how our previous lives have prepared us to be with each other in this one. Maybe. So what was Eve doing in her last life?

But Eve isn't on this trip. No one else from Asylum is here; no Shirley, no Jerry, no Ecaterina, no Simon, not even Sandra or Sam. The person I really needed to set limits on was myself.

Zoe told me she was looking forward to medical school. She might as well. There's a lot to be said for it.